Join Rick Martínez on a once-in-a-lifetime culinary journey throughout México that begins in Mexico City and continues through 32 states, in 156 cities, and across 20,000 incredibly delicious miles. In *Mi Cocina*, Rick shares deeply personal recipes as he re-creates the dishes and specialties he tasted throughout his journey. Inspired by his travels, the recipes are based on his taste memories and experiences. True to his spirit and reflective of his deep connections with people and places, these dishes will revitalize your pantry and transform your cooking repertoire.

Highlighting the diversity, richness, and complexity of Mexican cuisine, he includes recipes like herb and cheese meatballs bathed in a smoky, spicy chipotle sauce from Oaxaca called Albóndigas en Chipotle; northern México's grilled Carne Asada that he stuffs into a grilled quesadilla for full-on cheesy-meaty food euphoria; and tender sweet corn tamales packed with succulent shrimp, chiles, and roasted tomatoes from Sinaloa on the west coast. Rick's poignant essays throughout lend context—both personal and cultural—to quilt together a story that is rich and beautiful, touching and insightful.

RICK MARTÍNEZ

MI COCINA

Recipes and Rapture from My Kitchen in México

Photographs by REN FULLER

Clarkson Potter/Publishers
New York

PARA MÉXICO

CONTENTS

BAJA CALIFORNIA

SONORA

CHIHUAHUA

6

BAJA CALIFORNIA SUR

SINALOA

DURANGO

ZACAT

NAYARIT

7

8

JALISCO

COLIMA

CHAPTER 1

BÁSICOS

STAPLES OF THE MEXICAN TABLE p. 17

Introduction p. 8
Agradecimientos p. 296
Index p. 298

CHAPTER 2

EL BAJÍO

AND CENTRAL MÉXICO p. 67

CHAPTER 3

OAXACA

AND THE SOUTH PACIFIC COAST p. 105

CHAPTER 4

YUCATÁN

PENINSULA p. 145

CHAPTER 5

EL GOLFO

CENTRAL p. 173

CHAPTER 6

EL NORTE

THE NORTHERN STATES p. 205

CHAPTER 7

PACÍFICO

CENTRAL p. 239

CHAPTER 8

BAJA

CALIFORNIA PENINSULA p. 273

AHUILA

NUEVO LEON

ASCALIENTES

TAMAULIPAS

SAN LUIS POTOSI

NAJUATO

QUERETARO

HIDALGO

CHOACAN

MÉXICO

CD MX

TLAXCALA

MORELOS

PUEBLA

GUERRERO

VERACRUZ

OAXACA

TABASCO

CHIAPAS

CAMPECHE

YUCATÁN

QUINTANA ROO

INTRODUCTION

><

WHEN I WAS GROWING UP in Austin, Texas, my mom and I spent a lot of time watching cooking shows. I'd stretch out on the hideous gold plaid sofa in front of our rear-projection big-screen TV (that took up half of the living room) and Mom would watch from the kitchen, usually while sweeping the floor with one of the superior Mexican brooms she'd buy across the border and bring home.

We loved *Two Fat Ladies* on the BBC and *Emeril Live*, but our favorite show was Diana Kennedy's. We'd watch her make chorizo with green and red chiles from a mercado in Michoacán, and were deeply envious of her sun-drenched kitchen full of red clay bowls. It all just seemed so magical. And dammit, I wanted all of those things, too! I decided then and there that I would grow up to be just like her.

Now I know that this desire was masking a deeper one: the desire to understand myself. Sure, part of me wanted the ego recognition of being "the best" or "the authority," but what was so devastating to me as a Mexican American boy growing up in Texas was that she knew more about my culture and my people than I did. That a British woman and Rick Bayless, a white man

from Oklahoma, got to represent the culinary diversity of México while my Mexican American family tried to enculturate with meatloaf and Chef Boyardee.

MY GREAT-GRANDFATHER Andrés Castruita was a dairy farmer in Torreón, a city in the northern state of Coahuila. He sold his farm in 1910, moved his family, including my five-year-old grandfather Agustín Flores Castruita, across the border and bought a small farm just south of Austin. Even though my grandfather only spent the first five years of his life in México, somehow, he was able to hold on to it—from the intense sea-green color of his house to his embellished style of handwriting to the mariachi songs he'd sing when he drank. I didn't know at the time how Mexican all these things were, but in the years since, as I've explored the country myself, I've recognized them all. To this day, I'm not sure how he picked them up from such a young age.

Agustín would grow up in Austin, eventually marry and have five children, the first of whom was my mom, Gloria. While he wasn't the best father in the world (he had a tendency to play

Grilling for my
friends at their ranch
in El Huajote, Sinaloa.

favorites), he was a good grandfather. He liked me, probably because I looked like him. I have a lot of the Castruita features, but more important, I am dark, like he was. My mom, dad, and brother are all light-complected. When I was born, the nurse who delivered me said to my mom, "Gloria, your baby has a tan!"

From that moment on, I was different. I didn't want to be, but I had no choice. I was brown, and in Texas in the 1970s that meant you were labeled Mexican. Neither of those things—being brown and being Mexican—was bad to me, but to many of the parents, students, and teachers at the all-white preschool and elementary school in a small town south of Austin (where I was the first Mexican American to attend and my younger brother was the second), they were bad. So my parents decided not to teach us Spanish as kids because they were worried we'd develop accents and would be made fun of or be held back in school as a result.

When I was in first grade, the school administration tried to put me in the free-lunch program. Both my parents worked; we were middle class; we had a swimming pool and lake property. But the assumption was that I needed it. When I was in second grade, the PTA tried to start a coat collection for me. I had two coats; they were new and both fit well. I didn't need more coats. But the assumption was that I needed it. When I was in third grade, my homeroom teacher asked the class what we wanted to be when we grew up. I eagerly raised my hand and said I wanted to be President of the United States. The little boy who sat next to me looked me in the eye. "You can't be President," he said. "You're not white." I was so confused. I didn't understand. I went home that night and asked my parents and they said he was wrong; as an American-born citizen, I had every right to be president. But that eight-year-old boy was taught that I couldn't be. Someone

he trusted said those words to him. And his assumption was that I needed to hear them.

Back when my parents bought their first home in Austin in 1963, the neighborhood association called a vote on whether to allow them, a Mexican American couple, into the community or not. Eleven years later, they were forced to finance their second home on their own because no mortgage company would lend money to a Mexican American family wanting to build a custom-home in an all-white suburb. Texas was a brutal place for people of color.

AS I GREW OLDER, my mom started to explore her own identity. We took weekend trips across the border to an unassuming little town called Nuevo Progresso, about five hours from Austin. My mom loved it, and I would later fall for Nuevo Progresso as well. It only had one paved street, but it was there that I got to experience for myself the vibrant mercados I'd only ever seen on Diana Kennedy's and Rick Bayless's shows. Whole animals from farms five miles away would arrive in the morning, get butchered on-site, and be sold fresh to people who would go home and cook the meat that afternoon. At the comida corrida stalls, the mercado version of fast food, there was such an immediacy to the connections people had to one another, from farmers and ranchers to cooks and eaters.

My mom was taken by the spices and dried chiles she found there. At a time when everyone, even Mexican Americans, were using chili powder (used to flavor the dish of the same name), canned sauces, and jarred moles, she experimented with chiles anchos, pasillas, and guajillos. My aunts saw it as the equivalent of churning your own butter; if you had access to McCormick's, why would you take the time to buy a whole dried chile, reconstitute it, and puree it? But as you'll see in the recipes that follow, this process is at the very heart of Mexican

My mom is the reason that I cook.

cuisine, and the flavor is clearly superior. (Try my Birria estilo Aguascalientes on p. 216 and I think you'll agree.)

We never talked about it, but I think that during this time my mom was longing for a connection to México and to her heritage. Immigrants and first- and second-generation Mexican Americans often live in two different worlds. One world is wholly white American, where you feel compelled to fit in to the point of sacrificing your own identity. The other is Mexican, which for immigrants is the world you left behind and always miss, but for first- and second-generation Mexican Americans it is the world you don't fully understand because you are so far removed from it. My mother was first generation, and her food reflected that.

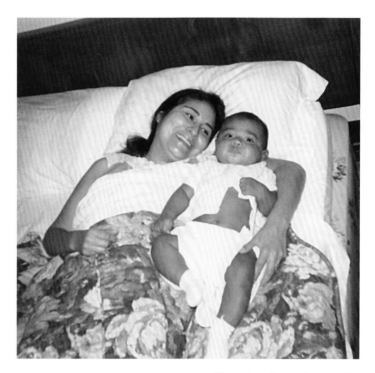

▲ My mom and me, a few months after I was born, in Austin, Texas.

She learned a lot of what she knew from her mother (who was known for her epic Thanksgiving feasts and the oyster cornbread dressing she'd serve) as well as from the home ec classes that she had to take in high school where she learned classic mid-century American dishes like cheeseballs, fondue, and chicken and dumplings. When she got married she bought the 1963 edition of the *Betty Crocker Cookbook* (which I still have to this day) with lobster thermidor and the gelatin molds and the sugar cookies (only Mary's, never Ethel's) as well as the complete set of the Time-Life Foods of the World cookbooks. She was passionate about food and loved to cook.

When she was in the kitchen, she never tasted her food, which drove me crazy when I got to culinary school, where one of the core tenets is to taste as you go. But she had the keenest sense of smell of anyone I have ever known; all she had to do was sniff and she'd know exactly what a dish needed and could balance it perfectly. She'd

call in me or my brother or my father at the end and have us taste, only for salt. "Why don't you try it?" I would ask, and she'd give me that disgusted-but-not-disgusted mom face. "Why would I need to?"

Above all, my mom cooked to express her love. The biggest insult you could ever give her was to not like her food. In the thirty-nine years that I knew her, there were probably only two times I didn't like what she made. (Sorry, but nobody needs salmon croquettes made with canned salmon.)

My mom is the reason that I cook. When I was four years old, I would push a chair to the kitchen, climb up, and stir the pots simmering on the stove. I'd watch her and learn. When I was in sixth grade, she took two weeks off of work during my winter break so we could learn how to make tamales together. She had only ever seen her aunts and her mother make them, all of whom had died by that point. There was no one in our family who could pass the recipe down, so she decided to restart the tradition and pass it to her sons. Every year after that, she hosted a tamalada—a tamale party—with all of the family helping to make (but mainly helping to eat) her tamales. Family and friends gathered at nine in the morning and stood side by side, eating donuts and making fun of each other while spreading masa on husks and filling them with my mom's recipe for the pork filling consisting of a hog's head and shoulder slow-roasted until the meat was literally falling off the bone, ancho-pasilla puree made from the mercado chiles, and (exactly) thirty-seven cloves of garlic. After an entire year of waiting in anticipation of that first bite of a tamal since the last year's tamalada, pulling the first batch of tamales from the steamer was like plucking the first ripe tomato off the vine in late summer.

Years later, when I was in culinary school, I wanted to make sure that I could correctly make tamales on my own, so I pitched them for one of my class projects. My mom sent me all of her notes and her handwritten recipe. We had several conversations about the method and why she did what she did. I took detailed notes and in the end, I succeeded. My tamales reminded me of home and of her.

The next year, a few months after she attended my graduation, she died.

That first Christmas without her was horrible. And my dad said that he did not want to host the tamalada. At first I agreed; doing it without her felt too painful. But as the holidays got closer, I couldn't let it pass. I couldn't let the tradition she'd worked so hard to restart die with her. So I told my dad we were going to host but that I wanted all the kids in the family to cook with me and learn how to make tamales. Gathering around the kitchen island with them, watching them smear masa onto husks with their tiny hands (and seeing them covered head to toe with masa), was one of the most incredible experiences. Here was the next generation, keeping the family tradition intact—keeping my mother's memory and her recipe alive.

BEFORE I STARTED WRITING this book, I had a very scattered, incomplete picture of México. As a kid, all I had to go on was a few old books and photos and a lot of negative news coverage, telling me

▼ My mom and me in our boat on Lake Travis in Austin.

how bad and scary México was. As an adult, I took many trips, but it was never enough; I never seemed to understand it fully, there was so much more to experience and learn. What I did know, however, is that I always felt more connected to the people in México than I ever have to people in the US. Here was a place where I wasn't the only Brown person in the room. Here was a place where I was surrounded by people who look and think and talk like me, who love the same food I do, who like me for who I am and don't consider me a foreigner. When I came here I used to apologetically tell the locals I was American. But they would say, "No, tu corazón es Mexicano." Your heart is Mexican.

The deep yearning to return to this place and feel connected to it is something I liken now to the process of coming out as gay. You have this burning knowledge inside you, knowing that you are different but too scared to acknowledge it. But at some point you have to either embrace your truth or repress it forever, which is far more difficult. I came out at twenty, but at forty, I found myself asking the same questions again: Who am I? What am I? Where do I belong? And luckily, this time, there was a place I could go to find answers. A whole country, in fact.

So, in October of 2019, I flew to Mexico City, bought a car, and set off on the journey that would change my life. All 32 states, 156 cities, and more than 20,000 miles of distance.

I was going to México to seek out the flavors I love: fatty and spicy and sweet. I chose my meals by what smelled the best and looked the best, which puestos had the most locals sitting in front of them, eating and laughing as the juice of slow-braised pork and bright green salsa de aguacate dripped down their faces. I'd ask the cooks a single question: Out of everything you make, what do *you* like best? With this as my criterion, 99.9 percent of what I ate was delicious.

Out of the countless dishes I got to try this way, I selected a hundred of my favorites and created my own interpretation of each, not as an archetype or a be-all and end-all "best" version, but as a highly personalized love letter to that dish, with my own unique sazón, of course—my personal flair and signature that makes these dishes my own. All of the food in this book I re-created from my memories of eating the dish for the first time, but each recipe is influenced by my own preferences—preferences that the events of 2020 have taught me are worth considering.

You have this burning knowledge inside you, knowing that you are different but too scared to acknowledge it.

BACK IN THE EARLY 1960s, my mother was the second person of color ever to attend the nursing school at the University of Texas at Austin. She told me about how the white woman who headed up the program didn't like her because she was a Brown person, even wanted to fail her and remove her from the program. My mother was ninety-eight pounds and five feet four inches tall, very slight and soft-spoken. But she told this woman: "You can't fail me unless I fail myself." And she didn't let that happen. She worked twice as hard, finished the program, graduated, and became a nurse.

I think about those words often: You can't fail unless you fail yourself. In many ways, I feel that I've failed myself for forty-eight years. As a public-facing cook in this industry, I was complicit in the game of labeling certain dishes, cuisines, and recipes as "authentic" because at the time I thought that I had to.

But I have come to hate the word "authentic" as well as "genuine," "cookable," "modern," "easy," and "simple." When you're a person of color, these words are like cattle prods. They're what people use when they want to extract something—the truth, the real story, the universal flavor—from you, a single person forced to represent an entire country, an entire culture, an entire people. They're the place where marketing and racism intersect. They're what people have been trying to use on me my entire life.

When you call something authentic, you're necessarily saying that everything else is not. You're saying there is only one true version of a dish and therefore everyone else is making it wrong. Whether you're an acclaimed chef in Mexico City or a home cook in Tabasco, you've been summarily dismissed because some random guy from Texas says his version is the clinical archetype, arbitrarily decided upon because he traveled to every state and you didn't. For so long, this has been the lexicon of publishing—if something isn't American, if it's not centered around whiteness, then we have to qualify it, so white people know they're getting the "real" version. "Sure, there are a billion people in China, but there's only one authentic and correct way to make a soup dumpling."

I even started off marketing this very book as "simple, modern Mexican you can cook right now." I didn't realize at the time how much those words limited me. I agonized over how to develop these recipes in ways that would represent the whole country correctly. "Authentically." I tortured myself, feeling like I had to extricate myself, my personality, and my passion from the food to make it more sellable. The book lost its point of view—my point of view. And the joy that I felt traveling around México, exploring the food and the culture was replaced with a deep anxiety and the fear of misrepresenting the country that I had fallen in love with.

The recipes I was writing didn't feel like mine. I felt forced out of the equation entirely. But that's what living in the US as a person of color has always been: putting yourself aside completely in order to compete. It was never about me and what I liked, but about what would sell.

This is a garden-variety story for any person of color in any industry who wants to get ahead or be successful or even just survive. This is the constant battle we live with. To take one step forward, we have to figure out how to compromise, who to pander to, and when to bite our tongues.

But then, in May 2020, a Black man named George Floyd was murdered on camera. He wasn't the first or the last, but his death—the slow, agonizing brutality of it, the initial lack of any real consequences faced by those responsible for it—shook something loose in the American psyche. And at first, everything else felt inconsequential. Who cared about my stupid little book when people were dying in the streets?

When this country's racial reckoning began to spread to other industries, checking the corporate gatekeepers that have dominated with impunity for decades, I started confronting all the compromises I'd made for so long in my own work. Suddenly it became clear that everything I'd done in my entire life to feel like I could exist in this country (the country I was born in)—whether it was dressing a certain way, cooking a certain way, or pitching a certain type of story a certain way—was designed to fit in rather than be true to myself.

When my employer, Condé Nast Entertainment, refused to give me a fair and equitable contract relative to what they were paying my white co-workers in August 2020, I knew it was

> **I fell in love with a beach town in México and decided to buy a house there.**

▲ Modeling my culinary school uniform for my mom in our kitchen in Austin.

time to stop compromising. So I left. It was one of the most empowering things I've ever done. Walking away—even without another job lined up—was worth more to me than anything they could have offered.

It was then that everything else began falling into place. No, I wouldn't write a book with "simple, modern Mexican" as its subtitle. No, I wouldn't make a 30-minute "Tuesday night" tamal. No, I wouldn't stop using lard because some people think it's unhealthy. And if that meant nobody would read or buy or cook or watch me ever again, fine.

I felt so free. Free to be and do whatever I wanted. Without fear. Without a concern for consequence. I surrounded myself with the things that I loved. I fell in love with a beach town in México and decided to buy a house there. I filled it with furniture and art made with love

and passion by Mexican hands. I grow flowers and vegetables that thrive in the tropical sun. I rescued a chocolate lab, named him Choco, and he has become my best friend. I cook, write, and live in a paradise that I created by deciding to be me.

And at that moment, I found the joy in writing this book again. I knew exactly what this book was going to be: a book filled with recipes that are authentic to *me*. I wanted to write it, I wanted to cook this food and, more important, I wanted to eat it. The recipes in *Mi Cocina* are inspired not only by my travels but also the road to self-acceptance and, finally, my happiness.

Mi Cocina is the story of where I went, who I met, what I learned, what I ate, and how to make it. It's also the story of who I am, and who I am becoming—past, present, and future.

Provecho!

BÁSICOS

STAPLES OF THE MEXICAN TABLE

▼ Tacos de carnitas with pico de gallo; Quiroga, Michoacán

The recipes in this book represent the food that I loved eating the most

during the 586 days I spent traveling throughout México. It wasn't easy paring down the list; I ate *a lot* of amazing food. The 104 dishes you are about to flip through are my favorites. They are the recipes that I cook over and over again for myself, friends, and family. They are the recipes that mean the most to me because every single one of them is connected to a memory—the moment in the trip where I first tasted that dish. The moment I fell in love and knew that it needed to be a part of *Mi Cocina*.

I chose to divide these recipes into two camps: the staples, which you'll find in this chapter, and the iconic regional recipes—the ten or so dishes I believe are *must-eat* foods in each part of the country—which are organized by region in the chapters that follow. Here, in the Básicos chapter, you'll find your building blocks: recipes that exist universally throughout México, organized by key ingredients: corn and wheat, rice, beans, and chiles (which is where you'll find all the salsas, ready to be paired up with all the other recipes). How you use this book is up to you; mix and match the quick and easy recipes with others like tamales, which are definitely a weekend project, like a lasagna—and they're so incredibly worth it. Before we get started, you'll find some notes (p. 24–32) about the way I cook and the way you can make the most of this book, however you decide to use it.

THE RECIPES

CORN AND WHEAT

Tortillas de Maíz
corn flatbread made
from ground corn,
p. 38

**Tortillas de
Harina de Maíz**
corn flatbread made
from instant corn
flour, p. 39

**Tostadas de Maíz
(Fried or Baked)**
crispy corn flatbread,
p. 40

Gorditas de Maíz
stuffed corn flatbread,
p. 43

Pan Árabe
yeasted wheat flour
flatbread, p. 44

**Tortillas de Harina
con Mantequilla**
wheat flour flatbread
made with butter,
p. 46

**Tortillas de Harina
estilo Sinaloa**
Sinaloan-style wheat
flour flatbread,
p. 47

RICE AND BEANS

Arroz Rojo
toasted rice with
tomato, carrots, and
serrano, p. 49

**Arroz Blanco
con Mantequilla**
buttery rice with
poblano, carrots, and
corn, p. 50

Arroz Verde
herbed rice with
scallion and cilantro,
p. 51

Frijoles de Olla
simple beans with
scallions and herbs,
p. 54

Frijoles Refritos
porky refried beans,
p. 55

SALSAS, CONDIMENTS, AND SEASONINGS

Salsa Blanca
serrano cream with
lime and cilantro,
p. 58

**Chiles Habaneros
Encurtidos**
charred pickled
habaneros, p. 58

Salsa Tatemada
charred tomato,
onion, and serrano,
p. 58

**Cebolla Morada
Encurtida**
pickled red onions
with habanero, p. 59

Curtido
lightly fermented
cabbage with carrots,
onion, and jalapeños,
p. 59

**Chiles Chipotles
en Escabeche**
pickled chipotles with
cinnamon and cloves,
p. 59

Salsa de Aguacate
avocado cream with
serranos and
jalapeños, p. 60

**Salsa de Papaya y
Tomatillo Cruda**
papaya and tomatillos
with habanero, orange
juice, and mint, p. 60

Salsa Macha
oil-roasted cashews,
garlic, and chiles
anchos, p. 60

**Salsa de Chipotle
y Chile de Árbol**
smoky dried jalapeños
and chile de árbol
stewed with tomatoes,
p. 62

**Salsa de Chile
de Árbol**
chiles de árbol
simmered with tangy
tomatillos, p. 62

Salsa de Tomatillo
tomatillo, avocado,
and poblano, p. 62

**Aceite de Habanero
Quemado**
charred habanero oil,
p. 63

Salsa Chipotle
smoky dried jalapeños
stewed with garlic
and a touch of sugar,
p. 63

**Salsa de Zanahoria
y Habanero**
fermented carrot and
habanero, p. 63

**Chiles Jalapeños
en Escabeche**
pickled jalapeños with
carrots, p. 64

Guacamole
smashed avocado,
jalapeño, and lime,
p. 64

**Recado de
Todo Clase**
ground spice blend
with allspice,
cinnamon, clove, and
chile de árbol, p. 64

Recado Rojo
annatto seed paste
flavored with citrus,
herbs, and spices,
p. 65

▲ Tomates del país del
Rancho Los Olivos,
El Huajote, Sinaloa.

▼ Outdoor food market in Capula, Michoacán.

Why do I measure in grams?

→ Because I love you, I have measured out almost (okay, so I didn't weigh out a teaspoon of cumin seeds) every ingredient of every recipe in volume, grams, *and* ounces, so please use them! I do this because produce size and weight can vary widely, especially between countries, and when you dry out produce it varies even more. For example, using 5 chiles anchos to thicken a sauce or stew in México, where they're usually quite fresh and retain a lot of moisture and sugar even when they're dried, may give you a very different consistency than using 5 chiles anchos in the United States, where they'll likely be older and drier, and thus produce a thinner sauce. By weighing your ingredients out to match mine, you'll get as close to the result that I got when I created the recipe, which is why I recommend investing in a good kitchen scale (a digital one) before diving into the recipes. While a digital scale is definitely not required to cook this book, I often get asked questions like "Why is my sauce so thin?" or "Is it supposed to be this thick?"—I am here to tell you that you will never have that problem if you use a scale and use the gram amounts that I have written in the recipes.

What equipment do you need in your kitchen?

→ Aside from the aforementioned kitchen scale, these recipes don't require much by way of equipment. Just make sure you have a decent blender, a large heavy pot, and a heavy skillet, which can stand in for a tortilla press if you're running low on kitchen space.

What's with all the salt?

→ Salt, to me, is the most essential ingredient. You'll find it in nearly all of my recipes, and the amounts may be quite startling to you—they're sometimes startling to me, too! But using plenty of salt (like restaurants do) is the key to maximizing all your other flavors. I typically use sea salt since I live near the sea, but I've weighed out conversions for Morton and Diamond Crystal (the two most common brands of kosher salt, which are actually quite different from each other) so you can work with what you have. My general rule of thumb is 4 grams of salt (which is ¾ teaspoon of Morton kosher or 1 teaspoon of Diamond Crystal kosher salt) for every 1 pound of food or 1 quart (4 cups) of water, whether you're cooking meat, masa, or vegetables. If the meat has bones in it, this will throw off your measurements (a pound of ribs isn't a pound of meat), so I'll take out 25 percent of the weight in relation to the amount of salt I add. For example, if I'm cooking 4 pounds of ribs, I'll add 1½ teaspoons of Morton salt (or 3 teaspoons of Diamond Crystal). If I'm adding 1 pound of tomatoes, in goes another ½ teaspoon Morton or 1 teaspoon Diamond Crystal salt. If you're scared of the volume of salt I use (for health reasons or any other), use less. Or start at half of what I call for and season up—because while you can always add more, you can't take salt away.

Can you make these recipes vegetarian?

→ People think Mexican food is all about pork and lard (and, to be clear, I love pork and lard), but before the Spaniards came and brought domesticated animals with them, the indigenous cuisine in this area was mostly plant-based. Think nuts, seeds, vegetables, and fish. You can convert any of the dishes in this book to be vegetarian if you simply sub in vegetables for the meat, brown your veggies in your favorite oil (instead of lard), and cook until tender. Just remember to adjust the cook times accordingly. All the chile sauces in this book should be cooked for at least 30 minutes to bring out their full flavor, so if you're using a vegetable that takes less than half an hour to cook, simmer the sauce without the vegetables and add them at the end and cook them to your desired doneness.

Why do I love lard?
(And what should you do if you don't?)

→ Lard is amazing and, in my opinion, the best fat to cook with. In my house growing up, we always saved our bacon drippings, which added rich flavor to everything that went into our skillet. (Don't believe me? Try refrying beans in vegetable oil versus bacon fat and tell me you can't taste a difference.) Lard is what home cooks in México use, and it's what I recommend for you: Any time you cook bacon or really any meat, save your drippings (the liquefied fat leftover in the pan) in a jar and refrigerate or freeze for later.

I think of lard like butter: Sure, if you ate a whole stick you'd probably get sick, but a couple tablespoons in a dish that serves eight people means you're consuming just under 1 teaspoon at the most, so there's no cause for alarm. Plus, using leftover animal fat to cook other dishes is economical and efficient—and far more sustainable than buying separate (and often inferior) oils to cook with. And if that wasn't enough to convince you, lard is *lower* in saturated fat than butter and significantly lower in cholesterol:

15 g butter = 32 mg cholesterol
15 g lard = 14 mg cholesterol

High-quality lard is rendered from a pig during a slow cooking process where the fat melts from the meat. It is a light caramel color—not white (like hydrogenated shortening). Good lard has a high smoke point and an umami-rich, almost nutty flavor. But if you're vegetarian or just not comfortable cooking with lard despite all my attempts to convince you, that's fine. I will clarify in each recipe exactly what kind of cooking fat will serve you the best: rendered lard, something hydrogenated like Crisco, or extra-virgin olive oil.

What's in my pantry?

→ My pantry is a big source of creativity for me. When I'm trying to decide what to cook for dinner or developing a recipe for work, I often open the doors and let the contents of the pantry (or the garden, or the refrigerator) tell me what it wants me to make and what flavors should be included. Here, I present to you the items I always keep stocked, and encourage you to keep on hand as well so that you can be as fearless in the kitchen as I am.

MY PANTRY

DRIED CHILES
- Ancho
- Chipotle
- Guajillo
- Pasilla
- Chile De Árbol
- Cascabel

FRESH CHILES
- Jalapeño
- Serrano
- Habanero
- Poblano

DRIED HERBS
- Mexican Oregano
- Bay Leaves
- Mint
- Avocado Leaves

FRESH HERBS
- Cilantro
- Mint
- Basil
- Epazote
- Mint
- Parsley
- Thyme
- Scallions

SPICES
- Cumin
- Coriander
- Canela/Cinnamon
- Allspice
- Clove
- Anise
- Cardamom

SUGARS, SYRUPS, AND FLAVORINGS
- Piloncillo
- Agave Syrup
- Granulated Sugar
- Vanilla Bean
- Vanilla Extract

FATS
- Extra-Virgin Olive Oil
- Vegetable Oil
- Lard
- Butter

SALT
- Kosher Salt
- Sea Salt
- Olives
- Capers
- Anchovies

NUTS AND SEEDS
- Pepitas (Hulled Pumpkin Seeds)
- Almonds
- Pecans
- Peanuts
- Sesame Seeds
- Hazelnuts
- Cashews

DRIED FRUIT
- Dates
- Apricots
- Prunes
- Raisins
- Cherries
- Figs

SOUR
- Limes
- Oranges
- Pineapple
- Vinegars

DAIRY
- Crema
- Milk
- Queso Fresco
- Cotija
- Quesillo
- Queso Chihuahua

BAKING
- Wheat Flour
- Nixtamalized Harina de Maíz or Masa Harina (such as Bob's Red Mill or Maseca)

ALCOHOL
- Mezcal
- Tequila
- Beer (Lager)

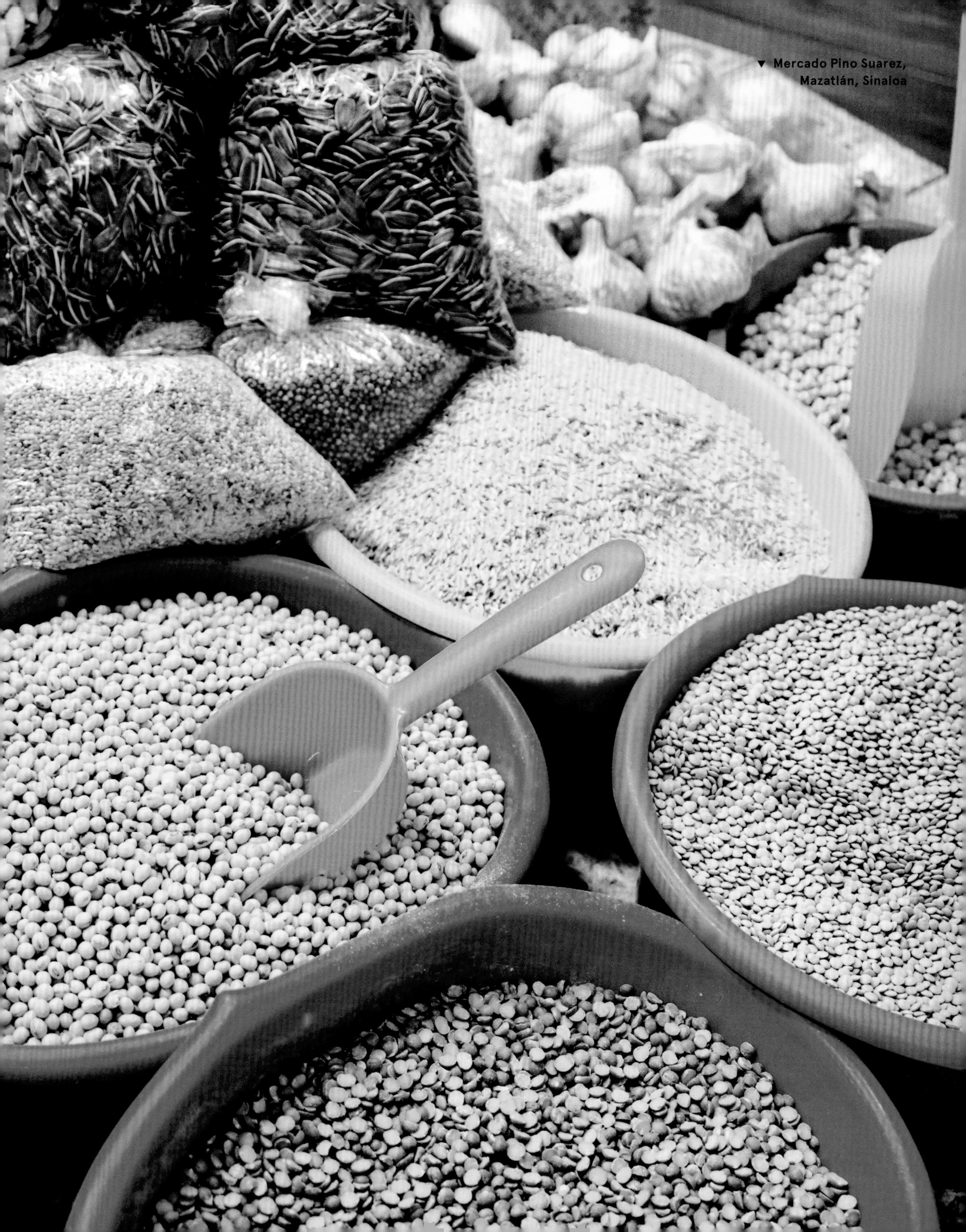

▼ Mercado Pino Suarez,
Mazatlán, Sinaloa

Fresh Produce

→ Tomatillos, tomatoes, white onion, garlic, and poblanos are always in my kitchen. They are the building blocks for almost every dish in this book—and, more important, they are the flavor base for two of my favorite salsas, verde and roja. Salsa emergencies are real, and when the craving strikes you have to be ready to go *now*—not 5 minutes from now! Having these ingredients at the ready means that a quick blender salsa is literally 60 seconds away and your naked tacos can be sauced and eaten as the universe intended.

All About Herbs

→ I prefer to grow my own herbs because it's cheaper than constantly buying them fresh, and I never feel guilty about letting them wilt into mush in the fridge because I only cut what I need. These days, growing just about anything on my sunny roof in Mazatlán is a snap, but even when I lived in a small New York City apartment, I kept cilantro, basil, mint, parsley, and thyme plants on my windowsill at all times. When cooking, I like to use the more tender herbs (cilantro, basil, mint, and parsley) as a garnish or stir them into a pot of beans or a spicy, rich guiso (stew or braise) before serving to add a pop of freshness and color. Hardier herbs like thyme stand up to heat better and can be added earlier in the cooking process to bring a mellow back note to soups and sauces.

HOW TO STORE FRESH HERBS

If you don't have the space, light, or climate to grow herbs year-round and need to buy them in bunches at the store, I get it. Here's how to keep them fresh and looking their best:

Wash the herbs in a large bowl or sink filled with cool water, gently agitating to remove any sand or dirt. Let soak for 5 minutes to allow all of the dirt and sand to sink to the bottom. Lift the herbs out of the water leaving all the dirt behind and use a salad spinner to remove excess water. Gently pat dry with clean kitchen towels.

• **TENDER HERBS** have problems with excess moisture and can easily start to decompose and get soggy if they are too wet. To help absorb excess moisture, arrange your herbs in a single, even layer (stems all pointing in the same direction) on a dry paper towel and top them with another dry paper towel, sandwich style. Gently roll up into a loose log so that the stems are lying flat, place in a large resealable freezer bag, and store in your refrigerator's crisper drawer.

• **HARDY HERBS** have the opposite problem; they suffer from not enough moisture and tend to wilt when stored. So you'll want to use a damp paper towel instead, placed inside a large, resealable freezer bag so that it can lie completely flat. Arrange your herbs on top, seal the bag, and store it in the crisper drawer.

TENDER HERBS
- Cilantro
- Epazote
- Basil
- Mint
- Chervil
- Parsley
- Dill
- Hoja Santa
- Tarragon
- Chives
- Scallion (not an herb, but I store it like one)

HARDY HERBS
- Rosemary
- Thyme
- Sage
- Oregano
- Marjoram

DRIED HERBS WORTH BUYING

I don't generally like using dried herbs because they tend to lose their flavor as they sit (and who knows how long they have been sitting on the shelf at the store), but the three that I do keep in my pantry are Mexican oregano, avocado leaves, and bay leaves. Oregano is very pungent both fresh and dried and holds onto its flavor longer than most herbs. I prefer using Mexican oregano because the flavor is truer to what you would find in México: less bitter, slightly more floral, and sweeter than Italian. You can find McCormick's version at most grocery stores. But if you can't find it, Italian oregano is a good substitute.

Avocado leaves are used a lot in the southern part of México, similar to the way that we use bay leaves here. They have a bright, spicy citrus flavor, like orange, allspice, and cinnamon. They are almost always cooked with black beans in Oaxaca but can also brighten soups and moles. You'll find them fresh and dried in mercados across México, but most home cooks will buy a bunch of fresh leaves, use what they need, and dry the rest. They also hold onto their flavor much better than other dried herbs.

Bay leaves in México actually have flavor, unlike many of those I have sadly bought and used in the United States. If you can find fresh bay leaves, I prefer California bay over Turkish; I have found that they have a much stronger menthol/eucalyptus flavor that will last but mellow over long cooking times, which is normally how I use them. And if you have to buy a large box of them, use what you need and dry the rest. Lay them out on a sheet pan and put them in your (cold) oven. Toss them every morning until they are completely dry, then store in an airtight container in your pantry.

All About Spices

→ I always buy whole spices. Spices are like coffee beans: Once you grind them they immediately begin to lose their flavor. Unless you are using that whole jar of ground nutmeg or black pepper in the next month, I would recommend buying whole spices and grinding your own. Spice grinders are pretty inexpensive or you can just buy an inexpensive coffee grinder (or use your blender) to grind small amounts of spices.

If I am cooking from a recipe that calls for 1 teaspoon ground cumin, for example, I will use 1 teaspoon cumin seeds and just throw them in my grinder. The aroma and flavor is so much more intense than what you would get with preground. Freshly grinding spices may take an extra 30 seconds, but the way they transform a dish is immeasurable.

Chiles guajillos and chiles anchos, Mercado Pino Suarez, Mazatlán, Sinaloa

All About Chiles

→ Out of everything in my pantry, chiles are my favorite, both dried and fresh. They grow in almost every pueblito and absolutely define the flavor of Mexican food, which is why you'll find them in almost every recipe in this book. The flip side of that ubiquity is that so many regional dishes are made with chiles that *only* grow in that part of the country, which can make re-creating them hard, even in México. However, I have found that keeping my kitchen stocked with six different types of dried chiles (ancho, chipotle, guajillo, pasilla, chile de árbol, and cascabel) and four fresh (jalapeño, serrano, habanero, and poblano) allows me to approximate the regional flavors of each dish without having to special-order chiles every time I get a craving. These are all pretty easy to source in grocery stores around the US and México.

• **FRESHLY DRIED CHILES** are incredibly aromatic, flavorful, and delicious. They are soft and pliable and should smell almost like a spicy, apricot jam. These chiles are dried either when they are fully ripe and red or while they are still green and underripe. Because the red chiles have been allowed to fully ripen on the plant, they develop more sugars, giving the dried version a sweeter, almost raisin or dried apricot-like flavor—though they can still be very spicy. These chiles are used both for their flavor and for their color. Sauces and stews made with dried red chiles will have more red tones, from bright brick red (guajillo) to a deep red mahogany (ancho).

• **DRIED GREEN CHILES** are more vegetal and grassy than their red counterparts. They are picked before they are fully ripe, therefore they develop less sugar and aren't usually sweet at all. Their flavors tend to be a little sharper and they often complement the flavors of dried red chiles. Fresh green chiles, such as chilaca, turn black when dried and are called pasilla. They are used to add an spicy earthiness and darken the color of soups, stews, and moles.

• **WHEN SHOPPING,** look for dried chiles that are soft, pliable, and deeply colored (brick red, mahogany, or black). They should be fragrant and should feel like a raisin or prune—firm but fleshy. If you find chiles that are dry, dusty, or brittle, they are probably old and will have little flavor (just like a bottle of old, discolored/muted-colored paprika or cayenne—which are both chile powders made from dried chiles). Leave that store immediately and buy your chiles elsewhere (or order them online).

• **STORE YOUR DRIED CHILES** in an airtight container or resealable plastic bag, or extend them further by freezing them in airtight containers or freezer bags. Just be sure to let the chiles come to room temperature before using— this takes about 1 hour.

• **FRESH CHILES** should be bright, firm, and crisp (think bell peppers). If they sit too long on the market shelf, they'll start to get soft, wrinkle, and discolor. Keep in mind, when making your selections, that green chiles are not fully ripened and thus lack the complexity and depth of red chiles. They'll taste grassy, herbaceous, and less sweet than red chiles; the difference in flavor being similar to that of a green tomato versus a vine-ripened red one. For that reason, I find that a green salsa that is fresh and bright pairs nicely with red chorizos or guisos.

HOW TO PREP CHILES

Most of the recipes in this book will specify what type of chile to use and how to treat or prep it, but here are some general guidelines.

• **SEEDS** When it comes to seeds, those in larger chiles tend to be harder, woodier, and more tannic, and should be removed before using the chile. The seeds in smaller chiles are smaller, softer, less woody, and can easily be chopped fine or pureed into a smooth sauce.

• **SKIN** Many larger chiles also have very tough skin. The skin on a dried chile can be easily pureed into sauces, but when fresh, chiles are often roasted both to enhance flavor and to allow for easy removal of the skin.

• **GROUND CHILE POWDER** If you have difficulty finding the dried version of a chile, you can substitute the powdered equivalent—ancho powder, chipotle powder, etc. Check the ingredient label to ensure that the powder is pure dried chile and doesn't have added salt, spices, or other chiles. As a rule of thumb, use 1 tablespoon of powder per whole chile, adding more as necessary. For hotter chiles, such as chipotle, use 1 teaspoon per whole chile. And remember that the color of the chile powder should always be bright and vibrant—not dull.

HOW TO USE DRIED CHILES

TYPE	COLOR	HEAT	FLAVOR	USES
Chile Ancho	Mahogany red	Mild to medium	Sweet, jammy, raisin-prune flavor and texture	Salsas, guisos, moles, jams, stuffed with a filling
Chile Pasilla	Black	Mild to medium	Dried currant, earthy	Salsas, guisos, moles, jams
Chile Guajillo	Brick red	Mild to medium	Slightly acidic, earthy, dried tomato	Salsas, guisos, moles, stuffed with a filling, jams
Chile Chipotle	Dark reddish brown to reddish black	Hot	Smoky, chocolaty, slightly nutty	Salsas, guisos, moles, stuffed, jam, pickled
Chile de Árbol	Bright red	Extremely hot	Slightly acidic, nutty	Salsas, guisos, moles (toasted, fried, or ground)
Chile Cascabel	Reddish brown to black	Hot	Nutty, woodsy, slightly smoky	Salsas, guisos, moles (coarsely and finely ground)

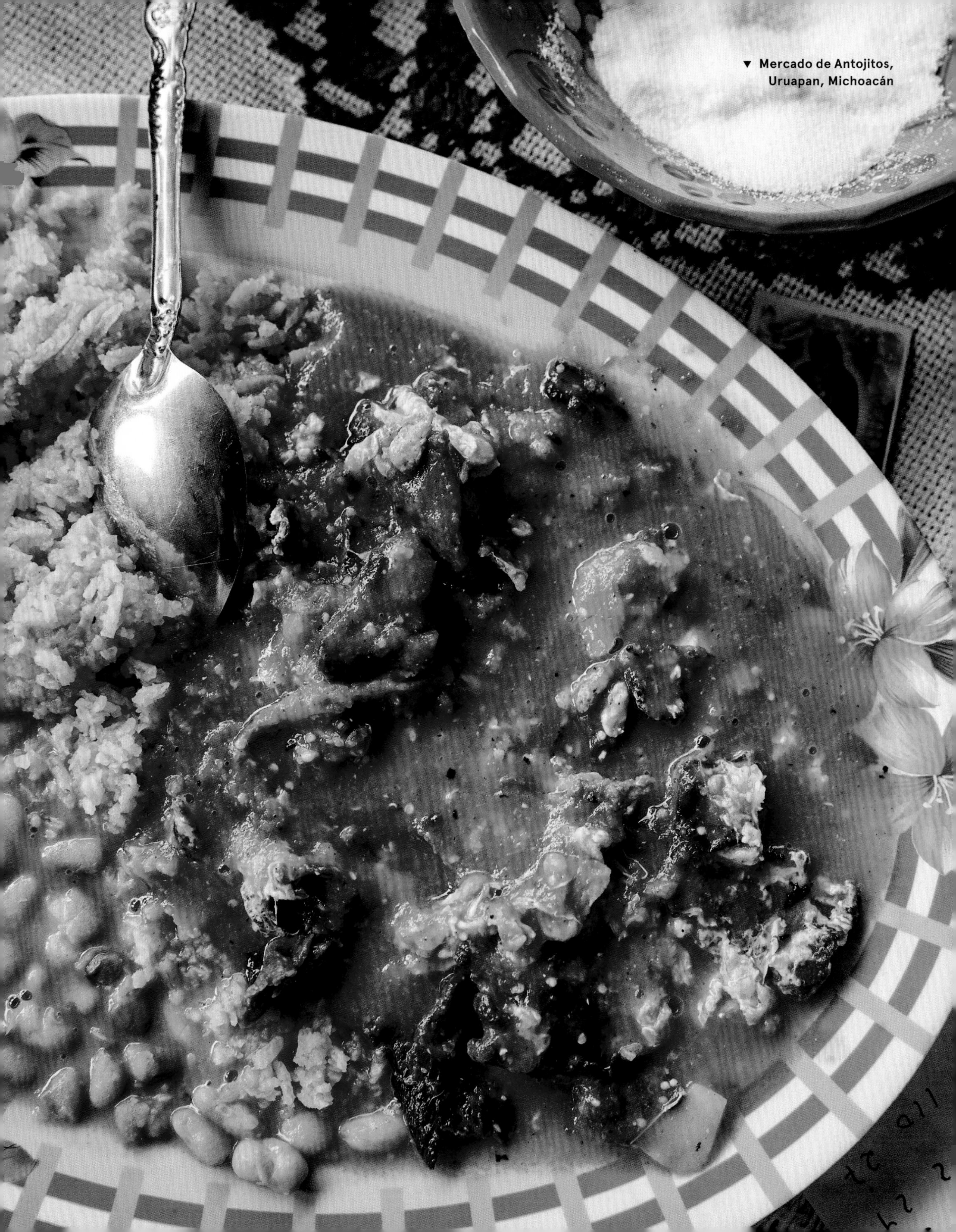

▼ Mercado de Antojitos,
Uruapan, Michoacán

Corn and Wheat

→ Growing up, I did not like corn tortillas. But to be fair, we only ever ate store-bought corn tortillas, and they were awful. The problem is that the corn used to make tortillas is highly perishable and only lasts about 12 hours without refrigeration before it starts to develop off-flavors and odors. To compensate, tortilla manufacturers add preservatives to the masa (dough made from ground, dried corn kernels) to stabilize it and lengthen the shelf life. You might have noticed that most corn tortillas are not refrigerated and seemingly last forever on that grocery store shelf. It is true that they will not spoil for weeks or months with all of those additives. The downside is all the additives and the sour flavor and odor they give the tortillas. Another downside is that they start to dry out, get brittle, and crack.

That said, 90 percent of the corn tortillas I have consumed in the US I bought from that sad grocery store shelf. My culinary hack for reviving them is to get a hard toast or char on them by cooking them directly on the grates of your stove or grill or over high heat on a comal or skillet. The charring or toasted spots will counter that sour-preservative taste. Or if you really want to transform a prefabricated corn tortilla, fry it (see fried Tostadas de Maíz, p. 40)! After they are fried they start to taste like corn again, and even better, toasted corn.

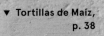

▼ Tortillas de Maíz,
p. 38

Tortillas de Maíz

Corn flatbread made from ground corn

I was in my early twenties when I finally tasted a real corn tortilla made with fresh corn masa. Before that moment, I thought of corn tortillas as mere delivery vehicles for taco fillings. And then I took a bite of a taco made with a good tortilla and I understood. The tortillas had an almost custardy mouthfeel on the inside with a toasted exterior that contributed to the different textures of a taco. And the flavor of the corn was earthy and nutty and was balanced out by the acidity of the salsa. Imagine you had only ever eaten sliced, white sandwich bread your entire life and then were introduced to a sourdough boule. Find fresh masa and make these tortillas and you will be amazed how much better your food is with the flavor of freshly ground corn in every bite.

You can source fresh masa at Mexican grocery stores or at tortillerias (tortilla bakeries).

MAKES 12 TORTILLAS

- 1½ pounds (680 g) fresh yellow, blue, pink, or white fine-grind corn masa for tortillas
- ¾ teaspoon Morton kosher salt (0.14 oz/4 g)

SPECIAL EQUIPMENT
- → 1-gallon zip-top freezer bag
- → Tortilla press, a smooth-bottomed 10-inch skillet, or a glass pie plate

1. In a large bowl, knead the masa, salt, and ⅓ cup water with your hands until well incorporated and the mixture is soft and pliable but doesn't stick to your hands, for about 4 minutes. If it's still dry or crumbly or sticks to your hands, add a tablespoon or two more water and continue to mix. Cover the bowl with plastic and let the masa sit for 30 minutes to rest.

2. Cut and remove the zip-top from a 1-gallon freezer bag. Cut two opposite sides of the bag, leaving the bottom intact so that the bag can open and close like a book. If you're using a tortilla press, trim the cut sides of the bag to fit the flat surface of the press.

3. Divide the dough into 12 portions the size of Ping-Pong balls (about ¼ cup or 54 g each). Arrange on a sheet pan and keep covered with a damp kitchen towel while you press and cook the tortillas.

4. Heat a comal, medium cast-iron skillet, or griddle over medium-high heat (you'll cook the tortillas one at a time unless you have a large cast-iron skillet or griddle). Place the prepared plastic bag inside the press so that the folded side of the bag is on the hinged side of the press. Working with one dough ball at a time, open the press and bag and place one ball in the center. Fold the bag over and gently press, holding steady, firm pressure for a few seconds, and flatten the dough to a 7-inch round. Open the press and remove the plastic with the dough pressed inside. Peel one side of the bag from the dough. Place the dough on your open palm so it is plastic-side up, and peel off the second side.

5. Cook the tortillas one at a time (unless you're using a large griddle), flipping it every 30 seconds. You'll flip it two times, cooking each tortilla until it just starts to brown in spots, for about 90 seconds total. Stack and wrap the cooked tortillas in a clean kitchen towel to keep them warm. Repeat with the remaining dough balls and serve warm.

DO AHEAD: The tortillas can be made 3 days ahead. Wrap tightly in plastic wrap. Reheat in a medium cast-iron skillet or griddle over medium heat until heated through, for about 60 seconds per side.

Tortillas de Harina de Maíz

Corn flatbread made from instant corn flour

If you can't find fresh masa, the next, most flavorful way to make and enjoy corn tortillas is with instant corn masa flour called harina de maíz (corn flour) in México and masa harina (dough flour) in the US. Harina de maíz is made from the same fresh corn masa used to make tortillas, but is dehydrated and ground into a powder. All you have to do is add water to rehydrate the corn and press into tortillas or whatever shape you want. This harina de maíz can be used to make anything that fresh masa can be used to make. For recipes that call for 1 pound of fresh masa, substitute 2 cups of harina de maíz mixed with 1½ cups of water; that will yield a little over 1 pound of masa. The most common brands you will find at most grocery stores are Bob's Red Mill and Maseca. I prefer Bob's Red Mill Masa Harina (golden corn) and Maseca Harina de Maíz Azul (blue corn). I think that these two harinas have the best flavor and very rich beautiful colors. I am not a fan of maíz blanco (white corn) in either fresh or dry/instant form. It has the least amount of flavor and it, obviously, doesn't have a rich color. Unfortunately for me, in Mazatlán, maíz blanco is the most common fresh and dry/instant masa available, so it is what I most often use to make my tortillas—if I don't have fresh masa.

MAKES 12 TORTILLAS

2 cups harina de maíz, such as Bob's Red Mill Masa Harina (7.05 oz/200 g)
¾ teaspoon Morton kosher salt (0.14 oz/4 g)

SPECIAL EQUIPMENT
→ 1-gallon zip-top freezer bag
→ Tortilla press or a smooth bottomed 10-inch skillet

1. In a large bowl, mix the masa flour, salt, and 1½ cups warm water with your hands until well incorporated and the mixture is soft and pliable but doesn't stick to your hands, for about 4 minutes. If the mixture is still dry or crumbly, add a tablespoon or two more water and continue to mix.

2. Cut and remove the zip-top from a 1-gallon freezer bag. Cut two opposite sides of the bag, leaving the bottom intact so that the bag can open and close like a book. If you're using a tortilla press, trim the cut sides of the bag to fit the flat surface of the press.

3. Divide the dough into 12 portions the size of Ping-Pong balls (about ¼ cup or 54 g each). Arrange on a sheet pan and keep covered with a damp kitchen towel while you press and cook the tortillas.

4. Heat a comal, medium cast-iron skillet, or griddle over medium-high heat (you'll cook the tortillas one at a time unless you have a large cast-iron skillet or griddle). Place the prepared plastic bag inside the press so that the folded side of the bag is on the hinged side of the press. Working with one dough ball at a time, open the press and bag and place one ball in the center. Fold the bag over and gently press, holding steady, firm pressure for a few seconds, and flatten the dough to a 7-inch round. Open the press and remove the plastic with the dough pressed inside. Peel one side of the bag from the dough. Place the dough on your open palm so it is plastic-side-up, and peel off the second side.

5. Cook the tortillas one at a time (unless you're using a large griddle), flipping it every 30 seconds. You'll flip it two times, cooking each tortilla until it just starts to brown in spots, for about 90 seconds total. Stack and wrap the cooked tortillas in a clean kitchen towel to keep them warm. Repeat with the remaining dough balls and serve warm.

DO AHEAD: The tortillas can be made 3 days ahead. Wrap tightly in plastic wrap. Reheat in a medium cast-iron skillet or griddle over medium heat until heated through, for about 60 seconds per side.

Tostadas de Maíz

Crispy corn flatbread

Frying tortillas is the best way to revive flavorless or old, stale tortillas. The hot oil makes the tortillas shatteringly crisp and gives them a deep golden color, even when you use tortillas de maíz blanco (white corn), and brings out the sweet and toasty nuttiness in the corn. I use fried tostadas whenever I am layering any wet fillings on top of them like frijoles refritos or a guiso (braised meat or vegetable). The fried tostadas will stay crispy and won't fall apart on you as quickly as baked tostada will.

I normally eat baked tostadas when I'm eating soup or stew—like how you'd eat crackers with soup. They provide a nice crunchy texture, and the toasty parts give you a slightly bitter and nutty counterpoint to your soup. To "bake" them, I usually use a large comal set on low heat on the stove. That's the way it is done here in México. But it takes a while, and you have to keep flipping and moving them from a cooler area to a warmer area to make sure they toast evenly. But most people don't have a large comal at home or even a large griddle, so here's a truly baked version that calls on the oven to do the work. This method is much faster and easier.

MAKES 6 FRIED TOSTADAS

- 1 cup vegetable oil
- 6 6-inch corn tortillas
  Morton kosher salt

1. In a small skillet set over high heat, heat the oil until it bubbles immediately when the edge of a tortilla touches the surface. Working with one tortilla at a time, fry the tortilla, turning once, until it's crispy, puffed in places, and deep golden brown, for about 1 minute per side.

2. Transfer the tostada to a sheet pan lined with paper towels to drain and season with salt while hot. Repeat with the remaining tortillas. Serve warm.

MAKES 6 BAKED TOSTADAS

- 6 6-inch corn tortillas
- 2 tablespoons vegetable oil
  Morton kosher salt

1. Arrange a rack in the center of the oven and preheat to 450°F.

2. Brush both sides of the tortillas with the oil. Season with salt and arrange on a sheet pan. Bake the tortillas until they're golden brown in spots and crisp, for about 10 minutes. Let cool before serving.

▲ Gorditas de Maíz filled with Frijoles Refritos, p. 55 and Morisqueta Michoacana, p. 80

Gorditas de Maíz

Stuffed corn flatbread

Gorditas are incredibly delicious, and I have eaten them for breakfast in almost every state in México. They are made from the same corn masa used for tortillas, but they are thicker than a normal tortilla and are split and stuffed with a variety of fillings, similar to a pita or arepa. The word "gordita" is used to describe something that is fat, and they are fatter than a normal tortilla: Depending on what part of the country you are in, they range from about ¼ inch thick to over an inch! Split them open after cooking and then fill them with just about anything you like to eat, from guisos to moles and almost any taco filling (about 90 percent of the recipes in the regional chapters would make amazing fillings in a gordita).

Griddled Gorditas

Alternatively, you can cook the gorditas without frying them. Heat a large cast-iron skillet or griddle over medium heat and cook the gordita until the center slightly puffs up and the gordita is browned in spots, for 3 to 4 minutes per side. Repeat with the remaining gorditas. Follow the instructions at right to create the pocket and stuff; serve warm.

MAKES 8 GORDITAS

1¾ pounds (794 g) fresh yellow, blue, pink, or white fine-grind corn masa for tortillas
2 tablespoons rendered lard or vegetable oil
1¼ teaspoons Morton kosher salt (0.28 oz/8 g)

IF USING INSTANT MASA
2⅔ cups harina de maíz, such as Bob's Red Mill Masa Harina (10.6 oz/300 g)
2 tablespoons rendered lard or vegetable oil
1¼ teaspoons Morton kosher salt (0.28 oz/8 g)

FOR THE GORDITAS
1 cup rendered lard
4 cups of the filling of your choice (about half a cup per gordita)

1. IF USING FRESH MASA: In a large bowl, knead the fresh masa, lard, salt, and ⅓ cup warm water until well incorporated and the mixture is soft and pliable but doesn't stick to your hands, for about 4 minutes. If the mixture is dry, crumbly, or sticks to your hands, add a tablespoon or two of water and continue to mix. Cover and let sit for 30 minutes to rest.

IF USING INSTANT MASA: In a large bowl, stir the instant masa, lard, salt, and 2 cups warm water until a soft and slightly sticky dough forms. If the dough seems dry, add another tablespoon or two of water and continue to mix. Cover the bowl with plastic wrap and let sit for at least 30 minutes and up to 3 hours.

2. FORMING AND COOKING THE GORDITAS: Divide the dough into 8 balls (about 98 g each), keeping them covered with a damp towel. Cut the sides of a small resealable plastic bag (or use a long sheet of parchment or wax paper) so that it opens up like a book. Place a ball on one side of the open bag, then fold the other side over to cover. Using a tortilla press or small skillet, gently press down on the ball to flatten into a 5-inch disk—about ¼ inch thick. Carefully peel open the plastic and transfer the disk to a parchment-lined baking sheet.

3. In a small skillet over medium, heat the lard for 2 minutes. Working with one at a time, fry a gordita, spooning the hot oil over the top, until it inflates and puffs out like a balloon, for 2 to 3 minutes. Flip and continue to cook, spooning the hot oil over top, until crispy and golden brown, for another 2 minutes. Transfer to a sheet pan lined with paper towels to drain and let sit for 10 minutes.

4. Insert a sharp paring knife into the edge of the warm gordita. Cut a pocket into the gordita leaving it intact on the other side to prevent the filling from leaking out. Repeat with the remaining gorditas. Stuff the gorditas and serve warm.

Pan Árabe

**Yeasted wheat
flour flatbread**

*Pan árabe is usually served
with Tacos Árabes (p. 93),
but any dish or taco you
would use a flour tortilla
with is a candidate for pan
árabe. It is similar in flavor
and texture to a pita but
thinner. I like retarding the
dough in the refrigerator for
at least 24 hours to develop
more depth of flavor and a
subtle tang, but if you have
the time, take it longer—
after 36 hours the dough
will develop a sourdough-
like texture and flavor that I
love. For full-on sourdough
flavor, let the dough
ferment for 3 days in
the refrigerator.*

MAKES 12 FLATBREADS

4 cups all-purpose flour
   (17.6 oz/500 g)
2 tablespoons extra-virgin olive oil,
   plus more for the bowl

1 envelope (0.25 oz/7 g) active dry
   yeast (about 2¼ teaspoons)
1¼ teaspoons Morton kosher salt
   (0.28 oz/8 g)

1. In the bowl of a stand mixer, combine the flour, oil, yeast, salt, and 1 cup
plus 2 tablespoons of warm water. (There's no need to proof the yeast unless
you worry that it's too old and want to test it.) Using the dough hook, mix on
medium-low speed for about 1 minute, or until the dough comes together but is
still slightly shaggy. Increase the speed to medium and knead until the dough is
smooth, elastic, and pulls away from the sides of the bowl, for about 10 minutes.

2. Lightly oil a large bowl. Scrape the dough into the bowl. Cover the bowl with
plastic wrap and let the dough rise in a warm, draft-free area until doubled in
volume, for 60 to 90 minutes. The visual cue is more important here than the
time. How long your dough takes to proof will depend on how warm your kitchen
is. You don't want to overproof the dough, so check it at 45 minutes. The finished
dough will smell grassy (from the olive oil) and yeasty and will have doubled in
size. If it isn't there, check every 15 minutes until it's ready.

3. Gently deflate the dough by lifting it up around the edges and letting it fall
back into the bowl, turning the bowl and repeating if needed. Cover the bowl
tightly with plastic wrap and refrigerate for at least 12 hours and up to 3 days
(making the dough in the evening and resting it overnight works great). Letting
the dough rise in the fridge for a longer period of time will produce a dough with
the best flavor, like a sourdough, but if you don't have the time, don't worry and
move on to the next step.

4. Remove the dough from the refrigerator. Gently deflate it and then knead it to
loosen and slightly warm it up. Divide the dough (it should weigh about 777 g) into
12 balls (about 64 g each). Working with one ball at a time, keeping the remaining
ones covered with a kitchen towel, roll out on a clean surface to 7-inch rounds.

5. Heat a comal, griddle, or a large cast-iron skillet over medium heat. Working
with one at a time, cook the pan árabe until browned in spots and air bubbles
form on the surface, for about 1 minute. Flip and cook on the second side until
browned, for about 1 minute (reduce the heat if it gets dark too quickly). Stack and
wrap in a kitchen towel as you go to keep warm. Repeat with the remaining dough.

6. Serve warm. Wrap any leftover pan árabe tightly in plastic and refrigerate.
Reheat on a comal, cast-iron skillet, or griddle until soft and warm.

FROM TOP LEFT:
Tortillas de Harina
con Mantequilla,
p. 46, Tortillas de
Harina estilo
Sinaloa, p. 47,
and Pan Árabe,
opposite

Tortillas de Harina con Mantequilla

Wheat flour flatbread made with butter

I love all tortillas, but tortillas de harina have a special place in my heart. My family is from Monterrey and Torreón in the north of México, where flour tortillas are more common than corn tortillas; the climate and geography of the northern states is more suitable for growing wheat than corn. When I was little, my mom would make flour tortillas from scratch, but by the 1980s, packaged flour tortillas were becoming more common. My mom started buying them and would only make homemade ones on special occasions. When I visited home from college, she always asked me what I wanted her to make. I always said chile colorado and flour tortillas. I remember opening the door to hear her rolling pin clicking on the granite countertop. I'd walk in and she'd greet me with a long hug, a kiss, and a warm tortilla.

To get a lighter and softer tortilla, I added a little baking powder for additional lift and some milk to tenderize the dough. And I swapped in butter for lard or shortening, which is more traditional, because I love butter and because butter is used in flour tortillas in communities with large dairy farms. But you can substitute vegetable shortening or lard if you prefer.

MAKES 16 TORTILLAS

- 1 cup plus 1 tablespoon whole milk
- 1 teaspoon Morton kosher salt (0.21 oz/6 g)
- 5 tablespoons unsalted butter (2.5 oz/70 g) or shortening
- 3 cups all-purpose flour (13.2 oz/375 g), plus more for dusting
- 2 teaspoons baking powder

1. In a small saucepan over medium heat, warm the milk and salt until tiny bubbles start to form around the edges of the pan (the milk should be 180°F), for 4 to 5 minutes. Immediately remove the pot from the heat and stir in the butter until it melts. Let cool for 15 minutes.

2. Meanwhile, in a large bowl, whisk the flour and baking powder until combined.

3. Pour in the warm milk mixture and stir using a rubber spatula until a shaggy dough forms. When cool enough to handle, knead the dough in the bowl until smooth, for about 3 minutes. The dough should be soft and only very slightly elastic but not sticky. Wrap the dough in plastic and let it rest at room temperature for 1 hour to relax the dough.

4. Divide the dough into 16 portions the size of Ping-Pong balls (about a scant 3 tablespoons or 46 g each). Arrange on a sheet pan and keep covered with a damp kitchen towel until ready to use. Working with one dough ball at a time, roll out on a lightly floured surface to a 7-inch round.

5. Heat a comal, medium cast-iron skillet, or griddle over medium-high heat. Cook the tortillas one at a time (unless you're using a large griddle), reducing the heat if they get dark too quickly, or until air bubbles form on the surface and there are brown spots on the bottom, for about 30 seconds. Poke any large bubbles with a fork to release the steam. Flip the tortillas and continue to cook until there are brown spots on the bottom of the second side, for about 30 seconds. Remove from the skillet and set in the center of a kitchen towel, wrapping it to keep warm. Repeat with the remaining dough balls, continuing to stack the tortillas as they finish cooking.

6. Serve warm. Wrap any leftover tortillas tightly in plastic and refrigerate. Reheat on a comal, cast-iron skillet, or griddle until soft and warm.

Tortillas de Harina estilo Sinaloa

Sinaloan-style wheat flour flatbread

Here in Sinaloa, the tortillas de harina are much thinner than the ones that I grew up with. They aren't quite as thin as the ones made in Sonora, where the dough is rolled, pressed, or stretched until paper thin and almost transparent. The tortilla sobaquera from the Northern Sonora can be up to 24 inches in diameter! It is used to make burros percherones—large burritos filled with carne a la plancha (griddled steak), avocado, tomato, onion, and queso Chihuahua.

I love thin Sonoran-style tortillas, but they typically have a higher fat to flour and water ratio than the thicker-style tortillas. They also require a little more work to get them that thin. In fact, many tortillerias use heated, electric presses to melt the fat and relax the gluten in the flour. In Sinaloa, the tortillas are about a millimeter or two thicker and use less fat, and that is what this recipe is based on. To be clear, I have no problems with fat and generally love more of it, but I like tortillas, both corn and wheat, with a little more heft and thickness. I find that they stand up to braised and saucy dishes much better than their thinner cousins. And if they are made well, they will have a nice, unleavened, toasted bread flavor.

MAKES 8 TORTILLAS

¾ teaspoon Morton kosher salt (0.14 oz/4 g)
½ cup (2 oz/60 g) hot water
Scant ¼ cup vegetable shortening or rendered lard (1.76 oz/50 g)

2 cups all-purpose flour (8.8 oz/250 g), plus more for the surface

1. In a small bowl, stir the salt in the hot water until it's dissolved.

2. In a medium bowl, toss the shortening into the flour and smash them together, squeezing in between your fingers and palms, until completely incorporated, no clumps of shortening remain, and the flour resembles damp sand.

3. Pour in the hot salted water and mix with your hands until a shaggy dough forms. Turn the dough out onto a lightly floured work surface and knead until the dough is smooth and elastic, for about 5 minutes. Wrap the dough in plastic and let it rest at room temperature for 30 minutes to relax the dough.

4. Divide the dough into 8 balls (about 50 g each) and place them on a sheet pan covered with a kitchen towel to prevent them from drying out. Working with one at a time and keeping the remaining balls covered with a kitchen towel, roll out on a clean surface to 8-inch rounds.

5. We are going to cook the tortilla in two stages. In the first stage, we will quickly cook the outside, but the inside will still be raw. In the second stage, the tortilla will puff out like a balloon as the water turns to steam, and that's how we know that it's cooked all the way through.

6. Heat a comal, large cast-iron skillet, or griddle over medium heat. Working one at a time, cook a tortilla until you see a few light brown spots, for 15 seconds; flip over and repeat. Flip again and continue to cook until the tortilla puffs and has golden brown spots, for about 45 seconds (reduce the heat if the tortilla gets dark too quickly). Flip one last time and cook until you see golden-brown spots, for 30 to 40 seconds more. Stack and wrap the tortillas in a kitchen towel as you go. This will keep them warm. Repeat with the remaining dough balls.

7. Serve warm. Wrap any leftover tortillas tightly in plastic and refrigerate. Reheat on a comal, cast-iron skillet, or griddle until soft and warm.

FROM TOP TO BOTTOM:
Arroz Verde, p. 51,
Arroz Rojo, opposite,
and Arroz Blanco con
Mantequilla, p. 50

Arroz Rojo

Toasted rice with tomato, carrots, and serrano

Compared to all the arroz that I have eaten across México, I still firmly believe that my tía Lorena made the best arroz rojo. When I was little I watched her make it, and she told me the secret was her pot. She had been using that same cast-aluminum Dutch oven to make arroz for fifty years. No one in our family made rice like she did. Whenever there was a family gathering, she always brought the rice.

I think her secret was that she toasted her rice in that pot, dry and unrinsed, until it was really browned. She told me that when you make rice, you are going to want to stop toasting because the pan will be smoking and you will think the rice is burning. "It's not," she would say. "Keep going." And so that is what I do and that is what you should do to coax a deep toasted and nutty flavor out of ordinary grocery store long-grain rice.

2 cups long-grain white rice (7 oz/200 g)

¼ cup rendered lard, bacon fat, or vegetable oil

½ medium white onion (5.4 oz/154 g), chopped

2 medium carrots (6.2 oz/175 g), finely chopped

3 garlic cloves, finely grated

2 teaspoons Morton kosher salt (0.56 oz/16 g)

¼ cup tomato paste

3 cups homemade chicken stock or store-bought low-sodium chicken broth

⅓ cup frozen green peas (1.97 oz/56 g), thawed

1 chile serrano (0.85 oz/24.3 g), halved lengthwise

1. Heat a large skillet over high heat. Cook the dry, unwashed rice, stirring constantly, until toasted and very brown and nutty smelling, for about 8 minutes. Transfer the rice to a heatproof bowl and set aside.

2. Meanwhile, in a large saucepan over medium heat, heat the lard. Add the onion, carrots, garlic, and salt and cook, stirring occasionally, until tender and just beginning to brown, for 6 to 8 minutes. Add the tomato paste and cook, stirring and scraping, until fragrant and it deepens to a brick red color, for about 1 minute. Add the stock and bring to a boil.

3. Stir in the rice and add the peas and chile serrano. Reduce the heat to low, cover, and cook, undisturbed, for 20 minutes. Quickly peek to see if all of the liquid has been absorbed; if not, replace the lid, continue to cook, and check again in 10 minutes. Once the liquid is absorbed, remove the pot from the heat and let sit, covered, for 20 minutes before fluffing with a fork to separate the grains. Serve warm.

Arroz Blanco con Mantequilla

Buttery rice with poblano, carrots, and corn

There are a few recipes in this book that have become my "go-to" and this is definitely one of them. It was very unexpected, too, because I love Arroz Rojo (p. 49) and eat it exclusively with all Mexican food. Or, rather, I used to. But this rice—slightly sweet from the carrots and onions and almost creamy thanks to the starchiness of the rice combined with the richness and incredible flavor of the butter—hit me hard and has stayed with me. I was in Durango and found an amazing restaurant that served regional dishes from around the state. One of the many things that I ate on my multiple visits were the enchiladas dulces, an iconic dish from Durango made with chile guajillo chocolate and piloncillo (dark brown sugar). Now, the enchiladas were good—a bit too sweet, even for me—but the star of that plate was the rice that accompanied them. I was blown away, and it was the butter that did it. Butter is not a commonly used ingredient in most of the country, but it is used in the dairy-rich regions of the northern states. Arroz blanco has since become my favorite Mexican rice.

SERVES 4

- 4 tablespoons unsalted butter (2 oz/57 g)
- ½ medium white onion (5.4 oz/154 g), chopped
- 2 medium carrots (6.1 oz/175 g), finely chopped
- 1 medium chile poblano (4 oz/125 g), stemmed, seeded, and finely chopped
- 1 cup fresh corn kernels (5.7 oz/164 g)
- 1 garlic clove, finely grated
- 2 teaspoons Morton kosher salt (0.56 oz/16 g)
- 2 cups long-grain white rice (7 oz/200 g)
- 3 cups homemade chicken stock or low-sodium chicken broth

1. In a large saucepan over medium heat, melt the butter. Add the onion, carrots, chile poblano, corn, garlic, and salt and cook, stirring occasionally, until tender and just beginning to brown, for 8 to 10 minutes.

2. Add the rice, stir to coat in the butter, and cook until the rice is opaque, for 4 minutes. Add the stock, stir to combine, and bring to a boil. Reduce the heat to low, cover, and cook undisturbed for 20 minutes. Quickly check to see if all of the liquid has been absorbed; if not, continue to cook and check again in 10 minutes. If the liquid has been absorbed, remove the pot from the heat and let sit, covered, for 10 minutes before fluffing with a fork to separate the grains and serving.

Arroz Verde

Herbed rice with scallion and cilantro

This rice is so beautiful and flavorful and, best of all, really easy. You are basically making a green blender broth to cook the rice and infuse it with flavor and color. You can substitute another leafy green herb in the same amount if you are not into cilantro.

SERVES 4

1 medium chile poblano (4.4 oz/ 127 g), stemmed, seeded, and coarsely chopped

1 large scallion (0.84 oz/24 g), root end trimmed, and coarsely chopped

1 garlic clove, peeled

2 teaspoons Morton kosher salt (0.56 oz/16 g)

1 cup (packed) fresh cilantro leaves and tender stems (4.3 oz/120 g), divided

2 tablespoons vegetable oil

2 cups long-grain white rice (7 oz/200 g)

1. In a blender, purée the chile poblano, scallion, garlic, salt, half of the cilantro, and 2½ cups water until smooth. Set aside until ready to use.

2. In a large saucepan over medium-high heat, heat the oil. Add the rice and cook, stirring occasionally, until opaque but not browning, for about 5 minutes. Stir in the cilantro mixture and bring to a boil. Cover the pot and reduce the heat to low. Cook until all of the water has been absorbed, for 20 to 25 minutes. Remove from the heat and let sit, covered, for 10 minutes.

3. Meanwhile, finely chop the remaining cilantro. Fluff the rice with two forks. Toss the chopped cilantro into the rice before serving.

FROM LEFT TO RIGHT:
Frijoles de Olla, p. 54,
and Frijoles Refritos,
p. 55

Frijoles de Olla

Simple beans with scallions and herbs

I do not soak beans. I have experimented with different soaking methods and different beans, and when you soak beans in water, guess what they taste like—water. My preferred method is to cook them from dry in a simple flavorful liquid over a low flame until they are tender. This method takes only slightly longer than soaked beans, about 1 hour longer depending on the age of your beans (older beans will take longer to cook even if you soak them). I also find that the broth is addictively delicious when you cook from dry. A longer cook time means greater flavor development and a richer broth.

If you can find avocado leaves (fresh or dried), I highly recommend trying them. They have a spicy cinnamon-allspice-citrus flavor that completely changes the way you will think of a pot of beans. They are commonly used in the southern part of México, where avocados are grown.

MAKES ABOUT 12 CUPS

- 1 pound (453 g) dried beans, such as black, pinto, cannellini, or kidney, rinsed and picked through
- 3 medium scallions (2.3 oz/67 g), roots trimmed, or ¼ medium onion
- 3 garlic cloves, lightly crushed
- 2 avocado or bay leaves, dried or fresh
- 3 fresh epazote sprigs or a combination of parsley, oregano, and/or mint sprigs
- 1 tablespoon plus ½ teaspoon Morton kosher salt (0.59 oz/ 17 g), plus more to taste

1. In a large pot, combine the beans, scallions, garlic, avocado leaves, epazote, salt, and 16 cups water and bring to a boil. Reduce the heat to medium-low and cook at a slow simmer, uncovered, skimming and stirring occasionally, and checking the beans every hour to see if they need more water (you want the beans to always be covered by water), until the beans are tender, for 2½ to 3½ hours. The cooking time will depend on how old the beans are; freshly dried beans might be fully cooked in as little as 1½ hours.

2. Remove and discard the scallions, garlic, and herbs. Taste and season the beans with more salt if desired.

DO AHEAD: The beans can be refrigerated for up to 2 days. Or, make them up to 3 months ahead and freeze in an airtight container.

Frijoles Refritos

Porky
refried beans

I grew up with my dad's amazing refried pinto beans. He had (and still has) a crock next to the stove where he would collect bacon fat and save it for the beans. I am convinced that the older he gets, the better his beans have become. I have a feeling it's because he uses a little more bacon fat each year, and I am not mad at that. (Note that in México, bacon is not that common and lard is the fat that is used most.) What is most important to the development of the beans' flavor is the frying. You need to start with a flavorful oil and it needs to be very hot before you add the beans and liquid. The heat will caramelize the sugars and brown the proteins in the beans. And the lard or bacon fat will add umami and richness. If you want a plant-based version, fry chopped onion and garlic in ½ cup of vegetable oil until deep golden brown, then use that oil with the vegetables to fry the beans.

MAKES 6 CUPS

½ cup rendered lard, bacon fat, or vegetable oil
6 cups (about ½ recipe) Frijoles de Olla, p. 54, and their liquid

1. In a large skillet, preferably cast-iron, over high heat, heat the lard. Add the beans and their liquid (they will splatter, so be careful) and fry until most of the liquid has evaporated, for about 10 minutes.

2. Smash the beans in the skillet with a potato masher until the mixture is thick and no whole beans remain (the refried beans should still be pourable at this point, but will thicken as they sit). Serve warm.

Salsas, Condiments, and Seasonings

→ Salsas are present in every taco stand, restaurant, and home kitchen in México. They add flavor, heat, and moisture to the dishes they are served with. I decided to put all of the salsas in the book in one place because I know that this will probably be the section of the book that you will use the most. I wanted to show the diversity of salsas that exist across the country. And there are so many more recipes that I wanted to include in this section, but I ran out of pages.

The ones that are here are incredibly delicious and really easy to make. I want you to try them all and I want you to personalize them with your favorite chiles, vegetables, fruits, and herbs. You will see as you go through them all that some are made with tomatoes and tomatillos, which are the most common. But there are also salsas that are cream-based and some that are oil-based. Some have fruit and some have nuts and seeds. Some are just made with water and chiles. I have included a wide range so that you can get comfortable with each style and then personalize to suit your taste or to the dish that you are planning to serve them with. The most important thing is to have fun and get creative!

CLOCKWISE FROM TOP LEFT: Salsa Blanca, p. 58, Chiles Habaneros Encurtidos, p. 58, Salsa Tatemada, p. 58, Cebolla Morada Encurtida, p. 59, Curtido, p. 59, Chiles Chipotles en Escabeche, p. 59, Salsa de Aguacate, p. 60, and Salsa de Papaya y Tomatillo Cruda, p. 60

Salsa Blanca

Serrano cream
with lime and cilantro

MAKES 1⅓ CUPS

1	oil-packed anchovy fillet
¼	teaspoon Morton kosher salt (0.07 oz/2 g), plus more to taste
¾	cup mayonnaise
¼	cup crema, crème fraiche, or sour cream
¼	cup finely chopped cilantro (0.7 oz/20 g)
2	chiles serranos (0.74 oz/21 g), stemmed and finely chopped
2	garlic cloves, finely grated
½	teaspoon finely grated lime zest
3	tablespoons fresh lime juice

1. Place the anchovy on a cutting board and sprinkle with the salt. Using the flat side of a knife, smash it until a paste forms. Scrape the mixture into a medium bowl.

2. Add the mayonnaise, crema, cilantro, chiles serranos, garlic, lime zest, and lime juice and whisk to combine. Season with salt to taste. Cover and refrigerate until ready to serve.

DO AHEAD: The salsa can be made up to 1 day ahead. Store in an airtight container in the refrigerator.

Chiles Habaneros Encurtidos

Charred pickled habaneros

MAKES 1½ CUPS

4	medium chiles habaneros (1.5 oz/43 g), stemmed, seeded, and halved
½	medium white onion (6.9 oz/ 196 g), thinly sliced
1	garlic clove, finely grated
½	teaspoon finely grated lemon zest
¼	cup fresh lemon juice (about 2 lemons)
½	teaspoon finely grated lime zest
¼	cup fresh lime juice (about 2 limes)
2	tablespoons extra-virgin olive oil
1	teaspoon sugar
¾	teaspoon Morton kosher salt (0.14 oz/4 g)
½	teaspoon dried oregano, preferably Mexican

1. Line a large cast-iron skillet with foil and heat over high until the pan is very hot, for about 2 minutes. Add the halved chiles habaneros and cook, turning occasionally, until charred on both sides, for 4 to 5 minutes. Transfer to a cutting board to cool.

2. When cool enough to handle, slice the chiles into thin strips and transfer to a medium bowl. Add the onion, garlic, lemon zest, lemon juice, lime zest, lime juice, oil, sugar, salt, and oregano and toss together. Let sit, uncovered, for 30 minutes for the flavors to develop.

DO AHEAD: The encurtido can be made up to 1 day ahead. Store in an airtight container in the refrigerator.

Salsa Tatemada

Charred tomato,
onion, and serrano

MAKES 3 CUPS

8	medium Roma tomatoes (2 lb/ 907 g), cored and left whole
½	medium white onion (6.31 oz/ 179 g), halved
2	chiles serranos (1.7 oz/48.6 g), stemmed
4	garlic cloves, unpeeled
¼	cup (packed) fresh cilantro leaves with tender stems (1.41 oz/40 g)
2	tablespoons fresh lime juice, or more to taste
¾	teaspoon Morton kosher salt (0.14 oz/4 g), or more to taste

1. Line a large cast-iron skillet with a sheet of foil and heat the skillet over high. Add the tomatoes, onion, chiles serranos, and garlic to the hot, foil-lined pan and cook, using tongs to turn occasionally, until everything is charred on all sides, for about 3 minutes for the garlic, 4 to 5 minutes for the chiles, 6 to 8 minutes for the onion, and 8 to 10 minutes for the tomatoes. Transfer to a plate to cool. Once cool enough to handle, peel the garlic.

2. Add the tomatoes, onion, chiles serranos, peeled garlic, cilantro, lime juice, and salt to a blender and puree on low speed, until the salsa is almost smooth but some small pieces remain. Taste and season with more salt and lime juice if desired.

DO AHEAD: The salsa can be made up to 2 days ahead. Store in an airtight container in the refrigerator, or freeze for up to 1 month.

Cebolla Morada Encurtida

Pickled red onions with habanero

MAKES 1 QUART

- 1 large red onion (12 oz/342 g), thinly sliced into rings
- 1¼ teaspoons Morton kosher salt (0.28 oz/8 g), divided
- 1 chile habanero (0.37 oz/10.7 g), stemmed, seeded, and halved
- 1 cup fresh orange juice (about 4 oranges)
- ½ cup fresh lime juice (about 4 limes)
- 6 allspice berries
- 1 teaspoon dried oregano, preferably Mexican

1. In a medium bowl, toss the onion and half of the salt until coated. Cover with hot water and stir to dissolve the salt. Let sit for 15 minutes.

2. Line a small skillet with foil to cover the bottom of the pan; heat over medium-high. Cook the chile skin side down, pressing down with a wooden spoon, until charred in spots, for 4 to 5 minutes (no need to char the flesh side). Transfer to a 1-quart glass jar or nonreactive container. If you like it extra spicy, chop the chile before adding to the jar.

3. Drain the onion, rinse with water, and add it to the jar. Add the orange and lime juices, allspice, oregano, and remaining salt. Cover and shake to combine. Chill for at least 3 hours before serving.

DO AHEAD: The encurtida can be made up to 1 week ahead.

Curtido

Lightly fermented cabbage with carrots, onion, and jalapeños

MAKES 2 QUARTS

- ½ large head green cabbage (23 oz/652 g), cored and thinly sliced
- 4 medium carrots (8.5 oz/244 g), cut into 3-inch-long sticks
- ½ medium white onion (6.9 oz/ 196 g), coarsely chopped
- 4 chiles jalapeños (4.4 oz/133 g), stemmed and quartered lengthwise
- 1 garlic clove, finely grated
- 3¾ teaspoons Morton kosher salt (0.7 oz/20 g)
- 2 teaspoons dried oregano, preferably Mexican
- 2 bay leaves
- 2 whole cloves

1. In a large bowl, toss together the cabbage, carrots, onion, jalapeños, garlic, salt, oregano, bay leaves, and cloves. Let sit for 30 minutes to wilt the cabbage.

2. Transfer to an airtight container (like a 2-quart mason jar) and press down firmly on the cabbage to release the juices; the liquid should be at or above the level of the vegetables. Fasten the lid and let sit at room temperature for at least 24 hours. The curtido will get tangier and funkier the longer it sits. I like it best after 4 days of fermentation. Refrigerate after 4 days.

Chiles Chipotles en Escabeche

Pickled chipotles with cinnamon and cloves

MAKES 1 QUART

- 30 dried chiles chipotles (2.89 oz/82 g)
- 1⅓ cups apple cider vinegar
- 4 garlic cloves, lightly crushed
- 2 fresh thyme sprigs
- 2 large bay leaves
- 4 whole cloves
- 1 3-inch stick canela or cassia cinnamon
- 2 teaspoons sugar
- 2 teaspoons Morton kosher salt (0.56 oz/16 g)
- 1 teaspoon dried oregano, preferably Mexican
- ½ teaspoon black peppercorns

1. In a medium saucepan, bring the chiles chipotles and 2 cups water to a boil over high heat. Remove from the heat, cover, and let sit for about 30 minutes to soften the chiles.

2. Strain and discard the liquid. Transfer the chiles chipotles to a jar and top with the vinegar, garlic, thyme, bay leaves, cloves, canela, sugar, salt, oregano, peppercorns, and 1⅓ cups water. Cover the jar and shake to combine and dissolve the sugar and salt. Set aside at room temperature for at least 24 hours and up to 4 days.

DO AHEAD: The escabeche can be made up to 1 week ahead. Store in an airtight container and refrigerate after 4 days.

Salsa de Aguacate

Avocado cream with serranos and jalapeños

MAKES 3 CUPS

- 2 medium avocados (12.6 oz/ 359 g), peeled and seeded
- 4 medium tomatillos (10.3 oz/ 294 g), husked, rinsed, and quartered
- 2 medium scallions (1.69 oz/48 g), coarsely chopped
- 1 to 2 chiles serranos (.4 oz/12 g each), stemmed and coarsely chopped
- 1 to 2 chiles jalapeños (1.1 oz/33.2 g each), stemmed and coarsely chopped
- 1 garlic clove, peeled
- 1¾ teaspoons Morton kosher salt (0.42 oz/12 g), plus more to taste

1. In a blender on medium-low speed, puree the avocados, tomatillos, scallions, chiles serranos, jalapeños, garlic, salt, and 1 cup water until smooth. Do not be tempted to blend above medium speed or your salsa will get airy and will have the texture of a smoothie. Taste and season with more salt if desired.

DO AHEAD: The salsa can be made 2 days ahead. Store in an airtight container in the refrigerator, or freeze for up to 1 month.

CLOCKWISE FROM TOP LEFT:
Salsa Macha, p. 60, Salsa de Chipotle y Chile Árbol, p. 62, Salsa de Chile de Árbol, p. 62, Salsa de Tomatillo, p. 62, Aceite de Habanero Quemado, p. 63, Salsa Chipotle, p. 63, Salsa de Zanahoria y Habanero, p. 63, and Chiles Jalapeños en Escabeche, p. 64

Salsa de Papaya y Tomatillo Cruda

Papaya and tomatillos with habanero, orange juice, and mint

MAKES 2 CUPS

- 3 medium tomatillos (8 oz/226 g), husked, rinsed, and cut into ¼-inch pieces
- ¼ firm-ripe papaya (8 oz/226 g), peeled, seeded and cut into ¼-inch pieces
- ¼ medium white onion (3.5 oz/ 98 g), coarsely chopped
- 3 chiles serranos (2.5 oz/72 g), stemmed and finely chopped
- 3 garlic cloves, finely grated
- 6 tablespoons fresh lime juice (3 to 4 limes)
- 3 tablespoons finely chopped fresh mint
  Morton kosher salt

1. In a medium bowl, toss the tomatillos, papaya, onion, chiles serranos, garlic, lime juice, and mint to combine. Season with salt to taste. Cover the bowl with plastic and refrigerate for 1 hour to allow the flavors to come together. Serve chilled or at room temperature.

DO AHEAD: The salsa cruda can be made up to 1 day ahead. Store in an airtight container in the refrigerator.

Salsa Macha

Oil-roasted cashews, garlic, and chiles anchos

MAKES 2 CUPS

- 1½ cups vegetable oil
- 5 garlic cloves, peeled
- ¾ cup raw cashews (4 oz/115 g)
- 5 large chiles anchos (2.7 oz/78 g), stemmed and seeded
- 7 large chiles cascabeles (0.95 oz/ 27 g), stemmed and seeded
- 2 tablespoons raw sesame seeds
- 2 dried bay leaves, crumbled
- 1 teaspoon dried oregano, preferably Mexican
- 1 teaspoon Morton kosher salt (0.21 oz/6 g)

1. Heat the oil, garlic, and cashews in a large saucepan over medium until the garlic is golden brown, for 6 to 8 minutes. Remove from the heat. Using a slotted spoon, transfer the garlic and nuts to a heatproof bowl to cool.

2. Add the chiles to the pan with the oil. Cook over medium heat until the oil is slightly reddish and the chiles are brick red colored, for about 30 seconds. Remove from the heat. Using a slotted spoon, transfer the chiles to the cashew mixture; let cool for 5 minutes.

3. Add the seeds to the hot oil and set aside; they will toast as they sit.

4. Puree the chile mixture with the bay leaves, oregano, and salt in a food processor until coarsely ground. With the motor running, slowly drizzle in the seed/oil mixture until the chiles are finely ground.

DO AHEAD: The salsa can be made 5 days ahead. Store in an airtight container at room temperature.

Salsa de Chipotle y Chile de Árbol

Smoky dried jalapeños and chile de árbol stewed with tomatoes

MAKES 1½ CUPS

- 4 medium Roma tomatoes (1 lb/453 g), cored and roughly chopped
- 2 chiles chipotles for mild or 4 for hot, stemmed
- 2 chiles de árbol for mild to 4 for hot, stemmed and seeded for a milder flavor
- ¼ medium white onion (3.5 oz/ 98 g), roughly chopped
- 1 garlic clove, peeled
- 1 teaspoon Morton kosher salt (0.21 oz/6 g), plus more to taste
  Fresh lime juice (optional)

1. In a medium saucepan, combine the tomatoes, chipotles, chiles de árbol, onion, garlic, salt, and ½ cup water. Bring to a boil over medium-high heat, reduce to a simmer, cover, and cook until the chiles and vegetables are soft, for about 15 minutes.

2. Remove from the heat, cover, and set aside for 10 minutes to cool slightly. Transfer to the jar of a blender and purée on medium-low until almost smooth. Taste and season with more salt and lime juice if desired.

DO AHEAD: The salsa can be made 2 days ahead. Store in an airtight container in the refrigerator, or freeze for up to 1 month.

Salsa de Chile de Árbol

Chiles de árbol simmered with tangy tomatillos

MAKES ABOUT 3 CUPS

- 8 medium tomatillos (13.2 oz/ 375 g), husked, rinsed, and quartered
- ¼ medium white onion (3.5 oz/ 98 g), coarsely chopped
- 3 to 5 chiles de árbol (0.12 oz/3.2 g), stemmed and seeded
- 1 garlic clove, peeled
- ¾ teaspoon Morton kosher salt (0.14 oz/4 g), plus more to taste

1. In a large saucepan over medium-high heat, bring the tomatillos, onion, chiles de árbol, garlic, salt, and ½ cup water to a boil. Cover and simmer until the tomatillos are soft and have turned olive green, for about 15 minutes. Remove the pan from the heat and let sit covered for 10 minutes.

2. Transfer to a blender and purée on medium-low speed until smooth. Do not be tempted to blend above medium speed or your salsa will get airy and will have the texture of a smoothie. Taste and season with more salt if desired.

DO AHEAD: The salsa can be made up to 2 days ahead. Store in an airtight container in the refrigerator, or freeze for up to 1 month.

Salsa de Tomatillo

Tomatillo, avocado, and poblano

MAKES 2 CUPS

- 7 medium tomatillos (12 oz/ 340 g), husked, rinsed, and quartered
- 1 medium chile poblano (4 oz/ 125 g), stemmed, seeded, and coarsely chopped
- 1 to 2 chiles serranos (0.85 oz/24.3 g each), stemmed and coarsely chopped
- ¼ medium white onion (3.45 oz/ 98 g), coarsely chopped
- ¼ medium avocado (1.48 oz/42 g), peeled and seeded
- 1 garlic clove, peeled
- ¼ cup (packed) fresh cilantro leaves with tender stems (1.41 oz/40 g)
- ¾ teaspoon Morton kosher salt (0.14 oz/4 g), plus more to taste

1. In a blender on medium-low speed, purée the tomatillos, chile poblano, chiles serranos, onion, avocado, garlic, cilantro, and salt until smooth. Do not be tempted to blend above medium speed or your salsa will get airy and will have the texture of a smoothie. Taste and season with more salt if desired.

DO AHEAD: The salsa can be made 2 days ahead. Store in an airtight container in the refrigerator, or freeze for up to 1 month.

Aceite de Habanero Quemado

Charred habanero oil

MAKES 1 CUP

- 1 cup vegetable oil
- 4 chiles habaneros (1.48 oz/42.8 g), stemmed, seeded, and halved
- 4 garlic cloves, thinly sliced

1. In a medium saucepan over medium-high, heat the oil for 2 minutes. Add the chiles habaneros and garlic and cook until the habaneros are black, for 15 to 20 minutes. Remove from the heat and let the habaneros and garlic cool in the oil. Once cool, transfer to a blender and purée until smooth.

DO AHEAD: The salsa can be made up to 2 weeks ahead. Store in an airtight container at room temperature.

Salsa Chipotle

Smoky dried jalapeños stewed with garlic and a touch of sugar

MAKES 1 CUP

- 9 medium chiles chipotles (0.7 oz/20 g), stems removed
- 1 teaspoon dried oregano, preferably Mexican
- 1 teaspoon sugar (0.1 oz/4 g)
- ½ teaspoon Morton kosher salt (0.1 oz/4 g)
- 1 garlic clove, peeled

1. In a small saucepan over medium-high heat, bring the chiles chipotles, oregano, sugar, salt, and 1 cup water to a boil. Reduce the heat to medium-low, cover, and simmer until the chiles have softened, for about 15 minutes. Let sit, covered, for 10 minutes to let cool slightly.

2. Transfer the mixture to a blender, add the garlic, and purée on medium-low speed until smooth.

DO AHEAD: The salsa can be made up to 3 days ahead. Store in an airtight container in the refrigerator, or freeze for up to 1 month.

Salsa de Zanahoria y Habanero

Fermented carrot and habanero

MAKES 2 CUPS

- 4 medium carrots (8 oz/226 g), peeled and grated on the large holes of a box grater
- 1 to 2 chiles habaneros (0.37 oz/10.7 g each), stemmed, seeded, and quartered
- 2 garlic cloves, lightly crushed
- ¼ cup fresh lime juice (about 2 limes)
- 1¼ teaspoons Morton kosher salt (0.14 oz/8 g)

1. In a blender, puree the carrots, chiles habaneros, garlic, lime juice, salt, and 1 cup water until smooth and no large chunks remain. Transfer to a 1-quart jar or a nonreactive container and cover loosely with plastic wrap. Poke a few holes in the plastic to allow the hot sauce to breathe. Let sit at room temperature for at least 24 hours and up to 3 days. After that, refrigerate for up to 1 week.

Chiles Jalapeños en Escabeche

Pickled jalapeños with carrots

MAKES 2 QUARTS

- 3 tablespoons extra-virgin olive oil
- 15 medium chiles jalapeños (17.5 oz/498 g)
- ½ large white onion (6.9 oz/198 g), cut into ½-inch wedges
- 2 large carrots (4.6 oz/130 g), peeled and cut crosswise into ½-inch-thick slices
- 5 garlic cloves, peeled
- 4 fresh thyme sprigs
- 4 bay leaves
- 2 whole cloves
- 1 teaspoon dried oregano, preferably Mexican
- ½ teaspoon black peppercorns
- 2 cups distilled white vinegar
- 1¼ teaspoons Morton kosher salt (0.28 oz/8 g)
- 1 teaspoon sugar

1. In a large pot over medium, heat the oil. Cook the jalapeños, onion, carrots, garlic, thyme, bay leaves, cloves, oregano, and peppercorns, stirring, until the jalapeños are bright green and the onion is translucent.

2. Add the vinegar, ½ cup water, the salt, and sugar and bring to a simmer. Cook, stirring, until the jalapeños are olive green and crisp-tender. Let cool.

3. Transfer to jars, seal, and refrigerate for at least 24 hours before serving.

DO AHEAD: The escabeche can be made 2 months ahead. Store in an airtight container in the refrigerator.

Guacamole

Smashed avocado, jalapeño, and lime

MAKES 3 CUPS

- 3 medium avocados (18.9 oz/538 g), peeled and seeded
- ¼ medium white onion (3.45 oz/ 98 g), finely chopped
- 2 chiles jalapeños (2.2 oz/66.4 g), stemmed (and seeded if desired), finely chopped
- 1 garlic clove, finely grated
- 2 tablespoons fresh lime juice, or more to taste
- ¾ teaspoon Morton kosher salt (0.14 oz/4 g)
- ¼ cup chopped fresh cilantro (.7 oz/20 g), plus more for serving

1. Use a potato masher or fork to smash the avocados in a medium bowl or with a molcajete (a Mexican mortar and pestle) until very coarsely mashed. Mix in the onion, chiles jalapeños, garlic, lime juice, salt, and cilantro. Taste and add more lime juice, if desired. Serve sprinkled with chopped cilantro.

DO AHEAD: The guacamole can be made up to 1 day ahead. Store in an airtight container in the refrigerator.

Recado de Todo Clase

Ground spice blend with allspice, cinnamon, clove, and chile de árbol

MAKES ¼ CUP

- 3 tablespoons dried oregano, preferably Mexican (1.2 oz/ 3.5 g)
- 2 tablespoons black peppercorns (0.77 oz/22 g)
- 8 allspice berries
- 5 whole cloves
- 1 1-inch stick canela or cassia cinnamon
- 1 dried bay leaf
- ½ teaspoon cumin seeds

1. In a spice mill or blender, grind the oregano, peppercorns, allspice, cloves, canela, bay leaf, and cumin until finely ground. Transfer to an airtight container and store in a cool, dark, dry spot for up to 3 months.

Recado Rojo

Annatto seed paste flavored with citrus, herbs, and spices

MAKES ½ CUP

- 2 chiles de árbol, stemmed
- 4 whole cloves
- 2 bay leaves
- ¼ cup annatto seeds
- 2 teaspoons coriander seeds
- 2 teaspoons cumin seeds
- 1 tablespoon dried oregano, preferably Mexican
- 1 teaspoon black peppercorns
- 1 teaspoon Morton kosher salt (0.21 oz/6 g)
- 4 garlic cloves, finely grated
- ¼ cup distilled white vinegar
- 1 teaspoon finely grated lime zest
- 1 teaspoon finely grated orange zest

1. In a blender, puree the chiles, cloves, bay leaves, annatto seeds, coriander seeds, cumin seeds, oregano, peppercorns, and salt until finely ground. Transfer to an airtight container and stir in the garlic, vinegar, lime zest, and orange zest until a thick paste forms.

DO AHEAD: The recado can be made up to 1 month ahead. Store in an airtight container in the refrigerator.

▼ Morisqueta
Michoacana,
p. 80, and Frijoles
de Olla, p. 54

EL BAJÍO

AND CENTRAL MÉXICO

I started my adventure in the center of the country

for a number of reasons. First being that Mexico City is the perfect hub and an easy direct flight to and from New York City, where I lived. But more important, I love it. It has the energy of the enormous international metropolis it is, but with the warmth, hospitality, and generosity of every small Mexican city that I have visited. Like New York, there is always something new happening—new restaurants, new art exhibits, theatre openings, parades, and festivals. Plus every state seems to be represented with the people, food, and culture of each state existing in various neighborhoods around the city. I realized this only after traveling throughout the entire country and then returning to Mexico City to discover that difficult-to-find ingredients, like Oaxacan chilhuacle chiles, and dishes like a three-foot-long tamal called zacahuil (from the Huastec civilization, which you can find in the states of Tamaulipas, Veracruz, Puebla, Hidalgo, San Luis Potosí, Querétaro, and Guanajuato) were all available in Mexico City .

Having lived in New York City for twenty years, I was used to, and craved, that energy, excitement, and newness—Mexico City satisfied me in the way that only NYC had been able to for so long. It is a city that is easy and comfortable to be in; it feels like slipping on your

THE RECIPES

Pollo al Pastor
spicy-sweet chipotle-roast chicken with onion and pineapple, p. 73

Enchiladas Mineras
salsa guajillo–dipped tortillas with roasted chicken and queso fresco, p. 74

Tlaltequedas
spinach and squash blossom fritters with roasted tomato and jalapeño salsa, p. 78

Morisqueta Michoacana
slow-cooked pork with roasted tomatoes and guajillos, p. 80

Carnitas estilo Ciudad México
slow-braised pork shoulder, ham hock, and pig's trotter, p. 82

Esquites
butter-roasted fresh corn with poblano and chile de árbol, p. 85

Chorizo Verde
fresh pork sausage with spinach, poblano, and pumpkin seeds, p. 86

Cemita Poblana
fried pork cutlet sandwich topped with strands of queso Oaxaca, p. 89

Gaspacho Moreliano
mango, pineapple, and jicama salad with an orange-lime dressing, p. 90

Tacos Árabes
seared pork steaks marinated with coriander and thyme and wrapped, p. 93

Pan de Muerto
orange-blossom-scented, brioche-style roll brushed with melted butter and sugar, p. 102

CENTRAL MÉXICO

States: México (State), Puebla, Morelos, Tlaxcala, Hidalgo, Distrito Federal, Michoacán, Guanajuato, San Luis Potosí, Querétaro

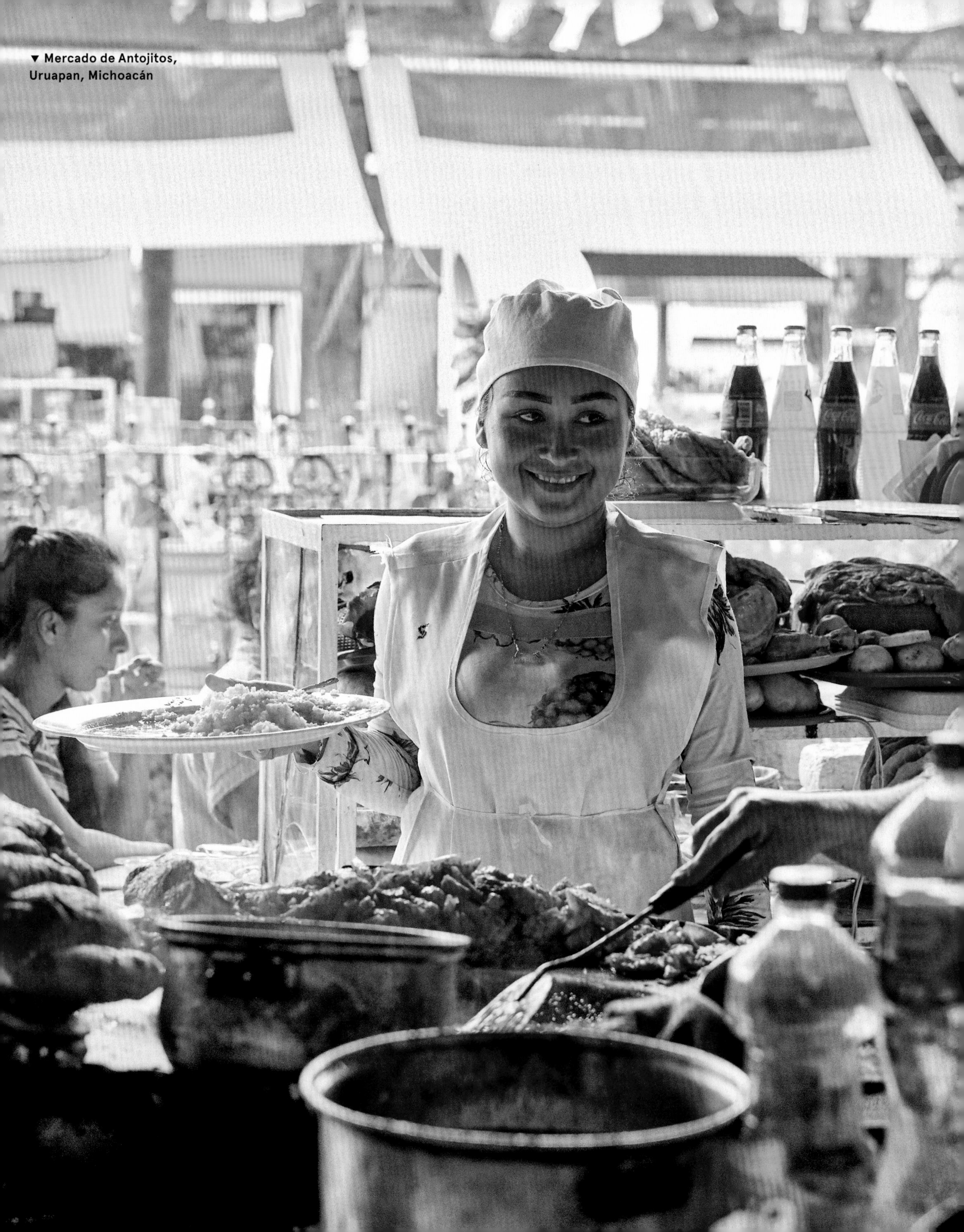

▼ Mercado de Antojitos, Uruapan, Michoacán

favorite pair of shoes. I found myself taking nine-hour walks in neighborhoods I had never visited before to more intimately explore its architecture, people, and food. It was great training for what I was about to begin: my trek across the country.

I flew to Mexico City on October 1, 2019, and straightaway met my friend Enrique Martínez (not a relative) at a car dealership in San Pedro de los Pinos, an urban and commercial neighborhood. I knew I'd need a car for my travels across the country and enlisted Enrique's help while I was still living in New York. We decided on a used cherry-red Nissan Versa, the same car all the Uber drivers in Mexico City seemed to have, so I figured it was a good choice to get me around the country. Armed with my car, a new iPhone, a new Canon Rebel camera, a MacBook Air, and a backpack, I drove out of the city and started almost two years of travel and research.

At first, I have to admit, I was a little scared. I love road trips, but I had no idea what to expect, especially after reading all the terrifying things that have been written by many American and European bloggers about traveling around México by car—all of their warnings about places you should not visit and things you should not do. But I also had a deep yearning for connection to the country and the culture, the kind that flying from city to city just can't give you. And as I watched the landscape fly past my windows—little wisps of smoke being belched out of the volcanoes and lush green valleys filled

◄

CLOCKWISE FROM TOP LEFT:
Capula, Michoacán;
freshly fried carnitas;
Janitzio, Michoacán;
Morisqueta Michoacana,
p. 80

with apple, peach, and pecan trees—my fears vanished and the excitement of exploration and discovery took over.

I drove to Puebla first, sixty-two miles southeast of Mexico City. The first thing I noticed was the architecture and how colonial-Spanish it was. And how much more pronounced the presence of Spain was there than even in Mexico City. This would be true for much of the central states more than in other parts of México, since the central part of the country was the epicenter of New Spain. Like the British who settled in New England and wanted to create an environment that reminded them of home, the Spanish left their colonial mark on this region—from architecture to religion, language, and even the animals they brought to México, like horses, cows, pigs, chickens, goats, and sheep. But what is equally if not more important is what existed *before* the Spanish arrived, like Teotihuacán, a cultural center and ancient city about an hour outside of Mexico City. It was the third largest city in the pre-Columbian Americas and the sixth largest in the world at its peak in 650 CE with a population estimated at 125,000. Teotihuacán is also home to the Pyramid of the Sun, the third largest pyramid in the world. Cities like this and the people who constructed them are a powerful reminder that México, the people, the culture, and the food are a centuries-old marriage of the indigenous people who first lived on this land and all of the immigrants who settled after them.

1941

Pollo al Pastor

Spicy-sweet chipotle-roast chicken with onion and pineapple

I was walking the streets in the city of Guanajuato and saw a rosticería that was selling rotisserie pollo al pastor. Al pastor is the meat filling of one of the most iconic tacos in the country. It's made by marinating thin cuts of pork steak in chiles, spices, and Recado Rojo (p. 65) and layering the steaks on a vertical spit called a trompo, which was actually brought to México by Lebanese immigrants in the late nineteenth century. The trompos are topped with onion and pineapple and spin around a propane fire; the pork chars and caramelizes as it spins.

At this rosticería, the vendor was using chicken instead of pork and had marinated the chicken in his version of an al pastor marinade. It was an incredible sight, hundreds of spinning brick-red chickens roasting over a live wood fire. I stood there mesmerized by the sight and the smell.

I knew I had to re-create this rotisserie-style al pastor for the book, and it has since become my favorite recipe. It is so good and has a totally unexpected flavor, being at once familiar because of the pastor marinade, but surprising because it's married to a perfectly roasted and juicy chicken with chile-stained meat that just falls off the bone.

SERVES 6 TO 8

2 tablespoons Recado Rojo, p. 65, or achiote paste
3 garlic cloves, finely grated
2 canned chipotle peppers in adobo sauce, finely chopped, plus 2 tablespoons adobo sauce
2 tablespoons apple cider vinegar
2½ teaspoons Morton kosher salt (0.7 oz/20 g), divided
1 tablespoon agave syrup or honey
¼ cup plus 2 tablespoons extra-virgin olive oil, divided

1 whole chicken (4 lb/1.8 kg)
1 medium pineapple (2.2 lb/988 g), peeled, quartered, cored, and thinly sliced crosswise
1 large white onion (14.6 oz/416 g), halved and thinly sliced

FOR SERVING
→ Warm Tortillas de Maíz, *p. 38*
→ Salsa de Aguacate, *p. 60*
→ Salsa de Chile de Árbol, *p. 62*
→ Cilantro leaves

1. In a medium bowl and using a fork, break up the recado rojo so no large clumps remain. Add the garlic, chiles, adobo sauce, vinegar, and 2 teaspoons of the salt and stir, using the fork to smash into a smooth paste. Vigorously whisk the agave syrup and ¼ cup of the olive oil into the achiote mixture until completely smooth.

2. Pat the chicken dry with paper towels. Place breast-side up in the center of a 13 × 9-inch baking pan. Liberally brush the chicken with the achiote sauce, getting into every nook and cranny, as well as inside the cavity. The chicken should be completely coated, and there shouldn't be any sauce remaining. Tie the ends of the drumsticks together with kitchen twine; tuck the wings underneath the back.

3. In a medium bowl, toss the pineapple, onion, and the remaining 2 tablespoons oil; season with the remaining ½ teaspoon salt. Arrange around the chicken. Let sit at room temperature for 1 hour; if you have more time, cover the pan (skip letting it sit at room temperature) and refrigerate for at least 3 hours and up to 12. Uncover and let sit at room temperature for 1 hour before roasting.

4. Arrange a rack in the center of the oven; preheat to 350°F. Roast the chicken, tossing the onion and pineapple with the juices in the pan halfway through, until the pineapple is lightly browned, the chicken is deep burgundy, and an instant-read thermometer inserted into the thickest part of the breasts registers 155°F (the temperature will climb to 165°F as the chicken rests), for 60 to 70 minutes.

5. Remove the pan from the oven and let the chicken rest uncovered in the pan for at least 20 minutes and up to 2 hours. Transfer the chicken to a cutting board and carve. Serve with roasted pineapple and onions, tortillas, salsas, and cilantro.

Enchiladas Mineras

Salsa guajillo-dipped tortillas with roasted chicken and queso fresco

Before driving northwest of Mexico City to Guanajuato, I asked all my friends and social followers to recommend their favorite places to eat. One hundred percent said, "You have to eat at Las Originales Enchiladas Mineras Doña Lupe." Enchiladas in México do not have any resemblance to the ones in the US. Don't get me wrong, I love a good Tex-Mex enchilada platter, but Mexican enchiladas are much lighter and easier to make.

Mexican enchiladas are almost never baked; occasionally they are put under the broiler to melt and brown cheese, but usually they are corn tortillas dipped in a chile sauce and then stuffed with a light filling. The word enchilada *means to be bathed or surrounded in a chile sauce or paste.*

Doña Lupe's restaurant seats about eight people at a communal table. She makes everything to order—and by everything I mean the three-item menu consisting of enchiladas mineras, with or without chicken, and on Saturdays and Sundays, pozole rojo. The intoxicating smell that wafted down the street made it easy to find this tiny spot. Years of practice have made her incredibly skilled at frying and bathing the tortillas. Like everyone said it'd be, eating at Doña Lupe's was a life-changing experience.

SERVES 4

- 8   Tortillas de Maíz, *p. 38*
- 5   tablespoons vegetable oil, divided
- 2¼ cups homemade chicken stock or store-bought low-sodium chicken broth
- 5   large chiles guajillos (1 oz/30 g), stemmed and seeded
- 2   medium chiles cascabeles (0.25 oz/5 g), stemmed and seeded
- 2   garlic cloves, lightly crushed
- 2   teaspoons Morton kosher salt (0.5 oz/16 g)
- ½   teaspoon dried oregano, preferably Mexican
- ¼   teaspoon freshly ground black pepper
- 4   large chicken thighs (6 oz/170 g each)
- 2   medium Yukon Gold potatoes (12 oz/340 g), peeled and cut into 2-inch pieces
- 3   medium carrots (8 oz/226 g), cut into 2-inch pieces
- ½   large white onion (7 oz/200 g), sliced
- 1   tablespoon apple cider vinegar
- 12 ounces (340 g) queso fresco or Cotija, crumbled

FOR SERVING
- → Shredded iceberg lettuce
- → Chopped onion
- → Crema
- → Chiles Jalapeños en Escabeche, *p. 64*

1. Brush both sides of the tortillas with 2 tablespoons of the oil. Heat a large skillet over medium-high. Working in batches, sear the tortillas until they're lightly browned and starting to crisp, for about 1 minute per side. Set the tortillas aside until you're ready to assemble.

2. In a medium saucepan, bring the broth, chiles guajillos, chiles cascabeles, garlic, salt, oregano, and pepper to a boil. Remove from the heat, cover, and let sit until the chiles are soft, for 30 minutes. Transfer to a blender and puree until smooth.

3. In a large heavy pot over medium-high, heat 2 tablespoons of the oil. Cook the chicken, skin-side down, until deep golden brown, for 5 to 6 minutes. Turn the pieces over and brown the other side, for 5 to 6 minutes more. Transfer the chicken to a plate. If there isn't at least 1 tablespoon of fat in the pot, add the remaining 1 tablespoon oil along with the potatoes, carrots, and onion. Cook, tossing occasionally, until the vegetables are lightly browned, for 4 to 6 minutes.

4. Pour the chile puree into the pot with the vegetables; scrape up any browned bits from the bottom of the pot. Nestle the chicken into the sauce and bring the mixture to a boil. Cover the pot, reduce the heat to low, and simmer until the chicken is completely tender and cooked through, for about 30 minutes.

5. Stir the vinegar into the pot and mound the chicken and vegetables on one side so there's room on the other side to dip the tortillas into the sauce.

6. Using tongs and working with one tortilla at a time, dip into the chile sauce, turning to coat, and cook in the sauce until softened (they will soften more as they sit), for about 3 seconds per side. Transfer the tortillas to a baking sheet as you go. Spoon 2 tablespoons of the queso fresco across the center of each tortilla and fold over like a taco.

7. Divide the enchiladas among four plates and spoon more chile sauce over top. Top with lettuce, more onion, crema, and any remaining queso. Serve with the chicken, vegetables, remaining sauce, and pickled jalapeños.

▲ Enchiladas
Mineras, p. 74

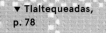
▼ Tlaltequeadas,
p. 78

Tlaltequeadas

Spinach and squash blossom fritters with roasted tomato and jalapeño salsa

One of my favorite pueblitos in México is Tepoztlán in the state of Morelos, south of Mexico City. The markets are known for pre-Hispanic food— food that existed before the arrival of Spanish colonialists. The Spanish brought pigs, cows, wheat, and methods for making cheese to México, but before their arrival, the indigenous people had a very plant-forward diet. They ate mostly vegetables like corn, beans, squash, amaranth, chia, chiles, nuts, and flowers as well as wild fowl and game, insects, fish, and shellfish.

Crispy-fried tlaltequeada fritters are beautiful and flavorful. I loved seeing the vendors at the market display all of the different kinds. Some were made with beets and were garnet red. Some, made with seasonal native wildflowers, were white, purple, and yellow. Others were made with quelites, different varieties of native leafy wild greens, and were emerald green. I even had one that was pink from red plums and served with a creamy nut-based sauce. Tlaltequeadas can be sweet or savory and spicy or not, depending on what is in season and what flavors you like. The fritters are held together by chia and flaxmeal, both of which mimic the consistency of eggs when added to a liquid.

MAKES 12 FRITTERS

- 7 large Roma tomatoes (1¾ lb/ 794 g), cored and left whole
- 2 large chiles jalapeños (2.5 oz/ 71 g), stemmed
- ¾ large white onion (10 oz/300 g), chopped
- 1 garlic clove, peeled Morton kosher salt
- 1 tablespoon fresh lime juice
- 2 tablespoons chia seeds
- 2 tablespoons golden flaxmeal
- 2 tablespoons sesame seeds
- 1 cup puffed amaranth
- ½ cup extra-virgin olive oil, plus more if necessary
- 8 ounces (225 g) mixed wild mushrooms, torn into small pieces (stemmed if using shiitakes)
- 2 medium carrots (5.6 oz/160 g), shredded on the large holes of a box grater
- 1 cup mung bean sprouts (4.58 oz/130 g)
- 3 garlic cloves, thinly sliced
- 12 ounces (340 g) mature spinach, torn into 1-inch pieces
- 16 squash blossoms (4 oz/113 g), stems, stamen, and pistils removed, blossoms torn

1. Arrange a rack in the center of the oven; preheat to 475°F. Line a sheet pan with parchment paper or foil.

2. Arrange the tomatoes and chiles jalapeños on the prepared pan and roast until the skin of the tomatoes and jalapeños is dark brown in places and starting to peel away from the flesh, for 30 to 35 minutes.

3. Transfer the tomatoes and jalapeños to a blender, add ¼ cup of the onion, the garlic, and 1½ teaspoons (0.2 oz/8 g) of the salt and process until completely smooth. Transfer the roasted tomato salsa to a small bowl, stir in the lime juice, and set aside (this can be made up to 8 hours in advance).

4. In a large bowl, stir together the chia seeds, flaxmeal, sesame seeds, and amaranth until combined.

5. In a large skillet, preferably cast-iron, over medium-high, heat 3 tablespoons oil. Add the mushrooms and cook, without stirring, until browned, for 3 to 4 minutes. Toss and continue to cook, stirring occasionally, until the mushrooms are browned on all sides and tender, for 4 to 5 minutes more. Season with salt and transfer to the bowl with the chia mixture.

6. In the same skillet, heat 1 tablespoon oil over medium-high heat. Add the carrots, sprouts, remaining onion, garlic, and 2¼ teaspoons (0.4 oz/12 g) salt. Cook, tossing occasionally, until all of the vegetables are tender, for 6 to 8 minutes.

7. Add the spinach, blossoms, and ¼ cup water. Bring to a boil, then reduce to a simmer, cover, and cook until the spinach is wilted and tender, for about 5 minutes. Transfer the spinach mixture to the bowl with the chia mixture and stir until completely combined. Set aside for 30 minutes to set. During this time, the seeds will absorb any excess liquid and the mixture should hold its shape when squeezed.

8. Using a large ice cream scoop or ¼-cup measure, scoop out the tlaltequeadas mixture and form it into small patties that are about ¾ inch thick and arrange them on a sheet pan.

9. Wipe the skillet clean and heat the remaining ¼ cup oil over medium heat. Working in batches to not overcrowd the pan, fry the tlaltequeadas until deep golden brown on both sides, for 4 to 5 minutes per side. Transfer to a large plate lined with paper towels. Continue to fry the remaining patties, adding more oil if necessary.

10. Serve the fried tlaltequeadas warm with the roasted tomato salsa.

Morisqueta Michoacana

Slow-cooked pork with roasted tomatoes and guajillos

Ren, the photographer who shot most of the photos for Mi Cocina, *and I had just wrapped our first shoot in Morelia, which is known for its Day of the Dead celebrations (see Día de los Muertos, p. 94). We had been shooting until about three in the morning the night before and were totally exhausted. Even though we had only gotten a few hours of sleep, the lure of eating a late lunch in Uruapan, a town about two hours southwest known for its Mercado de Antojitos (snack market) was enough to get us to rally and drive down.*

We ate tamales, atole, champurrado, and carnitas, but the dish that absolutely stole the show was the morisqueta, a dish of fork-tender pork shoulder simmered in a brothy tomato and guajillo sauce served over frijoles and arroz blanco. It was one of those meals that was not only so perfect because it was so delicious, but because it was exactly the kind of comforting meal we needed in that moment.

SERVES 6 TO 8

- 7 large Roma tomatoes (1¾ lb/ 794 g), cored, or one 28-ounce can diced fire-roasted tomatoes
- ½ large white onion (7 oz/200 g), halved
- 1 cup homemade chicken stock or store-bought low-sodium chicken broth
- 6 large chiles guajillos (1.26 oz/ 36 g), stemmed and seeded
- 6 garlic cloves, lightly crushed
- 3 chiles de árbol (0.18 oz/4.8 g), stemmed (and seeded for a milder flavor)
- 1 dried bay leaf
- 1 tablespoon Morton kosher salt (0.7 oz/20 g)
- 1 teaspoon dried oregano, preferably Mexican
- 1 teaspoon freshly ground black pepper
- 2 tablespoons rendered lard, bacon fat, or extra-virgin olive oil
- 3 pounds (1.36 kg) boneless pork shoulder, cut into 2-inch pieces

FOR SERVING
→ **Arroz Blanco con Mantequilla**, *p. 50*
→ **Frijoles de Olla**, *p. 54*
→ **Warm Tortillas de Maíz**, *p. 38*
→ **Crumbled queso fresco**

1. Arrange a rack in the center of the oven and preheat to 475°F. Line a sheet pan with parchment paper or foil. Arrange the tomatoes and onion on the prepared pan. Roast until the skin is browned in spots and starting to peel away, for 30 to 35 minutes. (Omit this step if you're using canned tomatoes; you'll use the onion raw in the next step.)

2. In a medium saucepan, bring the broth, chiles guajillos, garlic, chiles de árbol, bay leaf, salt, oregano, and pepper to a boil. Remove the pot from the heat, cover, and let sit until the chiles have softened, for 30 minutes. Transfer the chile mixture to a blender. Add the roasted tomatoes and onion (or canned tomatoes and raw onion) and puree until completely smooth.

3. In a large heavy pot over medium-high, heat the lard. Working in batches, cook the pork until browned on two sides, for 4 to 5 minutes per side. Transfer to a plate. Pour the chile puree into the pot with the pork fat. Using a wooden spoon, scrape up any browned bits from the bottom. Return the pork to the pot and bring the liquid to a boil. Cover, reduce the heat to low, and simmer until the pork is completely tender and can easily be shredded, for 2½ to 3 hours.

4. Serve with the arroz, frijoles, tortillas, and queso fresco.

DO AHEAD: The morisqueta can be refrigerated for up to 3 days (the flavor will improve as time goes on), or frozen for up to 3 months.

Carnitas estilo Ciudad México

Slow-braised pork shoulder with a ham hock and pig's trotter

I have eaten carnitas in almost every state and have watched the maestros in Michoacán make their masterpieces. After braising the pork until fall-apart tender, some fry their carnitas until very crispy; some season with oranges, onions, and aromatic spices like cinnamon and clove; and others prefer the simplicity of salt and pepper only.

I had been a fan of crispy carnitas until I tried them in Mexico City. Here they were incredibly tender, juicy, and pure in flavor: just pork, salt, and pepper. And that became all I wanted. The salsas blanketed the carnitas with the heat and acid to cut through all of that richness.

One of the reasons that the pork flavor of these carnitas was so prominent is because the whole pig was cooked in a giant copper pot, where it slowly braised in its own fat until all of the meat had come off the bones, essentially making the most ridiculously rich and lard-y broth on Earth. My recipe is a bit more manageable. I use a pork shoulder, one of the most flavorful parts of the pig, and a shank and trotter for added richness, flavor, and a little funk, which the best carnitas in México all have.

SERVES 8

- 2 pounds (907 g) boneless, skinless pork shoulder, cut into 1½-inch pieces
- 1 large ham shank or hock (1.9 lb/886 g)
- 1 large pig's trotter (11.3 oz/322 g)
- 1 cup homemade chicken stock or store-bought low-sodium chicken broth
- 2¼ teaspoons teaspoon Morton kosher salt (0.7 oz/16 g)
- 1 teaspoon freshly ground black pepper

FOR SERVING
- → Warm Tortillas de Maíz, *p. 38*
- → Salsa de Chile de Árbol, *p. 62*
- → Chopped white onion
- → Lime wedges
- → Dried oregano
- → Chopped cilantro
- → Chicharrones

1. In a large heavy pot, add the pork shoulder, ham shank, pig's trotter, broth, salt, and pepper. Bring to a boil over high heat, then reduce the heat to medium-low, cover, and simmer until the pork is tender and easily falls off the bone, for 2 to 2½ hours.

2. Uncover the pot and continue to cook, stirring occasionally, for 10 minutes to slightly reduce the liquid (but not completely). Remove the pot from the heat, cover, and let sit or until the pork is cool enough to handle, for about 30 minutes.

3. Carefully pour the cooking liquid from the pot into a large bowl and set aside. Transfer the pork shoulder, hock, and trotter to a cutting board and carefully remove the meat and skin from the bones. Discard the bones and tear or chop the skin into ½-inch pieces and set aside. Shred all the meat into bite-size pieces. Add the meat and skin to the bowl with the reserved cooking liquid. Season with salt to taste.

4. Serve the carnitas with tortillas, salsa, onion, lime wedges, oregano, cilantro, and chicharrones.

DO AHEAD: The carnitas can be made 3 days ahead. Store in an airtight container in the refrigerator.

Esquites

Butter-roasted fresh corn with poblano and chile de árbol

Esquites exist in every part of México, but there was one town that seemed to have not only the most esquites stands, but also the biggest variety of flavors and toppings of any place I visited. Bernal in the state of Querétaro is best known for having one of the largest natural monoliths in the world, the Peña de Bernal. My friends and I had driven to Bernal to hike to the top (1,421 ft/433 m) and sample the food from the stands lining the path to the Peña.

The esquites stands were everywhere. Each one had between six and twelve cazuelas of esquites cooking over open fires, each clay pot filled with different vegetables, herbs, and spices. The smell as you approached each stand revealed the sazón of each cook; the colors were vivid and rich. And the flavors—estilo pozole con guajillo, poblano mole verde, mantequilla, habanero, amarillo dulce, and asado con epazote y chile serrano—were the most common, but each cook had their own favorites and interpretations. This is mine.

Think of my recipe as your base to which you can add tomatoes or tomatillos for color and tang, switch out the chile de árbol for your favorite chile (dried or fresh), add meat or keep it plant-based. The main thing is to have fun with it and make it your own.

SERVES 4

- 4 tablespoons unsalted butter (2 oz/57 g) or extra-virgin olive oil
- 1 medium chile poblano (4 oz/125 g), stemmed, seeded, and chopped
- ¼ medium white onion (3.45 oz/98 g), chopped
- 2 garlic cloves, finely grated
- 4 chiles de árbol (0.12 oz/3.2 g), stems and seeds intact (it won't be too hot, I promise)
- 4 cups fresh corn kernels (19.4 oz/550 g; 4 large ears)
- 3 fresh epazote sprigs or a combination of fresh parsley, oregano, and/or mint sprigs
- 1¼ teaspoons Morton kosher salt (0.28 oz/8 g)
- ⅓ cup crema, crème fraîche, or sour cream
- ⅓ cup queso fresco or Cotija (1.4 oz/40 g), crumbled

FOR SERVING
→ Mayonnaise
→ Crushed chiles de árbol
→ Lime wedges
→ Chopped cilantro

1. In a large skillet over medium-high heat, melt the butter. Cook the chile poblano, onion, garlic, and chiles de árbol, tossing occasionally, until the onion is tender and just beginning to brown, for 6 to 8 minutes.

2. Add the corn, epazote, and salt and cook, tossing occasionally, until the corn is cooked through and just beginning to brown, for 6 to 8 minutes.

3. Serve the esquites warm with a drizzle of crema and a sprinkle of queso fresco and other desired toppings.

Chorizo Verde

Fresh pork sausage
with spinach, poblano,
and pumpkin seeds

*During the late 1960s and early
1970s, the price of dried chiles
and pimentón skyrocketed and
made chorizo rojo prohibitively
expensive to make for many
Mexicans. In Toluca, a city in
the state of México, residents
started using fresh green
chiles—specifically serranos—
fresh herbs, and tomatillos
to make chorizo, and chorizo
verde was born. The pork and
green chile filling is normally
stuffed into casings and tied
into small oval links, aged, and
grilled. I love the smoky flavor
of the grilled links, but I have
found that I am more likely to
make chorizo if I don't have
to pull out the sausage stuffer
and find casings. And
I love chorizo, so if having fresh
sausage in my house means
no casings, then that is the
sacrifice I am willing to make.
But feel free to stuff and grill.*

MAKES ABOUT 2 POUNDS

- 2 teaspoons coriander seeds
- 1 teaspoon black peppercorns
- 2 teaspoons cumin seeds
- 4 teaspoons dried oregano, preferably Mexican
- 5 ounces (184 g) mature spinach, washed, spun dry, and torn into 3-inch pieces
- 2 chiles serranos, stemmed and coarsely chopped
- 2 large scallions (1.9 oz/54 g), chopped
- ½ cup (packed) fresh cilantro leaves and tender stems (0.5 oz/15 g)
- 8 tablespoons rendered lard or extra-virgin olive oil, divided
- 6 tablespoons apple cider vinegar
- 4 garlic cloves, peeled
- ⅓ cup toasted pepitas (3.5 oz/100 g)
- 2 large bay leaves
- 2¾ teaspoons Morton kosher salt (0.42 oz/18 g)
- 2¼ pounds (1 kg) ground pork, preferably not lean

FOR SERVING
- → **Warm Tortillas de Maíz,** *p. 38*
- → **Nopales Enchilados,** *p. 292*
- → **Your favorite salsa**
- → **Sliced avocado**
- → **Chopped onion**
- → **Chopped cilantro**

1. In a small skillet over medium heat, toast the coriander seeds and peppercorns, swirling the pan often, until very fragrant and the coriander seeds are browned, for about 1½ minutes. Add the cumin seeds and oregano and cook until fragrant and beginning to brown, for about 30 seconds. Transfer to a heatproof bowl and let cool, then finely grind the spices in a molcajete or spice mill.

2. In a food processor, puree the ground spice mixture with the spinach, chiles serranos, scallions, cilantro, 6 tablespoons of the lard, the vinegar, garlic, pepitas, bay leaves, and salt until completely smooth. Transfer to a large bowl.

3. Mix in one-quarter of the pork (combining just a small amount of the meat in the beginning makes it easier to incorporate the rest without overmixing). Add the remaining pork and mix well to combine, but don't overwork it. Cover the bowl tightly with plastic wrap and refrigerate for at least 24 hours and up to 4 days. I like to marinate mine for 4 days for maximum flavor (see Cook's Note).

4. In a large skillet, preferably cast-iron, heat the remaining 2 tablespoons lard over medium-high heat. Cook the desired amount of chorizo, breaking it up with a wooden spoon, stirring, until browned and cooked through, for 7 to 9 minutes.

5. Make tacos with the chorizo, tortillas, nopales, salsa, sliced avocado, chopped onion, and cilantro.

Cook's Note

After the chorizo has
marinated, I like to cook half
right away and place the
other half in a freezer bag
and freeze for up to 3 months
so that I can have sausage
whenever the craving strikes.

Cemita Poblana

Fried pork cutlet sandwich topped with strands of queso Oaxaca

I had walked to the Mercado Municipal La Acocota in Puebla and was looking at ceramics when a crazy thunderstorm started. It shook the building and wouldn't let up. I had not intended to eat there, but I was trapped. I didn't want to walk in the rain and there were no taxis nor Ubers nearby.

I saw a woman at a cemita puesto (sandwich food stall) take balls of queso Oaxaca and pull them apart into long, thin threads of cheese—it was like watching someone pull apart a sweater into strands of fiber. Queso Oaxaca is similar in flavor to Monterey Jack with the string-like texture of fresh mozzarella—it is made by pulling the cheese into strands and rolling it up like a ball of yarn. After unraveling it, the vendor took a handful of the cheese strands and used them to top the cemitas before smashing the avocado into the bread and closing the cemita. I was in complete awe. I ordered a sandwich, of course.

This was also my first time tasting pápalo, an herb that has a flavor similar to the combination of cilantro, mint, and basil. It is pretty difficult to find, even in parts of México. So, if you can't find it, and you probably won't, just use a combination of herbs to mimic the flavor. But if you do see it, buy it and try it!

MAKES 4 CEMITAS

- 4 boneless center-cut pork chops (6 oz/170 g each), excess fat trimmed
  Morton kosher salt and freshly ground black pepper
- 1 cup all-purpose flour
- 3 large eggs, at room temperature
- 3 cups panko Japanese-style bread crumbs or unseasoned bread crumbs
- ½ cup vegetable oil
- 2 large avocados, peeled, seeded, and halved
- 4 cemitas poblanas, teleras, bolillos, or brioche rolls, halved and toasted

- Chiles Chipotles en Escabeche, p. 59, or sliced Chiles Jalapeños en Escabeche, p. 64, plus brine from the jar
- ½ medium white onion (5.6 oz/ 160 g), thinly sliced
- 1 cup (packed) pápalo (1 oz/30 g) or a combination of cilantro, basil, and mint
- 8 ounces queso Oaxaca or fresh mozzarella (226 g), pulled into thin strands or shredded
- 8 ounces thinly sliced smoked or cooked ham (226 g)

1. Place a pork chops between two sheets of plastic wrap and pound to a ¼-inch thickness. Unwrap and set aside on a plate. Repeat with the remaining chops, then season both sides with salt and pepper.

2. Add the flour to a shallow bowl (a pie plate works best). Place the eggs in another shallow bowl and beat to combine. Place the panko in a third shallow bowl. Season the flour, eggs, and panko with salt and pepper.

3. Working with one at a time, dredge a chop through the flour, shaking off any excess and making sure both sides are well coated. Transfer to the bowl with the eggs and turn to coat. Lift from the bowl, letting any excess drip off. Add the pork to the panko, pressing it into the crumbs on both sides to adhere, then transfer the pork to a sheet pan. Repeat with the remaining chops.

4. In a large skillet over medium-high, heat ¼ cup oil. Cook 2 cutlets at a time until the coating is deep golden brown and the pork is just cooked through, for about 3 minutes per side. Transfer to a plate lined with paper towels. Wipe out the skillet and repeat with the remaining ¼ cup oil and 2 cutlets.

5. Smash half of an avocado onto the top half of each toasted cemita so that it sticks to the bread. Set a pork cutlet on each bottom half. Top the pork with the chipotle, onion, pápalo, queso, ham, and a generous drizzle of chipotle brine. Top the cemita, cut in half, and serve.

Gaspacho Moreliano

Mango, pineapple, and jicama salad with an orange-lime dressing

When I started to write this headnote, my mouth began to water. West of Mexico City, in the city of Morelia, there is an area in el Centro, the historic district, near the cathedral where gaspacho (yes, it's spelled with an s) stands line the streets. Young men were working below each gaspacho sign, meticulously and quickly cutting not tomatoes and red bell peppers to make the famously chilled Spanish gazpacho soup, but instead mango, jícama, and pineapple into tiny and perfect cubes to make gaspacho, a sweet and salty fruit snack.

By midday, the streets are filled with people carrying large plastic cups mounded with tiny cut fruit and topped with chile and queso Cotija.

Gaspacho showcases the incredibly sweet mangoes that grow in the state and Cotija, the salty-sharp cheese that is produced there as well. My version is more like a summery side dish than a grab-and-go midday snack. Since I really don't want to spend a lot of time cubing fruit, I use larger slices. I love gaspacho so much that I pair it with everything from grilled meat to fish.

SERVES 4 TO 6

- 6 tablespoons extra-virgin olive oil
- ¼ cup fresh lime juice (about 2 limes)
- 1 teaspoon finely grated orange zest
- 2 tablespoons fresh orange juice
- 1 garlic clove, finely grated
- 1 chile de árbol (0.03 oz/0.8g), stemmed and finely chopped, or ¼ teaspoon red chile flakes
- 1 teaspoon Morton kosher salt (0.21 oz/6 g)
- 1 large Tommy Atkins mango (14.5 oz/416 g), or 2 Ataúlfo or champagne mangoes, peeled, seeded, and thinly sliced
- ¼ medium pineapple (10 oz/287 g), peeled, cored, and sliced into ½-inch pieces
- ½ large jícama (7.5 oz/214 g), peeled and thinly sliced
- ¼ medium white onion (3 oz/86 g), chopped
- ½ cup fresh mint leaves

FOR SERVING
- → Crumbled queso Cotija
- → Tajín
- → Lime wedges

1. In a liquid measuring cup, whisk together the oil, lime juice, orange zest, orange juice, garlic, chile de árbol, and salt until the salt has dissolved.

2. In a large bowl, gingerly toss the mango, pineapple, jícama, onion, mint, and half of the dressing. Let sit for 5 minutes to let flavors come together.

3. Serve with any additional dressing drizzled over and top with the Cotija, Tajín, and a squeeze of lime juice.

Tacos Árabes

Seared pork steaks marinated with coriander and thyme and wrapped

Puebla is known for many iconic dishes, but tacos árabes deserves more attention than they usually receive. They are a beautiful combination of Iraqi and Mexican culture and cuisine and represent the fusion of two beloved dishes, shawarma and the taco. The Tabe and the Galeana families emigrated from Iraq in the 1920s and settled in the city of Puebla. They brought with them their families' technique for making shawarma on the trompo (vertical spit) and the roasting technique of layering meat and spices and spinning it next to a column of burning coals. Originally, they used lamb, but it was hard to source and very expensive and, more important, no one in Puebla ate lamb. There is a saying in Puebla, "Tres cosas come el poblano: cerdo, cochino y marrano." (There are three things that Poblanos eat: pig, pork, and hog.) And so they began experimenting with pork and available herbs like the parsley and oregano brought over by the Spanish. They created a dish that is a bit closer in flavor to shawarma and wrapped it in a yeasted flatbread, called pan árabe, very similar to a pita only rolled thinner and filled and folded like a flour tortilla.

SERVES 4

- ½ cup fresh lime juice (about 4 limes)
- 4 garlic cloves, thinly sliced
- 3 bay leaves
- 1 tablespoon chopped fresh thyme leaves
- 2 teaspoons dried oregano, preferably Mexican
- 1 teaspoon cumin seeds
- 1 teaspoon Morton kosher salt (0.21 oz/6 g)
- ½ teaspoon coriander seeds, lightly crushed
- ½ teaspoon freshly ground black pepper
- 2 boneless pork shoulder steaks, ½ inch thick (9 oz/255 g each)
- ½ large white onion (6.98 oz/ 198 g), thinly sliced
- 4 medium scallions (3.7 oz/107 g), root ends trimmed
- 2 tablespoons extra-virgin olive oil
- ½ cup chopped fresh parsley (30 g /1 oz)
- 8 Pan Árabe, p. 44, or pita bread, lightly toasted

FOR SERVING
- → Salsa Chipotle, p. 63
- → Sliced radish
- → Sliced cucumber
- → Sliced onion
- → Lime wedges

1. In a large bowl, stir together the lime juice, garlic, bay leaves, thyme, oregano, cumin, salt, coriander, and pepper until combined. Toss the pork and onion in the lime marinade until completely coated. Cover the bowl with plastic and refrigerate for at least 1 hour and up to 4 hours.

2. Heat a large skillet, preferably cast-iron, over high heat for about 2 minutes, or until very hot. Cook the scallions in the dry pan until charred on both sides, for 3 to 5 minutes. Transfer to a plate and set aside.

3. Heat 1 tablespoon oil in the hot skillet (still over high heat) and cook half of the pork and onion mixture (no need to drain, the pork will soak up all of the marinade) until the pork is charred on both sides, for about 2 minutes per side. Transfer the cooked pork and onion to a large plate and repeat with the remaining 1 tablespoon oil and pork and onion mixture. Let rest for 10 minutes.

4. Just before serving, toss the pork and onion with the parsley. Serve the pork and onions wrapped in pan árabe topped with salsa chipotle, radish, cucumber, onion, and lime wedges for squeezing.

DÍA DE LOS MUERTOS

✕

I DIDN'T KNOW Día de los Muertos existed until I was sixteen years old. I had just started driving that summer. With my candy-apple red 1988 Buick Skylark, I had the freedom to pick up fresh-baked conchas and empanadas any time the mood struck—which was pretty often. Then one cool (for Texas) October afternoon, I stopped by La Reina in South Austin to find the panadería decked out with brightly painted calaveras (skulls) and sun-yellow cempasúchiles (marigolds).

This may sound strange, but I believe there are some things that we are hardwired or maybe even genetically predisposed to love, and for me, Día de los Muertos is one of those things. I don't know why, but from the moment I walked into the panadería, I felt so comfortable, so at home, and so excited—like I had just discovered a new part of myself. Inside the display case, there was a whole new section filled with breads I had never seen before. I ordered one of everything. For Texas in the '80s, they had a pretty impressive selection of pan de muerto. There were even loaves shaped like human figures with arms folded over their chests, similar to the panes (breads) I know about now from Guanajuato and Oaxaca. The panadero cut and folded a cake box to make it look like a coffin, placing the loaves inside it and tying it up like a present. I took it home to my parents, who were slightly horrified. I don't think they quite understood why I was so fascinated by this bread and this holiday, but from that moment, I was completely hooked. I started researching the significance and meaning of the holiday and how it was celebrated in

▼ Ofrenda, or altar, made with a collection of reminders of deceased loved ones; Morelia, Michoacán

▲ Cempasúchil, or marigold flowers, are used to decorate the graves of loved ones; Janitzio, Michoacán

México. I could not wait to travel across the border and see it for myself.

Día de los Muertos is a month-long celebration of the lives of lost loved ones (including pets) that culminates in a gathering of friends and family on All Saints' Day and All Souls' Day (November 1 and 2, respectively). While the holiday is a part of a larger global Catholic tradition, Día de los Muertos is very Mexican. It is an expression of love and remembrance rather than mourning that manifests itself in art, music, dance, and food. For Mexicans, on those two days, loved ones come back to visit them. As the living, you offer them things that you have made—a meal, a song, a drawing, an offering that you know they would love. Many Mexicans channel their grief into something creative, something positive and celebratory. It's not a replacement for tears, but it is incredibly empowering when you remove the finality from death and allow yourself to believe that your loved one is still there, in another form, existing peacefully in another place and that you will get to see them every October.

I was in Tzintzuntzán in Michoacán for Día de los Muertos a few years ago. It's a tiny town with some of the most beautiful cemeteries I have seen in México, all with elaborately carved tombstones, statues, and crypts. I went to a small and intimate cemetery and saw a group of six 19- to 20-year-olds gathered around a candlelit grave covered in marigold petals. They were drinking beer, playing guitars, and belting out some old cantina songs. I looked at the grave and saw that their friend had died four years earlier, when these kids were about sixteen. Even after four years, the bond that they shared hadn't waned. They were singing at the top of their lungs with tears rolling down their faces. They toasted the person they'd lost between songs, telling jokes and stories about the fun they had together as they laid photos and flowers down on the top of the grave. That person was there with them. And though I could not see that person, I could feel their presence, and even more powerfully, the love felt by every person gathered around that grave.

Standing there watching them, I thought about all of the people who I have loved and lost. How I tried so hard to forget them as a way to ease the pain. But here in México, it's the opposite. Here, you embrace the memories, and celebrate them every year, focusing on the person rather than the loss. And in this way, the loss becomes less painful. And I realized that I had done something similar, without realizing it, when my mom died.

I couldn't stand her not being in my life. We had talked on the phone almost every day. My life and even my food seemed so empty and devoid of passion without her. When I returned to New York from Austin, I decided that I needed to feel her presence in the kitchen with me. Like that little boy who stood at the stove to help his mom cook, I needed her now to help me cook. I pulled out every paper photo that I had of her and even printed some of the digital ones and taped them to the refrigerator. For months, when I passed the refrigerator, I cried. The photos were a reminder of loss. But eventually, they became a reminder of her presence in my life and in the kitchen. She will always be with me. Many of the spoons and ladles you see in the photos throughout *Mi Cocina* were hers, and now they are mine. I cooked the food in this book with the tools she used to cook for me. And in that way, I am passing her love to you.

> # Here, you embrace the memories, and celebrate them every year, focusing on the person rather than the loss.

▲ Flores de cempasúchil arriving from the farm

▲ Street art

▼ Me in Día de los Muertos face paint

▼ Detail of the ofrenda

▼ Pan de
Muerto

▲ Grave adorned
with Cempasúchil and
Pan de Muerto

Pan de Muerto

Orange-blossom-scented brioche-style roll brushed with melted butter and sugar

I ate my first pan de muerto from La Reina Panadería in Austin when I was sixteen. Immediately, I fell in love. Now, every October when I see the first pan de muerto in the windows of panaderías, my heart races and a smile spreads across my face in anticipation of the holiday, Día de los Muertos. It's like seeing the first pumpkin-spiced anything after Labor Day— you get flushed with the excitement of the approach of fall. Pan de Muerto is a scrumptious, soft, brioche-like, bun whose round shape represents the cycle of life and death. It's often adorned and baked with a small ball of dough and two or more bone-shaped pieces of dough crisscrossed on top representing a skull and crossbones. This bread is lightly sweetened and is perfumed with anise and orange blossoms and zest. You see it in panaderías across Mexico in the weeks leading up to Día de los Muertos, celebrated on November 1 and 2. My recipe uses a lot of butter and eggs to enrich the dough and is brushed with melted butter after it's baked to hold on to all of the sugar you sprinkle over the top.

MAKES 8 ROLLS

- ½ cup whole milk, warmed to 110°F
- 1 envelope (0.25 oz/7 g) active dry yeast (about 2¼ teaspoons)
- 3 large eggs, at room temperature
- 6 tablespoons (2.46 oz/75 g) plus 1 cup (6.98 oz/198 g) sugar, divided
- 1¼ teaspoons Morton kosher salt (0.28 oz/8 g)
- 1 teaspoon finely grated orange zest
- 1 teaspoon orange blossom water
- 3 cups bread flour (13.2 oz/375 g), plus more for the surface
- 3 tablespoons instant nonfat dry milk powder (1.19 oz/34 g)
- ¾ teaspoon ground allspice
- ¼ teaspoon ground anise
- 14 tablespoons unsalted butter (7 oz/198 g), at room temperature, plus 2 tablespoons (1 oz/28 g), melted
- Nonstick cooking spray

1. In the bowl of a stand mixer (or in a large bowl if kneading by hand), whisk the milk and yeast until combined. Let sit for 10 minutes to dissolve; you will see a few bubbles, but the mixture won't be foamy, and that's okay.

2. In a small bowl, whisk the eggs, 6 tablespoons of the sugar, the salt, orange zest, and orange blossom water.

3. To the yeast mixture, add the flour, milk powder, allspice, anise, and the egg mixture. Mix with a wooden spoon until a shaggy dough forms.

4. For the stand mixer, attach the dough hook and knead on medium speed until the dough comes together but is still slightly rough and shaggy, for about 3 minutes. Increase the speed to medium-high and add the 14 tablespoons butter, 1 tablespoon at a time (the dough will look broken after each addition, but it will eventually come together), and beat for about 1 minute between each addition, for a total of 14 minutes. The dough should be smooth, elastic, and very tacky but will pull away from the sides of the bowl. This may seem like a long time, but the texture of the bread improves with a long knead time. (If doing this by hand, knead the dough on a lightly floured surface, adding 1 tablespoon butter at a time, until smooth and elastic, for about 15 minutes.)

5. Lightly spray a large bowl with nonstick spray. Scrape the dough into the bowl. Cover with plastic wrap and let the dough rise in a warm, draft-free area until doubled in volume, for 35 to 50 minutes. The visual cue is more important here than the time. How long your dough takes to proof will depend on how warm your kitchen is. You don't want to overproof the dough, so check it at 35 minutes. The finished dough will smell buttery and yeasty and will have doubled in size. If it isn't there, check again in 10 minutes.

6. Gently deflate the dough by lifting it up around the edges and letting it fall back into the bowl, turning the bowl and repeating the process if needed. Cover the bowl tightly with plastic wrap and refrigerate for at least 12 hours and up to 3 days (an overnight rest works great).

7. Line two sheet pans with parchment paper. Lightly coat the parchment with cooking spray. Turn out the dough onto a clean work surface and divide it into 8 equal pieces. Tear off a tablespoon-size piece of dough from each piece and set those aside. Reshape the larger 8 pieces into smooth round balls and space them evenly apart on one of the lined pans.

8. Pinch off a ½ teaspoon-size piece of dough from each of the remaining smaller 8 pieces. Roll each tiny piece into a smooth round ball and transfer to the second prepared sheet in a single row, arranging them on one of the pan's narrow ends, spacing about 1 inch apart.

9. Divide the remaining 8 pieces of dough in half; you should now have 16 small pieces of dough. Working with one piece at a time, roll using the palm of your hand into a thin rope 3 inches long. Use your index finger to roll and press the center of the rope so that the middle is thinner and both ends are thicker.

10. Next, use your two index fingers to roll and press into the centers of the two thicker ends so that the centers are thin and the ends are thicker. The dough should look like a rope of 4 links of sausage; these are the bones. Carefully transfer the bones to the second lined pan and repeat with the remaining dough, spacing the bones evenly apart.

11. Spray two large sheets of plastic wrap with nonstick spray and loosely cover both pans. Let the dough rise in a warm, draft-free area until almost doubled in size, for 1½ to 2 hours.

12. Position a rack in the center of the oven and preheat to 350°F.

13. Remove the plastic wrap and carefully pick up one of the bones, lifting from the ends (it will stretch and deflate slightly). Drape over one of the larger dough rounds, positioning at 12 o'clock and 6 o'clock. Repeat with the second bone, positioning at 9 o'clock and 3 o'clock.

14. Carefully place one of the small balls in the center, at the point where bones overlap. Gently press the edges of the ball into the bones and larger ball, crowning the loaf. Repeat with the remaining bones and balls.

15. Bake until deep golden brown, for 20 to 25 minutes. Transfer the pan to a wire rack and let cool for 10 minutes. Remove the bread from the pan and brush with the melted butter. Immediately sprinkle with the remaining 1 cup sugar. Let cool on a wire rack for at least 1 hour before serving.

DO AHEAD: The breads can be made 3 days ahead. Let cool completely before tightly wrapping and storing at room temperature.

▲ Pescado a la Talla, p. 142

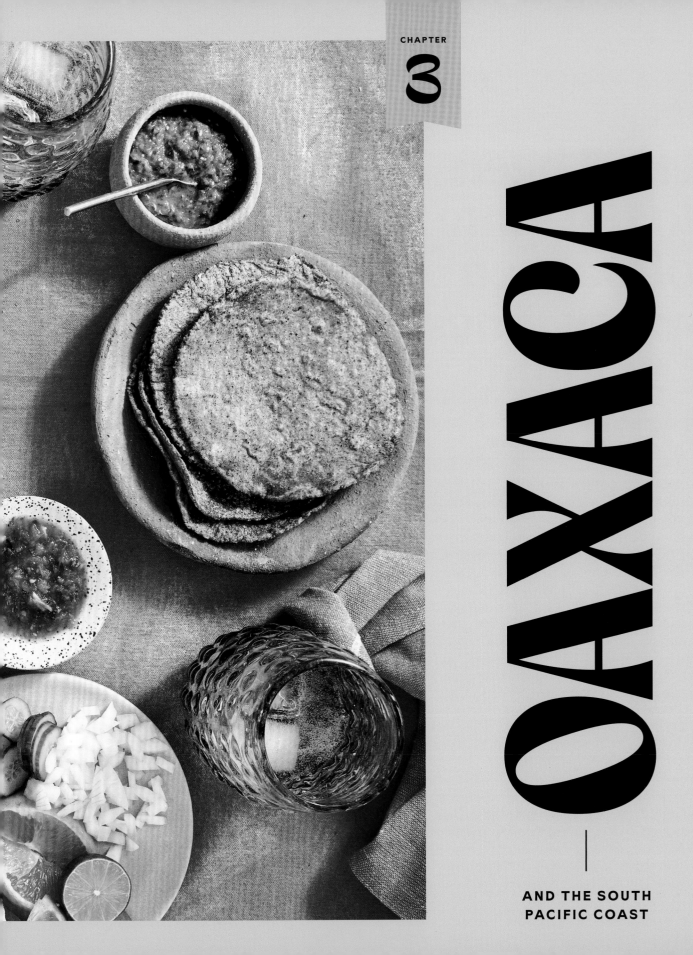

OAXACA

—

AND THE SOUTH
PACIFIC COAST

I had been to the state of Oaxaca many times. I thought I knew it.

But seeing it through the windshield of my car introduced me to the natural beauty of this area: semi-arid hills that morphed into verdant, majestic mountains with white water rapids rushing downriver to the valleys below. It turns out that I love driving through mountains. There is even a highway in Oaxaca, Carretera Federal 175, that is one of the most beautiful and breathtaking winding drives I have ever taken. It reminds me a lot of Pacific Coast Highway in California—both roads that wind so aggressively around the mountaintops that your arms ache from all of the sharp turns. I kept pulling over on the nonexistent shoulder to take pictures and breathe in the clean mountain air.

I knew that the food in the Oaxacan towns and cities that I had previously visited was really good—tlayudas so loaded with beans, tasajo (thin slices of seared semi-cured meat), and quesillo they would shatter from the weight—but I wondered if the food in the tiny pueblitos was going to live up to or even compare to what I had already eaten. My doubts were completely unfounded: The food in the smallest towns was in fact the *most* delicious because it was cooked without the intention to please a tourist. I have found that in larger cities with greater tourism, the food is less a reflection of the cook

THE RECIPES

Tamales Oaxaqueños
steamed corn dumplings filled with shredded chicken and sauce, p. 111

Pozole Verde estilo Guerrero
hearty hominy and chicken stew with poblano, tomatillo, and pumpkin seeds, p. 116

Tlayuda con Tasajo
large toasted corn tortilla topped with refried beans and grilled marinated flank steak, p. 119

Brochetas de Pulpo y Camarones
grilled orange, habanero-marinated shrimp, and octopus skewers, p. 122

Albóndigas en Chipotle
herb and cheese meatballs with a smoky tomato-chipotle sauce, p. 126

Mole Coloradito
rich chile sauce made with pasillas, dried fruits, seeds, and bittersweet chocolate, p. 130

Mole Amarillo con Chochoyotes
chicken and corn dumplings simmered in a velvety chile sauce, p. 134

Empanadas de Mole Amarillo
toasted corn turnovers filled with shredded chicken and mole, p. 137

Mojarra Frita
flour-dusted whole fried fish marinated in garlic and lime, p. 138

Chileatole Verde
roasted vegetables in a rich corn broth made from fresh and dried corn and green chiles, p. 141

Pescado a la Talla
guajillo chile and orange-marinated grilled red snapper, p. 142

SOUTH PACIFIC MÉXICO

States: Oaxaca, Guerrero, Chiapas

▼ Cintalapa, Chiapas

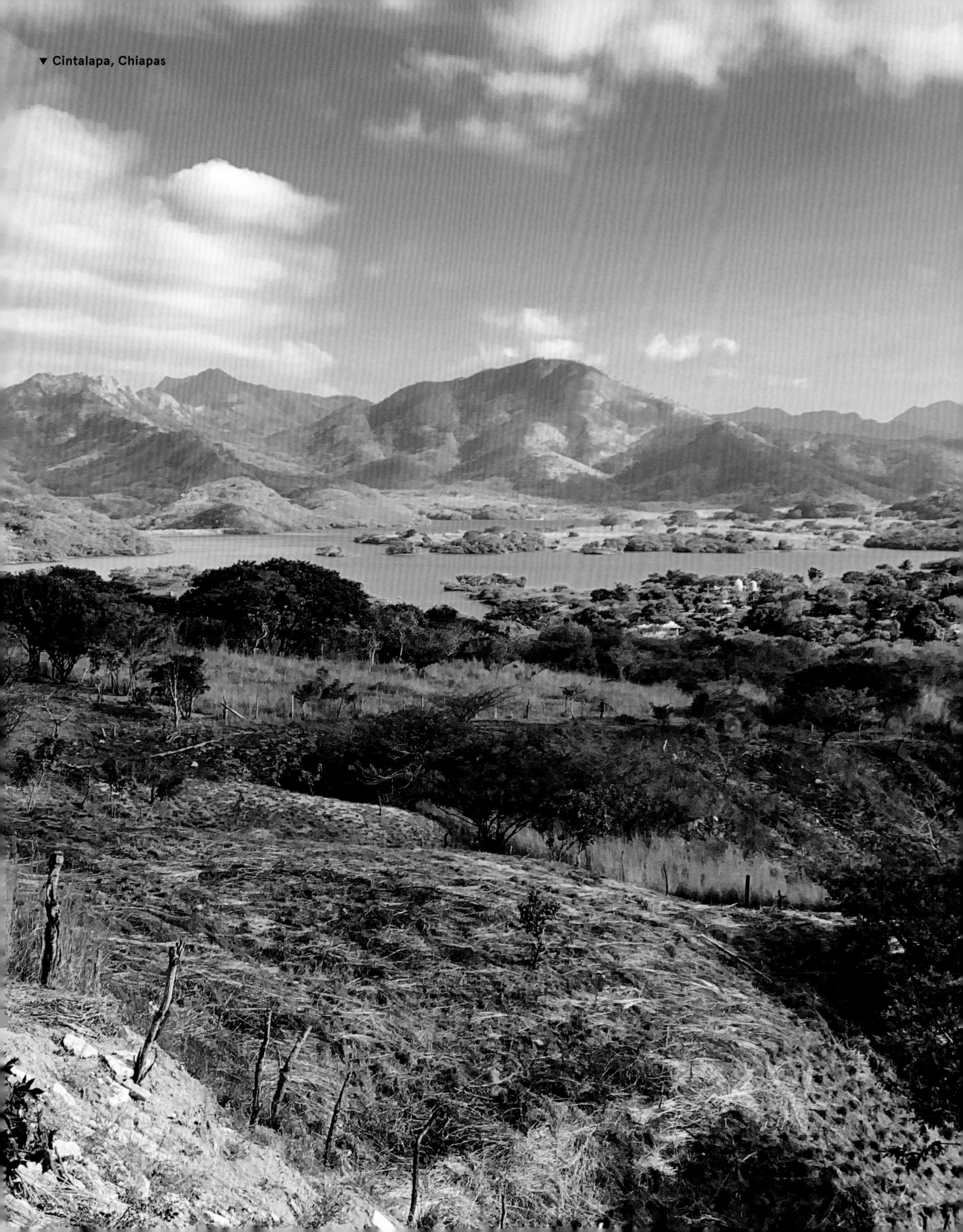

and more a reflection of what the cook thinks a tourist will buy. But in the smaller towns, the food seems more pure. It is truer to the place, using local fresh ingredients, as well as to the person who made it, pouring personal love into each serving.

One thing that I noticed that I believe contributes to the complexity of the flavors in Oaxaca is the desire to preserve food traditions and ancient agricultural practices. The mercados are filled with herbs, spices, and chiles that are particular to the region, like chile chilhuacle, which is used to make the most amazing moles for which Oaxaca is famous. It's really hard to find these chiles anywhere else in the country, and there is very little desire to commercialize agriculture and to mass cultivate and produce these native species of chiles and other fruits and vegetables. As a result, the food in much of the state remains as flavorful, and complex, and as full of indigenous tradition as it was a hundred—or even five hundred—years ago. While the traditional street food served in pueblitos is remarkable, innovative Mexican chefs in cities like Oaxaca and Puerto Escondido continue to expand the canon and create dishes using indigenous techniques and methods, with local produce, and with imagination and personal flair.

◄

CLOCKWISE FROM TOP LEFT:
Chiapa de Corzo, Chiapas;
Puerto Escondido, Oaxaca;
Miahuatlán de Porfirio Díaz,
Oaxaca; San José del
Pacífico, Oaxaca

As much as I loved the mercados in Oaxaca, the tianguis (outdoor markets) in Chiapas are even more incredible. Chiapas is a stunning state south and east of Oaxaca with kilometer-deep canyons, raging rivers, lush forests, and deep blue lakes. I walked through the tianguis in San Cristóbal for what seemed like hours, without ever managing to find the end. I was there during the Christmas holidays and the tianguis was packed with people preparing for their posadas (holiday parties), buying fresh fruits and cinnamon for their ponche (spiced fruit punch), and fresh masa to make tamales. The energy was intoxicating and overwhelming. The tianguis was huge, about four square city blocks, and it was packed full of holiday shoppers and vendors selling arts, crafts, produce, proteins, prepared food, and lots of preserved late-fall fruit and vegetables—it had the feel of a Moroccan bazaar. Tianguis can be roadside, too; I went to many that were about a kilometer long and sold nothing but salted, candied, pickled, jammed, and jellied fruits, vegetables, and chiles.

Guerrero, north of Oaxaca, is probably best known for its pozole, and its pozole verde did ruin me for all others. The inclusion of pepitas (pumpkin seeds) in the herby green broth creates a creamy and nutty counterpoint to the acidity of the tomatillos—something I knew I had to use in my Pozole Verde estilo Guerrero (p. 116). It is most often served topped with chicharrones, which always gets my heart racing.

Tamales Oaxaqueños

Steamed corn dumplings filled with shredded chicken and sauce

In this recipe, since I am using chicken as the main ingredient in the filling, I decided to include a recipe for a cooked chicken and homemade stock. Of course you can use your own homemade chicken stock or swap in a different filling for the chicken (roasted vegetables are also delicious in a tamal).

I am offering you three options for the salsa (sauce) for the filling. The most common Oaxacan tamales are made with mole, salsa tomatillo, or salsa guajillo.

For the 24 tamales in this recipe, you need a total of 6 cups of salsa. Each of the two salsa recipes makes about 6 cups, so choose only one salsa or cut each recipe in half and make half red and half green! Or, if you choose the mole (option 3), you can use 6 cups of that, too! Choose your own tamal adventure and make sure to invite friends and family to help you cook and eat them. Turn it into a tamalada (tamal party)—spread the masa and spread the love!

MAKES 24 TAMALES

**FILLING OPTION 1:
SALSA TOMATILLO**

- 4 cups Chicken Stock (recipe follows) or other low-sodium chicken stock
- 7 medium tomatillos (12 oz/ 340 g), husked, rinsed, and quartered
- ¼ medium white onion (3.45 oz/ 98 g), coarsely chopped
- 2 garlic cloves, lightly crushed
- 1 chile habanero, stemmed, seeded, and halved
- ⅓ cup (packed) fresh cilantro leaves with tender stems (1.76 oz/50 g)
- 1½ teaspoons Morton kosher salt (0.31 oz/9 g)

**FILLING OPTION 2:
SALSA GUAJILLO**

- 5 cups Chicken Stock (recipe follows) or other low-sodium chicken stock
- 6 large chiles guajillos (1.26 oz/ 36 g), stemmed and seeded
- 2 large chiles anchos (1.2 oz/35 g), stemmed and seeded
- ¼ medium white onion (3.45 oz/ 98 g), coarsely chopped
- 4 garlic cloves, lightly crushed

- 3 chiles de árbol, stemmed (seeded for less heat)
- 1½ teaspoons Morton kosher salt (0.31 oz/9 g)
- 1 dried bay leaf
- 1 teaspoon dried oregano, preferably Mexican

FILLING OPTION 3: MOLE

- 6 cups Mole Coloradito, *p. 130,* or Mole Amarillo, *p. 134*

FOR THE MASA

- 1¾ cups Chicken Stock (recipe follows) or other low-sodium chicken stock, warmed
- 1¾ teaspoons Morton kosher salt (0.42 oz/12 g)
- 3 pounds (1.36 kg) fresh coarse-grind corn masa for tamales, "unprepared" (see Cook's Note, p. 112)
- 1¼ cups plus 2 tablespoons melted lard or vegetable oil

FOR THE TAMALES

- 1 pound (453 g) fresh or thawed frozen banana leaves, washed and patted dry
- 3 cups shredded cooked chicken (recipe follows)

1. MAKE THE SALSA TOMATILLO: In a large saucepan over high heat, bring the stock, tomatillos, onion, garlic, habanero, cilantro, and salt to a boil, reduce to a simmer, cover, and cook until the vegetables are very tender and almost falling apart, for 20 to 25 minutes.

2. Transfer the tomatillo mixture to a blender and puree on medium-low speed until completely smooth. Set the salsa aside until you're ready to assemble.

RECIPE CONTINUES →

3. MAKE THE SALSA GUAJILLO: In a large saucepan, bring the stock, chiles guajillos, chiles anchos, onion, garlic, chiles de árbol, salt, bay leaf, and oregano to a boil. Cover the pot, remove from the heat, and let sit until chiles are tender, for about 30 minutes.

4. Transfer the chile mixture to the jar of a blender and puree on medium-low speed until completely smooth. Set the salsa aside until you're ready to assemble.

5. MAKE THE MASA: In a 2-cup liquid measure, whisk the stock and salt until the salt is dissolved. In a large bowl, mix the masa, stock mixture, and lard with your hands until the mixture looks shiny and smooth and is the consistency of thick cake frosting and is easily spreadable, for about 5 minutes. Cover the bowl with plastic wrap and set aside.

6. MAKE THE TAMALES: Unfold a banana leaf (it should be 2 to 3 feet long). If you have gas burners, heat one gas burner on high. (If you don't have a gas burner, see the Cook's Note on p. 167.) Hold the leaf at each end and very slowly move the leaf over the flame, leaving it in one place until you see light charring coming through the top. Continue moving the leaf slowly for 3 to 7 seconds to see char marks in one spot, or until the entire leaf is charred. Repeat with the remaining banana leaves.

7. Remove the center rib and cut the leaves into 12 × 14-inch pieces; reserve the ribs and scraps. If your leaves are narrow, double up and offset the leaves to get the right size.

8. Arrange the leaf so a long side is facing you. Measure out ½ cup of masa and place it onto the center of the leaf. Using a table knife, offset spatula, or rubber spatula, spread the masa into a thin, even layer, covering most of the leaf but leaving a 2-inch border on all sides; the edges don't have to be straight or neat. Visualize the tamal in the center of the leaf, about 6 inches long by 4 inches wide. Arrange 2 tablespoons of chicken in the center of that space. Top with ¼ cup salsa or mole.

9. Fold a long side of the leaf over the filling, then fold over the other long side to cover. Hold the tamal seam-side up and fold the two short ends over the tamal. Set the tamal on a sheet pan seam- and fold-side down. Repeat to assemble the remaining tamales.

10. Place a metal basket, steamer basket, or rack insert into a tamal pot, stockpot, or pasta pot. Fill with enough water so it comes up to just below the basket (you don't want the water to touch the tamales). Line the bottom of the basket with the reserved banana leaf scraps to cover any exposed metal. Arrange and stack the tamales, seam-side down, in the basket. Cover the tamales with a damp kitchen towel and tuck it inside the pot. Cover the pot and bring the water to a boil over high heat. Reduce the heat to medium-low to keep the water at a simmer and steam for 45 minutes, checking the water level occasionally and adding more water as needed to keep some liquid in the pot.

11. Carefully remove the kitchen towel and plastic. Remove a tamal and set aside to cool for 3 minutes. (If you don't let the tamal rest before checking, the masa will stick to the leaf and appear gummy.) Unfold the leaf—if the masa sticks, it's not ready. If it's not ready, carefully refold and return the tamal to the pot. Cook for 5 minutes more, then check again. If the leaf peels back easily and no masa sticks, your tamales are done. Remove from the heat, uncover the pot, and let sit for 10 minutes before serving.

COOK'S NOTE: If you are using fresh masa, look or ask for "unprepared" masa. This means that nothing has been added to the dough and the only thing in it is corn, water, and lime. "Prepared" masa has added lard and seasonings. I always use "unprepared" so that I can control the amount of lard, seasoning, and salt.

Shredded Chicken and Stock

MAKES ABOUT 3 QUARTS STOCK AND 4 CUPS SHREDDED CHICKEN

- 1 whole chicken (3½ lb/1.58 kg)
- ½ large white onion (7 oz/200 g), halved
- 4 garlic cloves, lightly crushed
- 1 tablespoon black peppercorns
- 1 teaspoon allspice berries
- 3 whole cloves
- 3 fresh epazote, oregano, marjoram, or thyme sprigs
- 2 hoja santa leaves (optional)

1. In a large heavy pot over high heat, bring 4 quarts water, the chicken, onion, garlic, peppercorns, allspice, cloves, epazote, and hoja santa (if using) to a boil; reduce to a simmer and cook, skimming occasionally, until the chicken is cooked through (if the chicken isn't completely submerged, you can turn it once or twice) and the legs wiggle easily in their joints, for 40 to 50 minutes.

2. Let the chicken cool slightly and transfer to a cutting board. Set the stock aside. When the chicken is cool enough to handle, remove the meat from the bones and shred into bite-size pieces. Discard the skin and bones. Transfer the meat to a bowl, cover with plastic wrap, and set aside until ready to use.

3. Strain the stock through a fine-mesh sieve and set aside until ready to use.

DO AHEAD: The stock can be made 3 days ahead. Store in an airtight container and refrigerate or freeze for up to 3 months. Chicken can be made 3 days ahead. Store in an airtight container and refrigerate.

1. Toast the banana leaves.

2. Spread with an even layer of masa.

3. Top with chicken and drizzle of salsa.

4. Fold the leaf over the filling.

5. Fold the ends over the tamal.

6. Arrange seam- and fold-side down.

▲ Pozole Verde estilo
Guerrero, p. 116

Pozole Verde estilo Guerrero

Hearty hominy and chicken stew with poblano, tomatillo, and pumpkin seeds

Taxco, which is just a couple hours south of Mexico City in Guerrero, is a beautiful colonial silver mining town built on the side of a mountain. It looks like a movie set with its cobblestone streets and old Spanish architecture. The best thing that I ate there was the pozole verde, which is unique compared to other areas in México. Here, the pozole has a richer, almost creamy broth because of the addition of pepitas (raw pumpkin seeds). And it's served with lots of crunchy chicharrones on top for added flavor and texture.

SERVES 8

- 2 15-ounce cans white hominy, rinsed and drained
- 2 tablespoons rendered lard or olive oil
- 4 whole chicken legs (8.8 oz/ 250 g each)
- 2 large chiles poblanos (13.6 oz/ 387 g), stemmed, seeded, and chopped
- 3 large chiles jalapeños (3.13 oz/ 89 g), stemmed, seeded, and chopped
- 1 large bunch of scallions (7.09 oz/201g), roots trimmed, green and white parts kept separate, roughly chopped
- ½ cup raw pepitas (2.2 oz/65 g) (raw pumpkin seeds)
- 4 garlic cloves, lightly crushed

- 1 tablespoon plus ½ teaspoon Morton kosher salt (0.84 oz/24 g)
- 1 teaspoon coriander seeds
- 1 teaspoon cumin seeds
- ½ teaspoon allspice berries
- 7 medium tomatillos (18.2 oz/ 516 g), husked, rinsed, and roughly chopped
- 1 medium bunch of cilantro (1.76 oz/50 g), roughly chopped

FOR SERVING
- → Chopped white onion
- → Sliced radish
- → Sliced avocado
- → Crushed chicharrones
- → Dried Mexican oregano
- → Crushed chile de árbol
- → Lime wedges

1. Arrange a rack in the center of the oven and preheat to 425°F. Line a sheet pan with parchment paper.

2. Spread the hominy in an even layer on the lined pan. Roast, tossing once, until lightly toasted, very fragrant, and just beginning to brown, for 12 to 18 minutes. Set aside until ready to use.

3. Meanwhile, in a large heavy pot over high heat, melt the lard. Working in batches if necessary, add the chicken legs, skin-side down, and cook until browned on both sides, for 8 to 10 minutes. Transfer to a plate and repeat with the remaining legs.

4. Reduce the heat to medium-high. To the same pot, add the chiles poblanos, chiles jalapeños, scallion whites, pepitas, garlic, salt, coriander, cumin, and allspice and cook, stirring occasionally, until the vegetables are just tender, for about 7 minutes. Add the tomatillos and continue to cook, stirring occasionally, until they begin to soften and brown, for 5 to 6 minutes. Remove from the heat, add 6 cups water, and stir and scrape up any browned bits from the bottom of the pot.

5. Carefully transfer the tomatillo mixture to a blender and puree until smooth. Pour the tomatillo puree into the pot (there's no need to wash the blender, you'll use it again). Add the reserved chicken and hominy to the pot and bring to a boil. Reduce the heat to medium-low, cover, and simmer until the chicken is cooked through and very tender and the flavors of the broth have come together, for 45 to 55 minutes. Remove from the heat and transfer the chicken to a large bowl. Set aside until cool enough to handle, then remove the meat from the bones and shred the meat into bite-size pieces. Discard the skin and bones and add the meat to the pot.

6. Add the cilantro, scallion greens, and 2 cups water to the blender and puree until smooth. Add the cilantro puree to the pozole in the pot and stir to combine. Let sit for 5 minutes to let the scallion mellow.

7. Serve the pozole in bowls topped with onion, radish, avocado, chicharrones, oregano, and chile flakes. Serve with lime wedges.

Tlayuda con Tasajo

Large toasted corn tortilla topped with refried beans and grilled marinated flank steak

SERVES 4

¼ cup white miso (fermented soybean paste)
1 canned chipotle pepper in adobo sauce, smashed, plus 2 tablespoons adobo sauce
1 garlic clove, finely grated
½ teaspoon Morton kosher salt (0.14 oz/4 g)
1½ pounds (680 g) flank steak
2 tlayudas oaxaqueñas or 6 baked Tostadas de Maíz, p. 40, warm
2 tablespoons rendered lard, warmed

1½ cups Frijoles Refritos, p. 55
12 ounces (340 g) quesillo or fresh mozzarella cheese, pulled into thin strands or shredded

FOR SERVING
→ Thinly sliced cabbage
→ Chopped white onion
→ Sliced avocado
→ Sliced tomato
→ Sliced cucumber
→ Salsa de Chipotle y Chile de Árbol, p. 62

1. In a small bowl, stir together the miso, chipotle pepper, adobo sauce, garlic, and salt until combined. Rub the miso mixture on both sides of the steak, working to get into the grain of the meat. Place the meat in a zip-top freezer bag and refrigerate for at least 30 minutes and up to 24 hours.

2. Prepare a gas grill or charcoal grill for high heat.

3. Brush off any excess marinade and cut the steak crosswise into 4 equal pieces. Use a meat mallet or heavy skillet to pound the steaks between two layers of plastic wrap to a ¼-inch thickness. Grill the steak, turning occasionally, for 1 to 2 minutes per side for medium-rare. Transfer the steaks to a cutting board and let them rest for 10 minutes. Cut or tear into 2-inch pieces.

4. Brush the tlayuda with lard. Spread a thin layer of frijoles on each. Top with the steak, quesillo, cabbage, onion, avocado, tomato, cucumber, and salsa.

COOK'S NOTE: To make homemade tlayudas, use the recipe for Tortillas de Maíz (p. 38), but instead of using ¼ cup masa for each tortilla, double the quantity to ½ cup. Flatten the masa as much and as evenly as you can with your tortilla press or skillet. After you press them, you can use the palm of your hand to continue to press the masa out from the center, making the disk even wider—it should be 12 inches in diameter. Peel one side of the plastic bag from the dough. Place the dough on your open palm and wrist so it is plastic-side up, and peel off the second side. Just cook it in a skillet as you would a tortilla. Meanwhile, arrange a rack in the center of the oven and preheat to 450°F. Place the tortillas on a sheet pan and bake until they're golden brown in spots and crisp, for about 10 minutes. Let cool before serving.

▼ Brochetas de Pulpo
y Camarones, p. 122

Brochetas de Pulpo y Camarones

Grilled orange, habanero-marinated shrimp, and octopus skewers

It was a hot December day on the Pacific coast and I had just driven into Puerto Escondido from the city of Oaxaca. I was very tired, and very hungry, but there is something about the beach that energizes me. I walked to the part of the beach where fishing boats come in and saw a stand with a grill. A man behind the grill (I later learned his name was Omar) waved me over. He said he made the best octopus. So of course I sat down and ordered his brochetas de pulpo y camarones. There was something so magical about sitting on the beach, listening to the waves crash, and smelling smoke and grilling seafood.

Omar's brochetas were pretty amazing. They were simple, with notes of garlic, lime, and smoke. And so fresh—the shrimp and octopus had been caught a few hours before I arrived and had traveled about twenty-five meters from the ocean to this man's grill on the beach. Of everything that I have eaten in México, this simple dish made the biggest imprint. Not just the food, but the moment and everything in it were perfect.

SERVES 4

- 2 tablespoons plus ¼ cup extra-virgin olive oil, divided, plus more for the grill
- 3 pounds (1.36 kg) octopus, cleaned, head separated from tentacles
- ½ medium white onion (6.7 oz/ 190 g), chopped
- 1 chile habanero (0.37 oz/10.7 g), halved, stemmed, and seeded
- 10 garlic cloves, finely grated, divided
- 4 wide strips orange zest
- 1 small bunch of fresh flat-leaf parsley
- ¼ cup fresh lime juice
- ¼ cup fresh orange juice
- ½ teaspoon ground chiles de árbol or red chile flakes
- 2¼ teaspoons Morton kosher salt (0.56 oz/16 g)
- 2 pounds (907 g) tail-on jumbo shrimp, peeled and deveined
- 1 large red onion (13.7 oz/389 g), chopped into 2-inch pieces
- 1 pint cherry tomatoes
- 2 large yellow bell peppers (13.8 oz/392 g), stemmed, seeded, and cut into 2-inch pieces

1. Arrange a rack in the lower third of the oven and preheat to 300°F.

2. In a large Dutch oven over medium-high, heat 2 tablespoons of the oil. Cook half of the octopus, turning with tongs occasionally, until browned on all sides, for 3 to 5 minutes. Transfer to a plate and repeat with the remaining octopus. To the pot, add the white onion, chile habanero, and half of the garlic and cook, stirring, until browned, for 5 to 6 minutes. Add 2 cups water; bring to a boil. Add the octopus, orange zest, and parsley. Cover the pot and transfer to the oven. Braise until the octopus is tender and a knife pierces the thickest tentacle with little resistance, for 1½ to 2 hours.

3. Uncover the pot and let the octopus cool in the liquid. Remove the octopus from the pot. Using a paper towel, wipe the skin off the tentacles, leaving the suckers intact. Cut the tentacles into 2-inch pieces, then cut the head into quarters. Discard the braising liquid.

4. In a large bowl, whisk the lime juice, orange juice, chiles de árbol, and the remaining garlic and ¼ cup oil. Transfer ¼ cup of the mixture to a small bowl; set aside. Whisk the salt into the remaining mixture in the large bowl. Add the octopus, raw shrimp, red onion, tomatoes, and bell peppers and toss to coat. Cover the bowl and let marinate for 15 minutes.

5. Thread the octopus and shrimp on metal skewers, alternating with the onion, peppers, and tomatoes, and transfer to a baking sheet.

6. Prepare a grill for high heat. Use tongs and an old, clean kitchen towel to brush the grates with oil. Grill the brochetas, turning occasionally, until lightly charred on all sides, for 4 to 6 minutes. Transfer the brochetas to a platter and brush with the reserved lime mixture.

▼ Albóndigas en Chipotle, p. 126

Albóndigas en Chipotle

Herb and cheese meatballs with a smoky tomato-chipotle sauce

I am a huge fan of meatballs no matter what country they come from. The best ones I had in Mexico were at the Mercado Juan Sabines in Tuxtla Gutiérrez in the state of Chiapas. It was a cool afternoon just before Christmas, and I had driven into Chiapas from Oaxaca. I was planning to eat only the typical foods from the region. When I saw albóndigas, I couldn't resist; I had to have them. They were brothy, spicy, and smoky from chile chipotle. I was so incredibly happy. Because I love them so much, I am also super critical of bad balls. I have made thousands of meatballs in my life and one of the most important things that I have learned over the years is you need to add fat and moisture to the ground meat. I like using dairy because it adds both moisture and milkfat, which also tenderizes the meat. I also add bread crumbs to hold on to the moisture and fat as the meatballs cook and prevent them from getting tough and dry (and no one wants tough, dry balls).

SERVES 4 TO 6

- 10 large Roma tomatoes (2 lb/ 990 g), cored
- 2 to 5 canned chipotle peppers in adobo sauce, plus 2 tablespoons adobo sauce
- Morton kosher salt
- 1 cup panko or fresh bread crumbs
- ⅓ cup finely chopped fresh cilantro (1.7 oz/50 g), plus more for serving
- ½ cup crumbled queso fresco (2.15 oz/61 g), plus more for serving
- ½ large white onion (5.7 oz/ 162 g), grated on the large holes of a box grater, divided
- 5 garlic cloves, finely grated, divided
- 1 teaspoon freshly ground black pepper
- ¾ teaspoon cumin seeds
- 1 cup crema or sour cream
- 1 pound (453 g) ground beef (20% fat)
- 1 pound (453 g) ground pork (20% fat if possible)
- 3 tablespoons extra-virgin olive oil, divided, plus more for shaping
- 1 teaspoon dried oregano, preferably Mexican
- 1½ cups homemade chicken stock or store-bought low-sodium chicken broth

FOR SERVING
- → Warm Tortillas de Maíz, *p. 38*
- → Arroz Rojo, *p. 49*
- → Frijoles de Olla, *p. 54*

1. Line a large skillet with a sheet of foil and heat the pan over medium-high (the foil prevents the tomatoes from burning and sticking to the bottom of the skillet and will keep the skillet clean as you roast them). Add the tomatoes and cook, turning occasionally, until charred on all sides, for about 16 minutes.

2. Transfer the tomatoes to a blender. Add the chipotle peppers (start with two), adobo sauce, and 1½ teaspoons salt (0.31 oz/9 g) and puree on medium-low speed until almost smooth. Don't be tempted to increase the speed or you will get an airy, smoothie consistency; it's better to have a chunky salsa than a smoothie! Taste, and if you want the salsa hotter, add more chipotles and puree to combine. Set the salsa aside until ready to use.

3. In a small bowl, whisk together the panko, cilantro, queso, ¼ cup onion, half of the garlic, 1½ teaspoons salt (0.31 oz/9 g), black pepper, and cumin until combined. Stir in the crema and set aside.

4. Add the beef and pork to a large bowl. Using two forks, begin "pulling" the ground meat apart as if you were shredding pulled pork, breaking up the clumps and bringing the two meats together without compacting the meat into a dense mass. Continue to pull the meat apart until thoroughly mixed and no clumps of beef or pork remain. Pour the crema mixture into the "pulled" meat and, using the same technique, mix until all of the ingredients are completely and evenly incorporated.

5. Lightly oil your hands. Working with one at a time, scoop out portions of the meat mixture with a ¼-cup measuring cup or very large ice cream scoop. Roll the meat mixture gently between your hands into balls and arrange them on a sheet pan.

6. In a large nonstick skillet over medium-high, heat 2 tablespoons of the oil. Add half of the meatballs and cook, using tongs or a fork to turn and roll them occasionally, until browned on all sides, for about 5 minutes. They will not be cooked through, just browned on the outside. Return the meatballs to the sheet pan and repeat with the remaining meatballs. Set aside until ready to add to the sauce.

7. In the same skillet, heat the remaining 1 tablespoon oil and cook the remaining onion, garlic, and oregano, stirring frequently and scraping up any browned bits on the bottom of the pan, until beginning to brown, for 3 to 5 minutes. Add the stock, reserved salsa, and meatballs with any accumulated juices. Reduce the heat to medium-low, cover, and simmer until the meatballs are cooked through, for 30 to 40 minutes. Taste and season with more salt if desired.

8. Serve hot with warm corn tortillas, arroz rojo, and frijoles de olla and topped with crumbled queso fresco and chopped cilantro.

▼ Mole Coloradito, p. 130

Mole Coloradito

Rich chile sauce made with pasillas, dried fruits, seeds, and bittersweet chocolate

I arrived in Oaxaca de Juárez late at night. I was tired. But it didn't matter—before giving in to sleep, I had to have mole. All the places I really wanted to try were already closed, but I managed to find a place that was still open, and they had mole negro. I ordered enmoladas, which are kind of like an enchilada but sauced with mole negro instead of a red enchilada sauce. And this hole-in-the-wall place, late on a Sunday night, served me one of the best moles I've ever eaten. I knew that I had to include it in my book.

Mole negro is made with chile chilhuacle negro, a chile native to the state of Oaxaca grown only in the Cuicatlán District in the northern part of the state. Sourcing this specialized chile can be hard, even in México. Still, I tried to make it by using chiles more common in Mazatlán and available in the US, but it just wasn't the same. It's like trying to make a marinara with a relative of the tomato. A potato perhaps? No, not the same. So, I decided to make a mole that I could successfully re-create and one that I know you can, too. Mole coloradito is very common in the central part of the state and showcases the flavor and color of chile pasilla, which is much easier to find both in México and in the US.

MAKES 2 QUARTS

- 1 tablespoon raw pumpkin seeds
- 1 tablespoon sesame seeds
- 1 teaspoon dried oregano, preferably Mexican
- 1 teaspoon dried or fresh thyme leaves
- ¾ teaspoon cumin seeds
- ½ teaspoon black peppercorns
- 2 allspice berries
- 1 whole clove
- 1 dried or fresh avocado leaf or 2 bay leaves
- ⅔ cup plus 2 tablespoons rendered lard or neutral oil, divided
- 8 large chiles pasillas (2.8 oz/81 g), stemmed and seeded
- 4 large chiles anchos (2.4 oz/70 g), stemmed and seeded
- 2 medium chiles cascabeles (0.5 oz/16 g), stemmed and seeded
- 1 Tortilla de Maíz, *p. 38*, or store-bought corn tortilla
- 4 large Roma tomatoes (12.5 oz/356 g), cored and chopped
- ¼ large white onion (3.9 oz/112 g)

- ½ large plantain (5.9 oz/170 g), black and very ripe, peeled and sliced crosswise into ½-inch rounds
- 3 garlic cloves, peeled
- 1 cup animal crackers (1.7 oz/50 g)
- ¼ cup raisins (1.4 oz/40 g)
- 2 tablespoons raw almonds (0.77 oz/22 g)
- 2 tablespoons raw peanuts (0.77 oz/22 g)
- 1 1-inch stick canela or cassia cinnamon
- 1 star anise
- 7 cups homemade chicken stock or store-bought low-sodium chicken broth
- ⅓ cup grated piloncillo or (packed) dark brown sugar (2.5 oz/71 g), plus more to taste
- 5¼ teaspoons Morton kosher salt (0.9 oz/26 g)
- 1.4 oz (40 g) bittersweet chocolate (70% cacao or higher), chopped

FOR SERVING
→ Roasted chicken or turkey
→ Toasted sesame seeds

1. Heat a large heavy pot over medium-high. Once the pot is hot, add the pumpkin seeds, sesame seeds, oregano, thyme, cumin, peppercorns, allspice, clove, and avocado leaf and stir constantly until everything is very fragrant and the seeds are beginning to brown, for about 1 minute. Transfer to a large bowl.

2. In the same pot still over medium-high, heat ⅔ cup of the lard until very hot. Working in batches, fry the chiles pasillas, anchos, and cascabeles, using tongs to turn them to coat in the lard, until fragrant, browned, and toasted on both sides, for about 30 seconds. Transfer to the bowl with the toasted spices.

3. Fry the tortilla, turning once, until deep golden brown and crispy, for about 2 minutes. Transfer to the bowl with the chile/spice mixture.

4. To the same pot, add the tomatoes, onion, plantain, and garlic and cook, stirring occasionally, until the vegetables are very soft and browned, for 7 to 9 minutes. Transfer to the bowl with the chile mixture.

5. In the same pot, fry the crackers, raisins, almonds, peanuts, canela, and star anise, stirring constantly, until the raisins puff and lighten and the crackers are browned, for 2 to 3 minutes. Add the stock, piloncillo, salt, and chile mixture to the pot. Bring to a boil, then reduce to a simmer, cover, and cook until the chiles and nuts are very tender and smash easily when pressed on the side of the pot, for about 30 minutes. Remove from the heat and set the pot aside, covered, for 20 minutes to cool slightly before blending.

6. Working in batches, carefully blend the chile mixture and liquid until completely smooth. Transfer to a large bowl, stirring to combine each new addition.

7. Rinse and dry the pot, set it over medium-high, and heat the remaining 2 tablespoons lard until it's very hot. Carefully pour the blended mole into the hot lard; it will spit and sputter, so an apron and long sleeves are a good idea. Stir, scraping up any fried bits from the bottom of the pot. Reduce the heat to medium-low and simmer, stirring frequently, until the mole is glossy and thick and the consistency of a cream gravy, for about 10 minutes. Stir in the chocolate and remove from the heat. Continue to stir until the chocolate is completely melted. Taste and season with salt or piloncillo if deisred.

8. Serve over chicken and sprinkled with the sesame seeds.

DO AHEAD: The mole can be made 2 days ahead. Store in an airtight container in the refrigerator, or freeze up to 1 month. Reheat in a medium saucepan over medium heat, stirring frequently until heated through.

▲ Choco and me,
Rancho Los Olivos,
El Huajote, Sinaloa

▲ Mole Amarillo
con Chochoyotes,
p. 134

Mole Amarillo con Chochoyotes

Chicken and corn dumplings simmered in a velvety chile sauce

This is another one of those dishes that is very hard to replicate because the chiles can be difficult to source outside of Oaxaca. But I have given substitutes because, unlike chiles for mole negro, I believe the chilhuacles amarillos used for mole amarillo can be substituted with the more common chile guajillo without compromising the flavor of the overall dish. This is also another case where I want you to make this dish and then immediately book your trip to Oaxaca to experience this mole on site, the way that it should be made.

I also love this dish because of the chochoyotes, which are masa dumplings with a dimple in them that holds onto the mole. Growing up in Texas, my mom made chicken and dumplings when it was cold and dreary out, and it was like getting a hug and kiss from her. This dish could be the Mexican comfort equivalent with chicken, a rich and thick, albeit spicy stew, and soft maíz dumplings cooked in that rich bright, spicy, and slightly sweet mole.

SERVES 6 TO 8

FOR THE CHOCHOYOTES
- 1 cup harina de maíz, such as Bob's Red Mill Masa Harina (3.6 oz/112 g)
- 1 tablespoon rendered lard or unsalted butter
- ¼ teaspoon Morton kosher salt (0.07 oz/2 g)

FOR THE MOLE AMARILLO
- 3 large chiles chilhuacles amarillos (0.63 oz/18 g) or chiles guajillos, stemmed and seeded
- 2 tablespoons rendered lard, olive oil, or vegetable oil
- 4 whole chicken legs (2.2 lb/1 kg)
- ½ medium white onion (6.7 oz/ 190 g), chopped
- 2 large fresh yellow chiles güeros/ caribes (5 oz/141 g), banana, wax, or bell peppers, stemmed, seeded, and chopped
- 3 medium tomatillos (4.23 oz/ 120 g), husked, rinsed, and chopped
- 6 garlic cloves, finely grated
- 2¼ teaspoons Morton kosher salt (0.56 oz/16 g)

- 1 teaspoon black peppercorns
- 1 teaspoon dried oregano, preferably Mexican
- ½ teaspoon cumin seeds
- 4 allspice berries
- 1 whole clove
- 1 hoja santa leaf or ¼ cup each mint and cilantro leaves
- 1 dried bay leaf
- 3 cups homemade chicken stock or store-bought low-sodium chicken stock
- 2 baked Tostadas de Maíz, *p. 40*, broken into small pieces
- 1½ pounds (680 g) summer or winter squash (such as zucchini or butternut), peeled if necessary, seeded, and cut into 1-inch pieces
- ½ pound (226 g) green beans, ends trimmed
- 1 medium chayote (7 oz/198 g) or large Yukon Gold potato, peeled (and seeded if using chayote) and cut into 1-inch pieces

1. **MAKE THE CHOCHOYOTES:** In a medium bowl, mix the corn masa flour, lard, salt, and ¾ cup warm water until combined. Cover with plastic wrap and let sit at room temperature for 30 minutes to allow the masa to hydrate.

2. **MAKE THE MOLE AMARILLO:** Meanwhile, soak the chiles for the mole: In a large saucepan over high heat, bring the chiles chilhuacles amarillos (or chiles guajillos) and ½ cup water to a boil. Cover the pot, remove from the heat, and let sit until the chiles have softened, for 30 minutes. Transfer the chile mixture to a blender and puree until completely smooth. Set aside.

3. To shape the chocoyotes, scoop tablespoon-size portions of masa and roll into balls. Gently press your thumb into the middle of the ball to create a large and deep dimple, then transfer to a sheet pan and repeat with the remaining masa. Loosely cover with plastic wrap until ready to cook.

4. In a large heavy pot over medium-high, heat the lard. Working in batches if necessary, cook the chicken, turning once, until browned on both sides, for 8 to 10 minutes. Transfer to a plate and set aside.

5. To the same pot, add the onion, chiles güeros, tomatillos, garlic, salt, peppercorns, oregano, cumin, allspice, clove, hoja santa, and bay leaf and cook, stirring occasionally and scraping up any browned bits from the bottom of the pan, until the vegetables are tender but just before they start to brown, for 6 to 8 minutes. Add the stock, tostadas, and reserved chicken. Bring to a boil, then reduce the heat to medium-low, cover, and simmer until the chicken is cooked through, tender, and falling off the bone, for 35 to 45 minutes. Transfer the chicken to a medium bowl and let cool slightly.

6. Working in batches, carefully add the chile mixture and the liquid to a blender and puree until completely smooth. Transfer the mole to a large bowl.

7. Rinse and dry the pot, then return the mole to the pot and bring to a simmer over medium-low heat. Add the squash, green beans, and chayote and cook until almost cooked through, for 10 to 15 minutes.

8. Nestle the chicken into the pot and gently add the chochoyotes. Cook until the chochoyotes float to the top and are cooked through, for 5 to 10 minutes.

Empanadas de Mole Amarillo

Toasted corn turnovers filled with shredded chicken and mole

One of the great things about leftover mole is all of the dishes that you can make with it. I first tried empanadas like these at a stand near a ceramic workshop outside of Santa María Atzompa in Oaxaca. I toured the workshop and after buying a number of pieces, I asked the ceramicist if there were any places nearby that he liked to eat. He told me I had to have the empanadas from the woman selling them on the corner a block and a half from his shop. So I went. They were absolutely amazing, and at 12 inches each . . . huge! My version at 7 inches is more hand-size, but if you want to graduate to the larger size, do it! You'll need to double the recipe and up the amount of mole. The larger empanadas can hold more of the mole without it leaking out.

MAKES 10 EMPANADAS

2 cups harina de maíz, such as Bob's Red Mill Masa Harina (7.93 oz/225 g)

½ teaspoon Morton kosher salt (0.14 oz/4 g)

1 cup shredded chicken

¾ cup Mole Amarillo, *p.134*

1. In a medium bowl, mix the corn masa flour, salt, and 1½ cups warm water until completely combined. Cover the bowl with plastic wrap and let sit at room temperature for 30 minutes to allow the masa to hydrate.

2. Divide the masa into 10 walnut-size portions (about 60 g each). Loosely cover with plastic wrap and set aside.

3. In a medium bowl, mix the chicken and mole until coated. Heat a comal, large skillet (preferably cast-iron), or griddle over medium-high until hot. Working with one ball at a time, using a tortilla press (or smooth, flat-bottomed skillet), press each portion of masa into a 7-inch round and cook in the center of the comal for 30 seconds.

4. Add 2 tablespoons of filling in a line down the center of the masa, leaving about ½ inch of space between the edge of the masa and the filling. Use a spatula to fold the masa in half over the filling. Use a fork to press the edges of the masa into the pan to seal the empanada. Cook until the empanada is browned in spots, for about 5 minutes; it's okay if the filling begins to bubble out. Flip and cook until browned in spots on the second side, for 5 to 6 minutes more. Transfer to a wire rack and repeat with the remaining masa and filling. Serve warm.

DO AHEAD: The empanadas can be made 1 day ahead. Store in an airtight container in the refrigerator.

Mojarra Frita

Flour-dusted whole fried fish marinated in garlic and lime

If there's one thing I discovered during my travels throughout México, it's that a city's most iconic and beloved dishes will always be served in the mercado. So when I found myself in Comitán, a beautiful small town in Chiapas, for New Year's, I immediately went to the mercado to see not only what people were buying and what farmers were selling, but also what everyone was eating.

One of the dishes that landed on the table next to me was a whole fried freshwater fish, a mojarra (the name also refers to saltwater fishes in other Latin American countries), which is native to several states in the southern part of the country. It was so dramatic and smelled so good I had to try it. My version is seasoned with garlic and lime and lightly dusted with flour for added crunch. If you are gluten-free, use cornstarch instead.

SERVES 4

- 1 teaspoon finely grated lime zest
- ¼ cup fresh lime juice (about 2 limes)
- 3 garlic cloves, finely grated
- 1 whole fish, such as tilapia, black sea bass, or red snapper (2 lb/ 907 g), scaled and cleaned
- Morton kosher salt and freshly ground black pepper
- 1 cup all-purpose flour (4.4 oz/125 g)
- 4 cups vegetable oil

FOR SERVING
- → Warm Tortillas de Maíz, *p. 38*
- → Sliced cucumber
- → Sliced radishes
- → Sliced avocado
- → Frijoles Refritos, *p. 55*
- → Chopped onion
- → Chopped cilantro
- → Salsa
- → Lime wedges

1. In a small bowl, whisk together the lime zest, lime juice, and garlic.

2. Place the fish on a sheet pan and thoroughly pat dry with paper towels. With a sharp knife, make cuts every 2 inches on a diagonal along the body of the fish on both sides, cutting all the way down to the bone. Brush the entire surface of the fish with the lime mixture, getting the garlic and lime into all of the cuts and inside the cavity of the fish. Season the fish generously inside and out with salt and pepper. Let the fish marinate for 15 minutes.

3. Holding a fine- to medium-mesh sieve over the fish, pour the flour into the sieve and evenly dust both sides of the fish.

4. Heat the oil in a large cast-iron skillet set over high. When the oil is hot and shimmering and registers 350°F on an instant-read thermometer (or drop a small piece of tortilla into the oil—if it sizzles immediately, then the oil is ready). Grip the fish firmly by the tail and carefully lower it, head first, into the oil, making sure to lay it down away from you. (If the tail sticks out of the pan a bit, it's not a big deal.) Fry until the flesh on the bottom side is cooked through and the skin is deeply browned and crisp, for 3 to 4 minutes. While the fish is frying, use a metal spoon to baste the top of the fish with the hot oil periodically. Use tongs and a fish spatula to carefully turn the fish over, making sure to turn the fish away from you so that if any oil splatters, it will splash away from you. Continue to fry until the flesh on the second side is cooked through and the skin is deeply browned and crisp, for 3 to 4 minutes. Transfer to a wire rack and season both sides with more salt.

5. Scoop the flesh (it will be tender enough to scoop with a spoon) onto the tortillas to build a taco with the desired toppings and serve.

Chileatole Verde

Roasted vegetables in a rich corn broth made from fresh and dried corn and green chiles

Chileatole is a pre-Hispanic dish whose origin is a broth of chile thickened with nixtamalized corn (corn treated with sodium hydroxide also called lime to soften it so it can be ground into masa). Today, every region has its own style of chileatole—some are served as soups, some as beverages, some are sweet instead of savory, some are made with meat. My version is green from fresh green chiles and similar to one I had in Oaxaca that was served as a sauce over roasted vegetables. I use both fresh corn and instant masa to thicken and flavor the dish. To turn it into a soup, increase the amount of water and reserve half of the corn kernels to add to the blended soup at the end, then stir in the roasted vegetables before serving.

SERVES 4

- 2¼ pounds (1 kg) summer or winter squash, cut into 2-inch pieces
- 1 medium head red cabbage (2 lb/907 g), cored and cut into 2-inch wedges
- 1 medium white onion (13.3 oz/ 392 g), cut into thin wedges
- ½ cup extra-virgin olive oil, divided Morton kosher salt
- 1 medium chile poblano (4 oz/ 125 g), stemmed, seeded, and chopped
- 1 chile jalapeño (1.1 oz/33.2 g), stemmed and chopped
- 1 medium tomatillo (1.73 oz/49 g), husked, rinsed, and quartered
- 3 medium scallions (2.68 oz/76 g), root ends trimmed, chopped
- 2 garlic cloves, finely grated
- 4 ears corn, kernels cut from the cobs, cobs reserved
- 3 fresh epazote sprigs or 1 fresh rosemary sprig
- 1 hoja santa leaf or 1 mint sprig
- ½ cup harina de maíz, such as Bob's Red Mill Masa Harina (1.76 oz/55 g)

1. Arrange a rack in the center of the oven and preheat to 450°F. Line a sheet pan with parchment paper.

2. On the prepared pan, toss the squash, cabbage, and onion with ¼ cup of the oil. Season generously with salt. Roast, tossing occasionally, until tender and browned, for 40 to 50 minutes.

3. Meanwhile, in a large heavy pot over medium-high, heat the remaining ¼ cup oil. Add the chile poblano, chile jalapeño, tomatillo, scallions, garlic, and 1 tablespoon kosher salt (0.70 oz/20 g) and cook, stirring occasionally, until tender and just beginning to brown, for 5 to 6 minutes.

4. Add the corn and cook, stirring, until the corn is tender, for about 7 minutes. Add 6 cups water, the reserved cobs (there is a lot of flavor in the cobs), epazote, and hoja santa; bring to a boil. Reduce the heat to medium-low and simmer until the vegetables are tender and the flavors have come together, for about 30 minutes.

5. Remove the cobs (and compost them). Transfer the chile mixture to a blender and carefully blend until completely smooth. Return the blended mixture to the same pot and bring to a boil over medium-high heat. Whisk in the masa harina, whisking constantly until incorporated and no lumps remain. Cook, stirring occasionally, until thickened to the consistency of a cream gravy, for about 5 minutes. If the chileatole is too thick, whisk in more water, ¼ cup at a time until that consistency is achieved. Season with salt.

6. Divide the chileatole verde among bowls. Top with the roasted vegetables.

Pescado a la Talla

Guajillo chile and orange-marinated grilled red snapper

I was in Puerto Escondido on the Pacific coast in Oaxaca and got a text message from my friend Kevin. "Look up Hotel de las Palmas and enter directly through the driveway onto the beach between 9 a.m. and 3 p.m. (the earlier the better). The fishermen are there selling the fish that they just caught. Turn right when you hit the sand and look for the people that fillet the fish. Ask for Flor and Fernando and ask them to show you how to make pescado a la talla."

I went at 9 a.m. on the dot, found Fernando, and bought a three-kilogram atún barrilete blanco (kind of like a small swordfish). I took it to his sister-in-law, Doña Mariana, who showed me her way of cleaning, dressing, and grilling it. She put it on a huge plastic platter with limes and warm corn tortillas. I was back on the beach by 10 a.m. eating some of the best grilled fish I have ever had.

SERVES 4

- 6 large chiles guajillos (1.26 oz/ 36 g), stemmed and seeded
- 3 chiles de árbol (0.12 oz/3.2 g), stemmed and seeded
- ¼ large white onion (4.3 oz/122 g), chopped, plus more for serving
- 3 garlic cloves, lightly crushed
- 2 ¼-inch-wide strips orange zest
- 1 tablespoon Recado Rojo, *p. 65*, or achiote paste
- 1 teaspoon dried oregano, preferably Mexican
- 1 bay leaf, dried or fresh
- 4 tablespoons unsalted butter (2 oz/57 g), at room temperature
- 2½ teaspoons Morton kosher salt (0.56 oz/16 g)
- 1 teaspoon freshly ground black pepper
  Vegetable oil, for the grill
- 1 whole red snapper (3 lb/ 1.3 kg), scaled, cleaned, and butterflied

FOR SERVING
- → Warm Tortillas de Maíz, *p. 38*
- → Your favorite salsa
- → Lime and orange wedges
- → Sliced cucumber
- → Chopped white onion

1. In a medium saucepan, bring ½ cup water and the chiles guajillos and chiles de árbol to a boil. Cover the pot, remove from the heat, and let sit for 30 minutes until the chiles are soft.

2. Transfer the chile mixture to a blender and add the onion, garlic, orange zest, recado rojo, oregano, bay leaf, butter, salt, and pepper. Puree until completely smooth. Set aside.

3. Prepare a grill for medium heat. Use tongs and an old, clean kitchen towel to brush the grates with oil. Pat the skin side dry with paper towels (this will help keep the fish from sticking). Using a sharp knife, score the flesh side of the fish at 1-inch intervals on a diagonal about ¼ inch deep. Season with the salt and pepper. Generously brush the chile guajillo puree onto the flesh side of the fish, making sure to coat the entire surface and pushing it into the score marks.

4. Grill the fish, skin-side down, until the skin is charred, for 7 to 10 minutes. Carefully turn the fish over with a wide spatula; continue to cook until the flesh side has char marks and easily releases from the grate and the flesh flakes easily, for about 2 minutes.

5. Place the fish flesh-side up on a platter. Serve with tortillas, salsa, limes, oranges, cucumbers, and onion.

▼ Cochinita Pibil, p. 149

YUCATÁN

—

PENINSULA

I miss the Yucatán.

The things that I miss the most: cenotes, the crystal-clear underground lakes nestled inside mossy and vine-lined caves carved deep inside the bedrock; Mayan ruins on the coastline; the stunning beaches; and, of course, the bright, citrusy food, which lends itself to the warm and humid-tropical climate. The amazing variety of citrus available there is incredible—like limas (an almost cinnamon-like, warm-tasting, sour lime) and naranja agria (bitter orange). In some of the markets and towns I visited, they were as common and as widely consumed as lemons and limes in the United States.

Another major flavor that exists throughout the region is smoke. One of the most popular regional dishes, Cochinita Pibil (p. 149), is made by slow-roasting pork in a pit (or pibil, a Mayan word that means buried or cooked underground). The pibil is lined with specific types of local wood such as chukum and catzín, chosen for their ability to burn long and slow and properly heat the rocks lining the pibil. The wood also adds its floral, allspice/clove-like characteristics to the cochinita or whatever is being cooked in the pibil. Small leaves and branches of other native trees, such as jabín and roble, can also be added to smolder and smoke, contributing an almost spicy, piney flavor.

THE RECIPES

Cochinita Pibil
grapefruit, lime, and orange slow-roasted pork shoulder, p. 149

Ceviche de Camarón y Leche de Coco
raw shrimp and watermelon tossed with coconut milk and lime juice, p. 150

Papadzules
toasted tortillas filled with jammy eggs and topped with a pumpkin seed sauce, p. 153

Relleno Negro
a rich chicken and pork meatball stew with chiles, tomatoes, and cloves, p. 156

Poc Chuc
orange- and lime-marinated grilled pork, p. 159

Ceviche de Pulpo y Habanero
citrus-infused octopus with tomatillos, radish, and a charred habanero oil, p. 160

Ha' Sikil P'ak
roasted pumpkin seed and habanero spread with orange and lime juice, p. 163

Salbutes
puffed fried corn and wheat tortillas topped with pulled pork and charred chile chicken, p. 164

Tikin Xic
grilled red snapper fillets rubbed with achiote paste and wrapped in banana leaves, p. 167

Pan de Cazón
toasted tortillas layered with beans, seared white fish, and a tomato-habanero sauce, p. 168

Sopa de Lima
rich chicken soup with chiles and lime topped with crumbled fried corn tortillas, p. 171

YUCATÁN PENINSULA

States: Yucatán, Campeche, Quintana Roo

▲ Mercado, Campeche, Campeche

▲ Valladolid, Yucatan

▼ Zona Arqueológica de Tulum, Quintana Roo

▼ Chetumal, Quintana Roo

Cochinita Pibil

Grapefruit, lime, and orange slow-roasted pork shoulder

While I was in Yucatán, I had the honor of meeting a maestro of the pibil, Silvio Campos, chef and owner of Pueblo Pibil in Tixkokob. He showed me his pits, and how he selects the wood, how he knows when the fire is ready to receive the cochinita. This is a hard dish to replicate at home because so much of the flavor comes from the wood, the fire, and the minerals in the soil and in the pit—but even so, this slow-roasted pork, marinated in lots of citrus and then braised in the marinade and wrapped in banana leaves—takes me right back to Yucatán. If you have a grill or a smoker, you can roast the pork in it to get a closer version of this dish.

SERVES 8

- 8 garlic cloves, peeled
- ⅓ cup Recado Rojo, p. 65, or achiote paste (3.5 oz/100 g)
- ⅓ cup fresh grapefruit juice (about 1 grapefruit)
- ⅓ cup fresh lime juice (about 3 limes)
- 8 wide strips orange zest plus ⅓ cup fresh orange juice (about 2 oranges)
- 4¼ teaspoons Morton kosher salt (0.9 oz/20 g)
- 2 teaspoons Recado de Todo Clase, p. 64
- 2 pounds (907 g) boneless pork shoulder, cut into 2-inch pieces
- 2 large fresh or thawed frozen banana leaves (optional)

FOR SERVING
→ Warm Tortillas de Maíz, *p. 38*
→ Cebolla Morada Encurtida, *p. 59*

1. In a blender, puree the garlic, recado rojo, grapefruit juice, lime juice, orange juice, salt, and recado de todo clase until smooth. Transfer to a large bowl. Add the pork and orange zest and toss to coat. Cover the bowl with plastic and refrigerate for at least 3 hours and up to 24. The more time, the better.

2. Arrange a rack in the lower third of the oven and preheat to 250°F.

3. Unfold a banana leaf (it should be 2 to 3 feet long). If you have gas burners, heat one gas burner on high (otherwise, preheat the oven to 475°F). Hold a leaf at each end and very slowly move the leaf over the flame, leaving it in one place until you see light char coming through the top, then continue moving slowly until the entire leaf is charred. It'll take 3 to 7 seconds to see char marks in one spot. Repeat with the remaining banana leaf. (If drying the leaves in the oven, unfold them and arrange on a sheet pan—it's okay if they are piled on top of each other—and bake until the leaves are browned and dried out in places, for about 20 minutes.)

4. Lay the leaves across the bottom and up the sides of a large heavy pot or Dutch oven, arranging them so there's about 6 inches of overhang draped over the rim.

5. Remove and discard the orange zest. Transfer the marinade and pork to the prepared pot. Fold the overhanging leaves over the top of the pork so it is completely covered. Cover the pot with a lid, transfer to the oven, and roast the pork until it's very tender and easily falls apart when poked, 2 to 2½ hours.

6. Remove the pot from the oven and set it aside, still covered, for 45 minutes or up to 2 hours. Using two forks, shred the meat and stir into the accumulated juices.

7. Serve with warm tortillas and cebolla morada encurtida.

Ceviche de Camarón y Leche de Coco

Raw shrimp and watermelon tossed with coconut milk and lime juice

I had this ceviche while lying on a secluded beach just outside Tulum. I had been driving for weeks and hadn't taken a day off, so I decided to get an Airbnb for the weekend, and I gave myself one beach day. I rented a cabana, ate ceviches, and swam all afternoon. It was one of the best days of my life.

The flavors of this ceviche were incredible, but what was most surprising was the burnt habanero chile oil drizzled on top. Its heat and bitterness cut through the bright and sweet flavors—it was at once sweet, spicy, and refreshing—in essence, everything I wanted at that moment.

SERVES 4

- 3 tablespoons virgin coconut oil or extra-virgin olive oil
- 1 medium white onion (14 oz/ 398 g), sliced into thin rings
- Morton kosher salt
- 2 pounds (907 g) large shrimp, peeled and deveined
- 2 cups watermelon (10.1 oz/ 304 g), cut into ½-inch pieces
- 1 medium cucumber (7.09 oz/ 201 g), halved and thinly sliced
- ⅓ cup coconut milk
- ¼ cup fresh lime juice (about 2 limes)
- 3 tablespoons finely chopped lemongrass (inner reed only), lemon balm, or mint

FOR SERVING
→ **Aceite de Habanero Quemado,** *p. 63*
→ **Totopos or baked or fried Tostadas de Maíz,** *p. 40*

1. In a medium skillet over medium-high heat, heat the oil. Add the onion and ¼ teaspoon salt (0.07 oz/2 g) and cook, stirring occasionally, until the onion is translucent, for about 2 minutes. Reduce the heat to medium-low and continue to cook, stirring frequently, until the onion is soft, caramelized, and golden brown, for about 12 minutes. Transfer to a small bowl and set aside to cool completely.

2. In a medium bowl, toss the shrimp, watermelon, cucumber, coconut milk, lime juice, lemongrass, and ¾ teaspoon salt (0.17 oz/5 g) until all are well coated. Let sit for 5 minutes, then gently stir in the cooled caramelized onions. Divide the shrimp mixture among four plates. Drizzle aciete de habanero quemado over top and serve with totopos or tostades.

Papadzules

Toasted tortillas filled with jammy eggs and topped with a pumpkin seed sauce

Before the arrival of the Spanish, the Mayans used quail and wild fowl eggs for this dish. There is also a black version of this dish that uses smashed black beans in place of the salsa de pepitas.

SERVES 4

10 large eggs
8 Tortillas de Maíz, *p. 38*
6 tablespoons extra-virgin olive oil, divided
1¾ cups pepitas (raw pumpkin seeds) (7.76 oz/220 g)
¼ large white onion (3.3 oz/94 g)
2 garlic cloves, thinly sliced
3 cups homemade chicken stock or store-bought low-sodium chicken broth

2 tablespoons chopped fresh epazote leaves or 1 tablespoon each chopped fresh oregano and mint
1¼ teaspoon Morton kosher salt (0.28 oz/8 g)

FOR SERVING
→ Salsa Tatemada, *p. 58* (see also Cook's Note)

1. Set up a bowl of ice and water. Bring a large saucepan of water to a boil over medium-high heat. Using a slotted spoon, carefully lower the eggs into the water one at a time. Cook, adjusting the heat to maintain a gentle boil, for 6½ minutes (for jammy eggs with a soft yolk). Transfer the eggs to the bowl of ice water and chill until just slightly warm, for 2 minutes. Gently crack the eggs all over and peel, starting from the wider end, which contains the air pocket, making it easier to peel. Cut the eggs into quarters. Set 8 quarters aside for serving.

2. Brush both sides of each tortilla with 2 tablespoons of the oil. Heat a large skillet over medium-high heat. Toast the tortillas one at a time until lightly browned and starting to crisp, for about 1 minute on each side. Set aside.

3. In the same skillet over medium-high heat, heat 2 tablespoons of the oil. Cook the pepitas, tossing occasionally, until browned and beginning to pop, for about 4 minutes. Reserve ¼ cup for garnish; transfer the remaining seeds to a blender.

4. In the same skillet over medium-high, heat the remaining 2 tablespoons oil. Cook the onions and garlic, tossing occasionally, until just beginning to brown, for 5 to 6 minutes. Transfer to the blender. Add the stock, epazote, and salt. Puree until smooth and the consistency of heavy cream. Return the pepita puree to the skillet and heat over low. Working one at a time and using tongs, dip a tortilla into the puree, turning to coat, until softened, for about 3 seconds per side. Transfer to a baking sheet as you go.

5. Arrange 4 egg quarters down the center of each tortilla. Fold one side over the eggs, then roll up the tortilla. Place seam-side down on a plate. Repeat with the remaining tortillas, dividing among plates and spooning the remaining pepita puree over. Top with the salsa and the reserved pepitas and egg quarters.

Cook's Note
For a more Yucatecan flavor, make the salsa tatemada, but substitute chiles habaneros for the chile serranos and omit the cilantro.

Relleno Negro

A rich chicken and pork meatball stew with chiles, tomatoes, and cloves

Years ago, when I tried relleno negro for the first time, I was at a taco stand on the side of the highway between Cancun and Tulum. There was a cazuela full of this incredibly fragrant guiso bubbling away over an open fire. It was jet black, which made me think it might be mole, but it looked too thin. The guiso had shredded turkey and broken-up pork meatballs, but at the time, I had no idea what it was—I just knew it smelled incredible, like a smoked turkey but with the fragrance of toasted chiles, and I had to try it. It came in a taco and was so amazing (and a little bit messy). The shredded turkey and broken meatballs held onto the broth, but after the first bite it was dripping down my chin. The friend who I was with saw how much I liked it, and just before I had to go back to New York, he gave me a bag of recado negro (a concentrated black spice paste similar to a curry paste used to make sauces and soups) to take home with me so that I could re-create the experience back in New York. Note that you need to start this dish at least the day before you plan on serving it.

SERVES 8

FOR THE RECADO NEGRO

- 7 large chiles anchos (4 oz/113 g), stemmed and seeded
- 9 large chiles guajillos (2 oz/56 g), stemmed and seeded
- 15 chiles de árbol (0.42 oz/12 g), stemmed
- 4 large Roma tomatoes (14.5 oz/ 412 g), cored and left whole
- 1 large fresh chile x'catik, cubanelle, banana pepper, or jalapeño (2.5 oz/72 g), stemmed
- ½ medium white onion (6.7 oz/ 190 g), halved
- 1 garlic head, peeled, cloves separated
- 1 tablespoon black peppercorns
- 6 whole cloves
- 6 allspice berries
- 1 tablespoon dried oregano, preferably Mexican
- ½ teaspoon cumin seeds
- 2 tablespoons Recado Rojo, *p. 65*, or achiote paste
- 2 tablespoons distilled white vinegar
- 1¾ teaspoons Morton kosher salt (0.42 oz/12 g)

FOR THE CALDO

- 1 tablespoon rendered lard
- 2¼ pounds (1 kg) whole chicken legs
- 1¾ teaspoons Morton kosher salt (0.42 oz/12 g)
- 6 cups homemade chicken stock or store-bought low-sodium chicken broth
- 8 large eggs

FOR THE ALBÓNDIGAS

- 3 ounces (85 g) totopos or 6 tostadas
- 1 large Roma tomato (3.5 oz/ 103 g), cored and finely chopped
- ¼ large white onion (2.8 oz/81 g), grated on the large holes of a box grater
- 1 large fresh chile x'catik, cubanelle, banana pepper, or jalapeño (2.5 oz/72 g), stemmed, seeded, and finely chopped
- 2 garlic cloves, finely grated
- 1 tablespoon chopped fresh epazote or oregano (preferably Mexican)
  Morton kosher salt
- 2 pounds (907 g) ground pork (20% fat if possible)
- ¼ cup vegetable oil, for shaping

1. MAKE THE RECADO NEGRO: Prepare a grill for high heat or place a rack in the center of the oven and preheat to 475°F.

2. On a sheet pan, grill or roast the chiles anchos, chiles guajillos, and chiles de árbol until completely black, slightly puffed, and charcoal-like in texture, for 1 hour. (An outdoor grill is preferable because of all the smoke—your kitchen will get *very* smoky, so if you use the oven, keep the vent on and your windows open—and you might want to disable your smoke alarm; the smoke will subside after the first 15 minutes.) Set aside to cool.

3. Transfer the cooled chiles to a large pot and lightly crush with a potato masher. Fill the pot with cold water and stir vigorously. Drain in a fine-mesh sieve, discard the water, and return the chiles to the pot. Cover the chiles with cold water, cover the pot, and let sit at room temperature for at least 24 hours and up to 48 hours. This step is critical and will remove all of the bitterness from the chiles.

4. Preheat the oven to 475°F.

5. Arrange the tomatoes, fresh chile, onion, and garlic on a sheet pan. Roast until the vegetables are soft and black in spots, for 30 to 40 minutes. Once cool enough to handle, peel the garlic cloves. Transfer everything to a bowl, cover with plastic wrap, and refrigerate until chilled.

6. In a dry small skillet over medium heat, toast the peppercorns, cloves, and allspice, swirling often, until fragrant and just beginning to smoke, for about 2 minutes. Add the oregano and cumin and toast until fragrant, for about 30 seconds more. Remove from the heat, cover, and set aside.

7. Drain the soaked blackened chiles in a fine-mesh sieve (discard the water). Transfer the chiles to a blender and add the chilled tomato mixture, toasted spices, recado rojo, vinegar, and salt. Puree until completely smooth. Measure out ½ cup recado negro and set aside for the albóndigas. The rest will be used to make the caldo (broth).

8. MAKE THE CALDO: In a large heavy pot over medium-high, heat the lard. Cook the chicken, starting skin-side down, until golden brown, for 4 to 5 minutes per side.

9. Add the recado negro, salt, and stock to the pot. Bring to a boil. Cover, reduce the heat to medium-low, and simmer until the chicken is tender, for about 30 minutes.

10. Meanwhile, set up a bowl of ice and water. Bring a large pot of water to a boil over medium-high heat. Using a slotted spoon, carefully lower the eggs into the boiling water one at a time and cook for 5 minutes, adjusting the heat to maintain a gentle boil. Transfer the eggs to the ice water and chill gently. Crack the eggs all over (starting from the wider bottom end, where the air pocket is) and peel. Set aside (they will finish cooking in the broth later).

11. MAKE THE ALBÓNDIGAS: In a food processor, pulverize the totopos until the crumbs are very fine, like breadcrumbs. Add the crumbs to a large bowl with the tomato, onion, chile x'catik, garlic, epazote, reserved ½ cup recado negro, and 1¾ teaspoons salt (0.42 oz/12 g) and whisk until combined. Add the pork and, using two forks, begin "pulling" the ground pork apart as if you were shredding pulled pork, breaking up the clumps and incorporating the totopos mixture until thoroughly mixed and the ground pork mixture is evenly colored black.

12. Lightly oil your hands. Working with one at a time, use a ½-cup measure to scoop out portions of the meat mixture and roll gently between your hands into balls. Transfer to a large platter.

13. After the chicken has simmered for 30 minutes, nestle the albóndigas into the pot. Cover and continue to cook until the chicken is falling off the bones and the albóndigas are cooked through, for 30 to 40 minutes more. Add the eggs, cover the pot, and cook until the eggs are just heated through, for about 5 minutes.

14. Serve the chicken, albóndigas, and eggs in bowls topped with caldo. (Alternatively, shred the chicken and break up the meatballs and eggs into the caldo and make tacos.)

Poc Chuc

Orange- and lime-marinated grilled pork

The first thing that drew me to this dish is how beautiful it is—charred onion, fresh radish, and avocado give a pop of color to the citrusy, charred pork steaks. The flavor of the meat is so bright and immediately takes me back to Valladolid, a beautiful town about an hour and a half inland from Tulum. It was there that I first tried poc chuc, a signature dish of the Yucatán with Mayan origins. The pork is sliced very thinly so it can absorb the fresh orange and lime marinade quickly and thoroughly—this also allows for a quick cook time on a hot grill.

SERVES 6 TO 8

- 2¼ pounds (1 kg) skinless, boneless pork shoulder (see Cook's Note)
- 1 teaspoon finely grated lime zest
- ⅔ cup fresh lime juice (about 5 limes)
- 1 teaspoon finely grated orange zest
- ⅔ cup fresh orange juice (about 3 oranges)
- 4 garlic cloves, finely grated
- 2¾ teaspoons Morton kosher salt (0.63 oz/18 g)
- 2 teaspoons Recado de Todo Clase, p. 64, or 1 teaspoon freshly ground black pepper
  Vegetable oil, for the grill
- 1 medium red onion (10.1 oz/ 287 g), quartered
- 8 medium radishes, thinly sliced

FOR SERVING
- → Sliced avocado
- → Cilantro leaves and tender stems
- → Warm Tortillas de Maíz, p. 38
- → Salsa de Zanahoria, p. 63
- → Chiles Habaneros Encurtidos, p. 58
- → Lime wedges

1. Place the pork shoulder on a parchment-lined sheet pan and freeze, uncovered, until almost completely frozen, for about 2 hours.

2. Using a very sharp knife, thinly slice the pork crosswise into ⅛-inch-thick pieces. Transfer to a large zip-top freezer bag set inside a large bowl and refrigerate until ready to marinate.

3. In a medium bowl, whisk the lime zest and juice, orange zest and juice, garlic, salt, and recado de todo clase. Pour over the pork, seal the bag, and squeeze the bag to coat the pork. Refrigerate for at least 30 minutes and up to 90 minutes.

4. Prepare a gas grill for high heat. Use tongs and an old, clean kitchen towel to brush the grates with oil. (Alternatively, prepare a charcoal grill for high heat.)

5. Remove the pork from the marinade, shaking off any excess; brush off the garlic and zests. Grill the pork, turning once, until charred, for 1 to 2 minutes per side. Transfer to a cutting board and let rest for 10 minutes. Cut into 2-inch pieces.

6. Grill the onion quarters, turning them occasionally, until charred on all sides, for 3 to 4 minutes per side. Transfer to a cutting board. Cut crosswise into 1-inch pieces and separate the individual layers of the onion.

7. Arrange the pork on a large platter. Top with the charred onion, radish slices, avocado slices, and cilantro leaves. Serve with the warm tortillas de maíz, salsa de zanahoria, chiles habaneros encurtidos, and lime wedges.

Cook's Note

Save yourself 2 hours and some hassle by asking your butcher to thinly slice your pork shoulder.

Ceviche de Pulpo y Habanero

Citrus-infused octopus with tomatillos, radish, and a charred habanero oil

I love octopus, so when it's on a menu I have to order it, no matter what. I once was on the beach in Tulum, and after eating the shrimp and coconut milk ceviche (see p. 150), I saw that there was an octopus ceviche offered. Even though I had just finished a ceviche, I had to try this octopus one—and I'm so happy I did. The orange and the lime play really well with the tomatillos and bring out their fruitiness. The octopus, when perfectly cooked, is super tender. Octopus can take a lot of that smoky habanero oil, so don't be timid!

SERVES 4

FOR THE OCTOPUS
- 2 pounds (907 g) octopus, cleaned, head and tentacles separated
- 4 fresh oregano sprigs
- 3 wide strips orange zest
- 3 wide strips lime zest
- 1 head garlic, halved horizontally
- 1 tablespoon black peppercorns
- ½ teaspoon Morton kosher salt (0.14 oz/4 g)
- 1 dried bay leaf

FOR THE CEVICHE
- 4 medium tomatillos (6.9 oz/ 196 g), husked, rinsed, and cut into ½-inch pieces
- ½ large red onion (6 oz/171 g), thinly sliced
- 4 medium radishes (1.26 oz/36 g), thinly sliced
- ¼ cup fresh lime juice (about 2 limes)
- ¼ cup fresh orange juice (about 1 orange)
- 1¼ teaspoons Morton kosher salt (0.28 oz/8 g)
- 2 medium avocados (12.6 oz/ 359 g), peeled, seeded, and cut into ½-inch pieces
- ¼ cup (packed) fresh cilantro leaves and tender stems (1.41 oz/40 g), finely chopped

FOR SERVING
- → Aceite de Habanero Quemado, *p. 63*
- → Totopos or baked or fried Tostadas de Maíz, *p. 40*

1. PREPARE THE OCTOPUS: In a large heavy pot, combine the octopus, water to cover, oregano, orange zest, lime zest, garlic, peppercorns, salt, and bay leaf. Bring to a boil. Reduce the heat to medium-low, cover, and simmer until the octopus is tender and a knife pierces the thickest tentacle with little resistance, for 1 to 1½ hours. Remove from the heat; let the octopus cool in the liquid.

2. Once the octopus is cool enough to handle, remove from the pot (discard the cooking liquid). Using a paper towel, wipe the purple skin off the tentacles, leaving the suckers intact. Cut the tentacles into ½-inch pieces and cut the head into bite-size pieces. Transfer to a large bowl, cover, and refrigerate until chilled.

3. MAKE THE CEVICHE: In a large bowl, combine the chilled octopus, tomatillos, onion, radishes, lime juice, orange juice, and salt. Stir and let sit for 5 minutes. Gently stir in the avocados and cilantro.

4. TO SERVE: Divide the ceviche among four plates. Drizzle aceite de habanero quemado over top. Serve with the totopos or tostadas.

Ha' Sikil P'ak

Roasted pumpkin seed and habanero spread with orange and lime juice

I debated on whether to include this recipe in the salsa section since it is often served as a starter and is becoming more and more common in Mexican restaurants in the US. But it is such an iconic Mayan dish and is featured so prominently throughout the Yucatán—everywhere from simple beach stalls to fine dining establishments—that I decided to keep it here. It is really delicious and can be served with totopos or as a condiment to fish or chicken.

MAKES 2 CUPS

- 1½ cups pepitas/raw pumpkin seeds (6.67 oz/189 g)
- 3 large Roma tomatoes (11 oz/ 314 g), cored and left whole
- ¼ large white onion (3.3 oz/94 g)
- 1 chile habanero (0.37 oz/10.7 g), stemmed, seeded, and halved
- 3 garlic cloves, unpeeled
- ¼ cup fresh cilantro leaves and tender stems (1 oz/30 g)
- ¼ cup fresh lime juice (about 2 limes), plus more to taste
- ¼ teaspoon finely grated orange zest
- ¼ cup fresh orange juice (about 1 orange), plus more to taste
- 1 teaspoon Morton kosher salt (0.21 oz/6 g), plus more to taste

FOR SERVING
- → Totopos de maíz
- → Plantain chips

1. Heat a large skillet over medium-high heat. Toast the pumpkin seeds, tossing frequently, until very fragrant and browned and beginning to pop, for 3 to 4 minutes. Transfer to a blender and blend on low speed until the seeds are finely chopped and beginning to turn into a paste.

2. Line the skillet with a large sheet of foil to cover the bottom (this will prevent the tomatoes from burning and sticking). Set over high heat and add the tomatoes, onion, chile habanero, and garlic and cook, turning occasionally, until charred on all sides, for about 5 minutes for the garlic, 9 minutes for the onion, and 16 minutes for the tomatoes. Transfer to the blender with the pumpkin paste. Puree on medium-low speed until smooth.

3. Add the cilantro, lime juice, orange zest, orange juice, and salt and puree until the cilantro is finely chopped and the mixture is the consistency of hummus. Taste and season with more orange and/or lime juice and salt if desired.

4. Serve with the totopos and plantain chips.

DO AHEAD: The ha' sikil p'ak can be made 2 days ahead. Store in an airtight container in the refrigerator.

Salbutes

Puffed fried corn and wheat tortillas topped with pulled pork and charred chile chicken

Anytime masa is fried, no matter the shape or size, you know it is going to be good. Salbutes are amazing, and you are going to love them. They are like a San Antonio puffy taco, but there is a little wheat flour added to the masa, which gives it a slightly chewy texture instead of a shatteringly crisp tostada or puffy taco. These are topped with cochinita pibil and relleno negro just like I had at the mercado in Campeche, but you could top it with your favorite taco filling. I considered putting this recipe in the Básicos chapter (p. 17), but it is yet another iconic Yucatecan dish, so important to the region, that I decided it belonged here.

<u>MAKES 8 SALBUTES</u>

4½ cups harina de maíz, such as Bob's Red Mill Masa Harina (16 oz/453 g)
½ cup all-purpose flour (2 oz/62 g)
¾ teaspoon Morton kosher salt (0.14 oz/4 g)
2 cups vegetable oil

FOR SERVING
→ Relleno Negro, *p. 156*
→ Cochinita Pibil, *p. 149*
→ Sliced avocado
→ Cebolla Morada Encurtida, *p. 59*

1. In a large bowl, knead the masa flour, all-purpose flour, salt, and ¼ cup water with your hands for about 4 minutes, or until incorporated and the mixture is soft and pliable but doesn't stick to your hands. If the mixture is still dry or crumbly or sticks to your hands, add a tablespoon or two more water and continue to mix. Cover the bowl with plastic wrap and let sit for 30 minutes.

2. Use scissors to cut off the zip-top from a plastic bag. Cut through the two opposite sides of the bag, leaving the bottom intact so that the bag can open and close like a book. If you're using a tortilla press, trim the cut sides of the bag to fit the flat surface of the press. (If you don't have a tortilla press, it's okay—you can use the bottom of a skillet.)

3. Divide the dough into 8 portions the size of Ping-Pong balls (about ¼ cup or 54 g each). Arrange on a sheet pan and keep covered with a damp kitchen towel until ready to use.

4. Heat a medium cast-iron skillet or griddle over medium-high heat. Place the prepared plastic bag inside a tortilla press so that the folded side of the bag is on the hinged side of the press. Working with one dough ball at a time, open the press and bag and place the dough ball in the center. Fold the bag over and gently press, holding steady, firm pressure, and flatten the dough to a 5-inch round; it should be slightly thicker than a tortilla. Peel one side of the bag from the dough. Place the dough on your open palm and peel off the second side.

5. Line a sheet pan with paper towels. In a small skillet over high heat, heat the oil until it bubbles immediately when the edge of a tortilla touches the surface. Working with one at a time, fry a tortilla until it inflates and gets crispy and golden brown, for 1 to 2 minutes. Flip and repeat on the second side. Transfer the salbute to the paper towels to drain. Repeat with the remaining pieces. Serve with relleno negro, cochinita pibil, avocado, and cebolla morada encurtida.

Tikin Xic

Grilled red snapper fillets rubbed with achiote paste and wrapped in banana leaves

I have a friend who was the chef at a beachside hotel in Tulum and when I told him I had just driven into town, he told me to come by and he would make me dinner. So I did. And this was one of the many incredible things I ate on the beach that night. I remember when it landed on the table and the aroma of charred banana leaf wafted up followed by grilled fish and oranges. I couldn't wait to peel back the banana leaves to see what was inside. The leaves do triple duty in this dish, providing an herby, charred vegetable flavor to the fish while also protecting it from overcooking and ensuring that all of the moisture stays inside the fish.

SERVES 4

- ¼ cup Recado Rojo, *p. 65,* or achiote paste
- ¼ cup fresh lime juice (about 2 limes)
- ¼ cup fresh orange juice (about 1 orange)
- 2 garlic cloves, peeled
- 1 tablespoon black peppercorns
- 1¼ teaspoons Morton kosher salt (0.28 oz/8 g)
- 1 teaspoon Recado de Todo Clase, *p. 64*
- ½ teaspoon cumin seeds
- 2 large fresh or thawed frozen banana leaves
- 4 large skin-on red snapper fillets (6 oz/170 g each)

- Vegetable oil, for the grill
- 1 large red onion (12 oz/342 g), sliced into ½-inch-thick rounds
- 2 large Roma tomatoes (7.97 oz/ 226 g), cored and sliced into ½-inch-thick rounds
- 1 large green bell pepper (7.79 oz/ 221 g), stemmed and sliced crosswise into ½-inch-thick rings

FOR SERVING
→ Grilled Tortillas de Maíz, *p. 38*
→ Sliced avocado
→ Lime wedges
→ Chiles Habaneros Encurtidos, *p. 58*

1. In a blender on medium-low speed, puree the recado rojo, lime juice, orange juice, garlic, peppercorns, salt, recado de todo clase, and cumin until smooth.

2. Unfold a banana leaf (it should be 2 to 3 feet long). If you have gas burners, heat one gas burner on high. Hold a leaf at each end and very slowly move the leaf over the flame, leaving it in one place until you see char coming through the top, then continue moving slowly until the entire leaf is charred. It'll take 3 to 7 seconds to see char marks in one spot. Repeat with the remaining banana leaf. Remove the center rib and cut the leaves into four 12 × 14-inch pieces. If the leaves are narrow, you can double up and slightly offset the leaves to get the right size.

3. Arrange a leaf piece with a long side facing you. Place a fish fillet in the center; brush all sides with the marinade. Drizzle a little more on top. Fold one long side of the leaf over the fish, then fold the other long side over to cover. With the packet seam-side up, fold the two narrow ends over. Set seam-side down on a sheet pan. Repeat with the remaining fish and leaves. Let sit for 30 minutes.

4. Prepare a grill for high heat. Brush the grates with oil. Grill the fish packets, seam-side down, until charred, for 5 to 6 minutes. Flip and grill the second side until charred, for about 5 minutes. Transfer to a sheet pan. Grill the onion, tomatoes, and bell pepper, turning, until tender and charred, for 6 to 9 minutes.

5. Serve with tortillas, avocado, lime wedges, and chiles habaneros encurtidos.

Cook's Note

If you don't have a gas burner to char the banana leaves, it's fine—you can blanch them in water instead. Unfold the leaves, place them in a large stockpot, cover with water, and bring to a boil. Cook for 10 minutes to soften, then drain and let cool completely. Pat dry before using.

Pan de Cazón

Toasted tortillas layered with beans, seared white fish, and a tomato-habanero sauce

I was at the mercado in Campeche when I tried Pan de Cazón. I had heard a lot about it; it's one of the dishes that locals tell tourists they have to try. Originally it was made with dogfish shark, but because of overfishing, other more sustainable fish are now used. I do love the spicy, bright flavor of the tomatoes and the habanero cut by the creaminess of the beans and the earthiness of the toasted tortillas. What I think is so unique about this dish is the way that it is constructed. When I first saw it looked like a stack of loaded tostadas. It's built with layers of tortillas, beans, fish, and salsa stacked on one another and topped with more salsa dripping down each layer.

SERVES 4

- 10 large Roma tomatoes (2 lb/990 g), cored and left whole
- ½ large white onion (7 oz/200 g), halved
- 2 chiles habaneros (0.74 oz/21.4 g), stemmed, seeded, and halved
- 5 garlic cloves, unpeeled
  Morton kosher salt
- 12 Tortillas de Maíz, p. 38
- 4 tablespoons rendered lard, bacon fat, or neutral oil, divided
- 1 pound (453 g) boneless swordfish steak or white-fleshed fish, such as cod
- 2 cups Frijoles Refritos, p. 55

FOR SERVING
→ Cebolla Morada Encurtida, p. 59
→ Chopped fresh epazote or oregano
→ Sliced avocado

1. Line a large skillet with foil (to prevent burning and sticking) and heat the pan over medium-high. Cook the tomatoes, onion, chiles habaneros, and garlic, turning occasionally, until charred on all sides, for about 5 minutes for the garlic, 9 minutes for the onion and habaneros, and 16 minutes for the tomatoes.

2. Peel the garlic, then transfer to a blender. Add the tomatoes, onion, half of the chiles habaneros, and 1½ teaspoons Morton kosher salt (0.31 oz/9 g) and puree on medium-low speed until almost smooth. Don't be tempted to increase the speed or you will get an airy, smoothie consistency; it's better to have a chunky salsa than a smoothie. Taste and, if you want it hotter, add the remaining chile habanero and puree to combine. Transfer to a medium bowl and set aside.

3. Brush both sides of each tortilla with 2 tablespoons of the lard. Heat the same skillet (remove the foil) over medium-high. Working in batches, cook the tortillas until starting to crisp, for about 1 minute per side. Transfer to a plate.

4. In the same skillet over medium-high heat, heat the remaining 2 tablespoons lard. Cook the fish, undisturbed, until golden underneath, for 2 to 3 minutes. Flip and cook until the fish is cooked through, for 2 to 3 minutes more. Transfer the fish to a medium bowl and flake it into ½-inch pieces. Add 1 cup of the charred tomato salsa and toss to combine. Season with salt. You should have about 2 cups of fish/salsa mixture plus 2 cups of the remaining charred salsa.

5. Arrange 4 tortillas on a sheet pan. Spread ¼ cup beans over each. Gently press ¼ cup of the fish mixture into the beans and top with another tortilla. Repeat with the remaining beans and fish, then top with the remaining tortillas.

6. Transfer each pan de cazón to a plate. Top with ¼ cup salsa and serve with cebolla morada encurtida, epazote, and avocado.

Sopa de Lima

Rich chicken soup with chiles and lime topped with crumbled fried corn tortillas

It has been a constant struggle of mine to create recipes representative of a place, knowing that the ingredients used in the place of origin do not exist anywhere else. For some recipes, like mole negro from Oaxaca, I feel more comfortable saying that it's best to go to the place and experience it for yourself firsthand the way it was meant to be served, rather than to make something that bears no resemblance to the original dish. This is not one of those dishes—and I'm so proud of how I was able to use grocery store limes and Recado de Todo Clase (p. 64) to replicate the allspice and clove, sour-lime flavor of the rich chicken soup. Traditionally limas are used, a variety of citrus that has a uniquely sour flavor while also tasting of cinnamon, allspice, and clove. They're hard to source outside of the Yucatán, but I have to say, this chicken and green chile soup is very close to what you would experience using limas.

SERVES 6

- 2 tablespoons extra-virgin olive oil
- 1⅓ pounds (600 g) bone-in, skin-on chicken thighs (about 4 large)
- ½ medium white onion (6.1 oz/ 175 g), chopped
- 1 large Roma tomato (5.9 oz/170 g), cored and chopped
- 1 large Anaheim, cubanelle, or green bell pepper (4.2 oz/ 120 g), stemmed, seeded, and chopped
- 2 garlic cloves, finely grated
- 1¾ teaspoons Morton kosher salt (0.42 oz/12 g)
- 1½ teaspoons Recado de Todo Clase, *p. 64*
- 6 cups homemade chicken stock or store-bought low-sodium chicken broth
- 2 limes, very thinly sliced

FOR SERVING
→ Chopped cilantro
→ Cebolla Morada Encurtida, *p. 59*
→ Sliced chile habanero
→ 6 corn tortillas, fried, or tostadas, broken into small pieces

1. In a large heavy pot over medium-high heat, heat the oil. Cook the chicken, skin-side down, until browned on both sides, for 8 to 10 minutes. Transfer to a plate.

2. To the same pot, add the onion, tomato, Anaheim pepper, garlic, salt, and recado de todo clase and cook, stirring occasionally, until the tomato begins to break down and the vegetables begin to brown, for 8 to 10 minutes.

3. Return the chicken and any accumulated juices to the pot, add the stock, and bring to a boil. Reduce the heat to medium-low and simmer until the chicken is cooked through and the flavors have come together, for about 30 minutes.

4. Use a slotted spoon to transfer the chicken to a cutting board and let sit until cool enough to handle. Shred the meat (discard the skin and bones). Stir the shredded chicken into the soup.

5. Divide the soup among six bowls and top each with 3 lime slices, cilantro, cebolla morada encurtida, habanero, and tortillas.

COOK'S NOTE The soup will become more acidic and take on more lime flavor as it sits, but after about 10 minutes, the pith will make soup go bitter, so it's best to discard the lime slices after the desired level of lime flavor is reached (kind of like steeping tea). Squeeze additional lime wedges into the soup for more tart lime flavor.

▼ Arroz a la
Tumbada, p. 176

EL GOLFO

CENTRAL

The mountains of Veracruz are so lush

and verdant; the vegetation dense and tropical like a mountainous rainforest. Their altitude and proximity to the coast make them the perfect place to grow some of the most amazing coffee, vanilla, canela, and allspice. Farther down the coast is the slightly flatter state of Tabasco, where cacao and tobacco dot the landscape.

I had always thought that plantains, peanuts, and sweet potatoes were native to the Mexican Gulf Coast, but they were actually introduced to the region by enslaved Africans working the sugarcane fields in Veracruz in the sixteenth and seventeenth centuries. When the Spanish arrived, the diseases they brought with them decimated the indigenous population and caused a labor shortage; African slaves were brought in to compensate for the loss.

The resulting fusion of Afro-Caribbean, Spanish, and pre-Hispanic cultures created foods like Puchero (p. 180), a soup made with cassava and taro, and Pescado a la Veracruzana (p. 198), made with parsley, thyme, capers, and olives. I met Nidia Patricia Hernández Medel in Los Tuxtlas. She is of Afro-Caribbean/Mexican descent and hosts dinners on her family's farm that showcase the food of her family, her culture, and the region. Foods like fried plantains and yuca, mogo mogo de malanga (a sweet and savory taro root puree), and mondongo frito (stewed and fried beef belly). Nidia's food, her family, and their history are examples of the important role immigrants played in shaping and defining Mexican cuisine.

THE RECIPES

Arroz a la Tumbada
fish and shellfish stew with tomatoes, jalapeños, and rice, p. 176

Horneado Tabasqueño
braised pork shoulder with tomato, chile ancho, fresh green chiles, and raisins, p. 179

Puchero Tabasqueño
beef stew with sweet green peppers, sweet potatoes, and plantains, p. 180

Uliche (Mole Blanco)
creamy chicken stew with oregano and coriander thickened with corn masa, p. 183

Café de Olla
fresh-brewed coffee with vanilla-cardamom spiced syrup, p. 184

Champurrado
hot corn and chocolate drink with cinnamon and dark brown sugar, p. 187

Chilpachole de Jaiba
blue crab stew with tomato, jalapeños, and chipotles, p. 188

Pambazos Rellenos de Huevos y Chorizo
chorizo, egg, and refried bean breakfast sandwiches, p. 191

Tamales con Chicharrones y Frijoles Negros
unfilled masa dumplings with black beans, chicharrones, and fresh chiles, p. 192

Jaibas Enchilpayadas
jumbo lump crabmeat in a garlic cream sauce with crushed red chiles, p. 197

Pescado a la Veracruzana
red snapper fillets in a tomato-bell pepper sauce with capers and olives, p. 198

EL GOLFO CENTRAL

States: Veracruz, Tabasco

▲ Coatzacoalcos, Veracruz

▲ Comalcalco, Tabasco

▼ Coatepec, Veracruz

▼ Mercado de Pescadería, Veracruz, Veracruz

Arroz a la Tumbada

Fish and shellfish stew with tomatoes, jalapeños, and rice

I first had this dish at the mercado de Pescados y Mariscos Arroyo in the city of Veracruz. I had been walking around early in the morning looking at all the seafood that had come in from the Gulf. One of the puestos (food stalls) had the most amazing smells wafting from it. There was a big crowd of locals eating there, and I took that as a sign that I needed to eat there as well. I talked to the cook, who told me that the seafood in the dish changes depending on what looks freshest that day. He told me who sells the best seafood in the market and where to find them. I remember thinking how amazing it must be to just walk the market each day and choose the best of the morning's catch and create stews like this one.

SERVES 8

- 7 large Roma tomatoes (1¾ lb/ 794 g), cored, or one 28-ounce can diced fire-roasted tomatoes
- ½ large white onion (7 oz/200 g), halved
- 2 chiles jalapeños (2.2 oz/66.4 g), stemmed (seeded for less heat)
- 4 garlic cloves, unpeeled
- ¼ cup extra-virgin olive oil
- 4 cups long-grain white rice (14 oz/400 g)
- 6 cups fish stock, crab stock, clam juice, or water
- 1 small bunch of fresh flat-leaf parsley (1.41 oz/40 g), tied together
- 3 bay leaves
- 1 tablespoon Morton kosher salt (0.7 oz/20 g)
- 1 teaspoon dried oregano, preferably Mexican
- 1 teaspoon freshly ground black pepper
- 2 pounds (907 g) whole crabs, halved, or shell-on king crab or Dungeness crab legs, cut into 2-inch pieces
- 2 pounds (907 g) littleneck clams or mussels, scrubbed well
- 1 pound (453 g) skinless firm white-fleshed fish fillets, such as red snapper, sea bass, or halibut, cut into bite-size pieces
- 1¼ pounds (566 g) jumbo shrimp (about 20), peeled and deveined
- ⅓ cup fresh epazote leaves (1.41 oz/ 40 g), torn, or a combination of fresh mint and oregano

1. Arrange a rack in the center of the oven and preheat to 475°F. Line a sheet pan with parchment paper.

2. Arrange the tomatoes, onion, chiles jalapeños, and garlic on the prepared pan; roast until the tomato skin is dark brown in places and starting to peel away, for 30 to 35 minutes. Let cool slightly. (Omit this step if you're using canned tomatoes.)

3. Peel the garlic and transfer to a blender. Add the roasted vegetables (and canned tomatoes, if using). Puree until completely smooth and set aside.

4. In a large heavy pot over medium-high, heat the oil. Cook the rice, stirring, until opaque, for about 5 minutes. Add the pureed vegetables, stock, parsley, bay leaves, salt, oregano, and pepper; stir and bring to a boil. Cover and cook for 10 minutes. Arrange the crab and clams on top, cover, and simmer until the crab shells are pink and the clam shells open, for about 10 minutes. Arrange the fish and shrimp on top; simmer, covered, until the fish is opaque and the shrimp are pink, for 2 to 3 minutes. Discard the parsley, bay leaves, and unopened clams.

5. Serve topped with the epazote.

Horneado Tabasqueño

Braised pork shoulder with tomato, chile ancho, fresh green chiles, and raisins

A friend told me about an amazing chef in Tabasco who had a restaurant whose kitchen was completely outdoors—she used only wood and fire to cook her food. I had already visited Tabasco, and with so much of the country to explore, I didn't want to make a habit of returning to a state twice, no matter how much I wanted to—but decided I needed to try this restaurant. I turned around and drove from Mérida to Comalcalco. I am so happy that I did, as this was one of the best meals I had in all of México. The chef, Nelly Cordova Morillo, is from Tabasco and has studied the food of the region and feels passionately about using all local ingredients, local ceramics, and local wood to cook her food. She took me into her kitchen and let me taste everything that she served. She was so sweet and so talented, and honestly I wanted to eat there again and put all of her dishes in my book (because I need her food in my life). This horneado (braised pork shoulder) was one of the many amazing dishes I tried there and is one of Nelly's signatures. To be clear, this is not her recipe, this is my homage to the amazing meal that she prepared for me, and I hope that I put as much love in making it for you as she did when she made it for me.

SERVES 6 TO 8

- 7 large Roma tomatoes (1¾ lb/ 794 g), cored and left whole
- ½ large white onion (7 oz/200 g), halved
- 1 medium green bell pepper (6.34 oz/180 g), stemmed, seeded, and quartered
- 4 large chiles anchos (2.68 oz/ 76 g), stemmed and seeded
- ⅓ cup raisins (2.64/75 g)
- ¼ cup sesame seeds (1.2 oz/40 g)
- 1 tablespoon plus 1 teaspoon Morton kosher salt (0.9 oz/28 g)
- 2 tablespoons distilled white vinegar
- 1 tablespoon piloncillo or dark brown sugar
- 1 tablespoon Recado Rojo, *p. 65*, or achiote paste
- 2 teaspoons dried oregano, preferably Mexican
- 1 teaspoon freshly ground black pepper
- 5 allspice berries
- 2 whole cloves
- 2 dried bay leaves
- 2 tablespoons rendered lard
- 3 pounds (1.36 kg) boneless pork shoulder, cut into 2-inch pieces, or 1 large rack of pork spareribs, sliced into individual ribs

FOR SERVING
→ **Arroz Rojo**, *p. 49*
→ **Tortillas de Maíz**, *p. 38*

1. Arrange a rack in the center of the oven and preheat to 475°F. Line a sheet pan with parchment paper.

2. Arrange the tomatoes, onion, bell pepper, and chiles anchos on the prepared pan; roast for 5 minutes. Remove the pan from the oven. Transfer the chiles to a blender with tongs. Continue to roast the remaining vegetables until the tomato skin is dark brown in places and starting to peel away, for 30 to 35 minutes.

3. Transfer the roasted vegetables to the blender. Add the raisins, sesame seeds, salt, vinegar, piloncillo, recado rojo, oregano, black pepper, allspice, cloves, and bay leaves and process until smooth. Set aside.

4. In a large heavy pot over medium-high, heat the lard. Working in batches, cook the pork (or a few ribs—take care not to overcrowd the pot), turning once, until browned on only 2 sides, for 4 to 5 minutes per side. Transfer to a plate. Into the same pot, pour the tomato puree and scrape up any browned bits from the bottom of the pan. Return the pork and any accumulated juices to the pot and bring the puree to a boil. Cover the pot, reduce the heat to low, and simmer until the pork is completely tender and can easily be shredded, 2½ to 3 hours.

5. Serve warm with the arroz rojo and tortillas de maíz.

Puchero Tabasqueño

Beef stew with sweet green peppers, sweet potatoes, and plantains

This soup is a great example of the Spanish, African, Cuban, and Caribbean influence in the culture and cuisine of the Gulf states. The use of plantains, sweet potatoes, taro, and yuca are all ingredients brought into México by other cultures, most notably African slaves during the sixteenth and seventeenth centuries.

SERVES 8

- 4 tablespoons rendered lard or extra-virgin olive oil, divided
- 1 medium white onion (10 oz/ 300 g), chopped
- 1 medium green bell pepper (6.34 oz/180 g), stemmed, seeded, and chopped
- 2 large chiles x'catik/güeros/ caribes, banana, or cubanelle (5.07 oz/144 g), stemmed, seeded, and chopped
- 6 garlic cloves, finely grated
- 2¼ pounds (1 kg) beef shanks, oxtails, or neck bones
- 1 tablespoon plus 1 teaspoon Morton kosher salt (0.9 oz/ 28 g)
- 1 teaspoon freshly ground black pepper
- 2 ears corn, shucked and cut into 2-inch lengths
- 2 large green plantains (24 oz/ 680 g), peeled and cut into ½-inch-thick rounds
- 1 pound (453 g) winter or summer squash, cut into rounds
- 1 large Yukon Gold potato (9 oz/ 255 g), peeled and cut into 1-inch pieces
- 1 medium sweet potato, preferably purple (9 oz/255 g), peeled and cut into 1-inch pieces
- 1 medium chayote (6.6 oz/188 g), peeled, seeded, and cut into 1-inch pieces
- 2 large Roma tomatoes (6.27 oz/ 178 g), cored and chopped
- 8 ounces (226 g) malanga or taro root, peeled and cut into 1-inch pieces
- 8 ounces (226 g) yuca, peeled and cut into 1-inch pieces
- 8 ounces (226 g) green beans, trimmed and cut into 3-inch pieces
- ¼ cup chopped fresh cilantro (1.41 oz/40 g)
- ¼ cup chopped fresh flat-leaf parsley (1.41 oz/40 g)

FOR SERVING
→ Warm baked Tostadas, *p. 40*

1. In a large heavy pot over medium-high, heat 2 tablespoons of the lard. Add the onion, bell pepper, x'catik, and garlic and cook, stirring occasionally, until beginning to brown, for 8 to 10 minutes. Transfer to a bowl; set aside. In the same pot, heat the remaining 2 tablespoons lard and cook the beef, turning occasionally, until browned on all sides, for about 4 minutes per side. Add the salt, black pepper, and 8 cups water and bring to a boil. Cover the pot, reduce the heat to medium-low, and simmer for 1½ hours. Add the reserved onion mixture, corn, plantains, squash, potatoes, chayote, tomatoes, malanga, and yuca. Cover and cook, stirring occasionally, until the beef is very tender and easily comes off the bone, for about 1 hour. Add the beans. Cover the pot and cook until the beans are crisp-tender, for about 5 minutes. Remove the pot from the heat and let the soup sit for 10 minutes.

2. Divide among bowls. Top with the cilantro and parsley. Serve with warm tostadas.

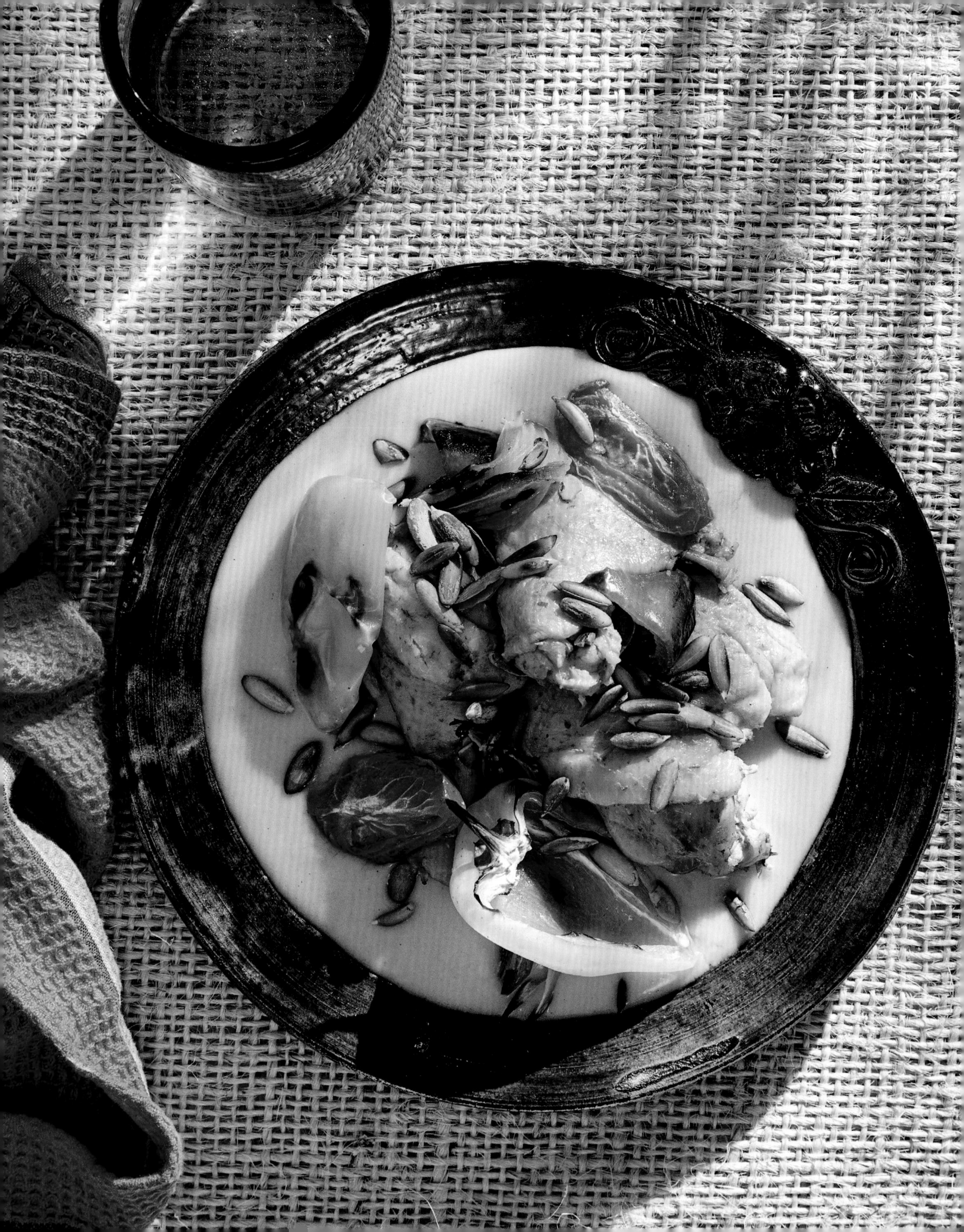

Uliche
(Mole Blanco)

Creamy chicken stew
with oregano and coriander
thickened with corn masa

I love this mole because it uses masa as the base, which adds not only flavor and richness but also thickens it to the consistency of a cream or pureed soup. Uliche is a pre-Hispanic dish and is very Tabasqueño. It was consumed by the indigenous people living along the Gulf Coast and is also an example of a white mole, which most Americans have never seen or tasted. It can be customized to your taste or to the season—you can make it vegetarian by swapping out the lard and chicken for olive oil and hearty winter squash or root vegetables.

SERVES 6 TO 8

- ½ cup (2.2 oz/63 g) pepitas/raw pumpkin seeds, plus more for serving
- 4 tablespoons rendered lard, olive oil, or vegetable oil, divided
- 8 large fresh yellow chiles güeros/caribes, banana, or cubanelle (1¼ lb/564 g), halved and seeded, stems on, divided
- 1 large white onion (14 oz/400 g), cut into thin wedges, divided
- 1 medium green bell pepper (6.34 oz/180 g), stemmed, seeded, and quartered
- 6 garlic cloves, lightly crushed
- 3¾ teaspoons Morton kosher salt (0.9 oz/26 g), plus more to taste
- 1 small bunch of fresh cilantro (1.76 oz/50 g)
- 3 fresh oregano or marjoram sprigs
- 1 tablespoon coriander seeds
- 1 teaspoon black peppercorns
- 1 whole chicken (3½ lb/1.5 kg), cut into 10 pieces
- 2 large Roma tomatoes (6.25 oz/178 g), cored and quartered
- 1.1 pounds (500 g) fresh white fine-grind corn masa for tortillas

1. Heat a large skillet over medium-high heat. Toast ½ cup of the pepitas, tossing, until fragrant and browned in spots, for 3 to 4 minutes. Transfer to a bowl.

2. In a large heavy pot over medium, heat 2 tablespoons of the lard. Cook half of the chiles güeros, half of the onion, and all of the bell pepper, garlic, and salt, stirring, until tender but not taking on any color (if they start to brown, reduce the heat), for 8 to 10 minutes. Add the cilantro, oregano, coriander seeds, and peppercorns; cook, stirring constantly, until very fragrant, for about 2 minutes. Add the chicken and 12 cups water. Bring to a boil, reduce the heat to medium-low, and simmer, uncovered, until the chicken is cooked through and pulls easily away from the bone, for 40 to 50 minutes.

3. Meanwhile, arrange a rack in the center of the oven and preheat to 425°F.

4. On a large sheet pan, spread the tomatoes and remaining chiles güeros and onion. Drizzle with the remaining 2 tablespoons lard. Roast, tossing the chiles once or twice, until browned, for 15 to 25 minutes. Season with salt; let cool.

5. Transfer the chicken to a plate. Strain the stock through a fine-mesh sieve set over a large bowl (discard the solids). Transfer 4 cups of the stock to a blender and add the masa and toasted pepitas. Puree until smooth.

6. Wipe out the pot. Pour in the masa mixture and the remaining stock and bring to a simmer. Season with salt and add the chicken to warm through.

7. Divide the stew among bowls. Top with the chiles, onion, tomatoes, and pepitas.

Café de Olla

Fresh-brewed coffee with vanilla-cardamom spiced syrup

Café de olla and Champurrado (p. 187) are two recipes that are odes to a few of my favorite things that grow in the state of Veracruz—coffee, chocolate, vanilla, allspice, cinnamon, cardamom, and mandarin. Sometimes all on the same farm. The first time I visited a coffee farm in Veracruz, I was taken aback because it looked like a jungle growing on the side of a mountain. In many of these farms complementary crops are planted adjacent to the cash crop to fight disease, attract beneficial insects, and to attract and repopulate honeybees. The crops create a biosphere where literally all of my favorite things grow—like Geisha coffee beans normally grown in Africa but also in Chiapas, Oaxaca, and Veracruz. The Veracruz variety, because of higher mountain altitudes and cooler temperatures, has a stronger fruit and berry flavor with a higher acidity that I love. I met a coffee roaster in Querétaro in 2019 who turned me on to this coffee and who later introduced me to the farmer who gave me a tour of his farm when I visited the state in early 2020. It's what I used to make café de olla—sweet, spiced coffee cut with farm-fresh whole milk.

SERVES 6 TO 8

¾ cup grated piloncillo or (packed) dark brown sugar
1 3-inch stick canela or cassia cinnamon
½ vanilla bean, split lengthwise
5 green cardamom pods, cracked
5 allspice berries
1 teaspoon black peppercorns
Pinch of Morton kosher salt

3 wide strips orange zest (or mandarin zest if you can find it)
5 to 8 cups freshly brewed coffee (I prefer Chemex), V60, espresso, or cold-brew coffee

FOR SERVING
→ Warm or cold milk, cream, half-and-half, coconut milk, or steamed milk

1. In a small saucepan, combine the piloncillo, canela, vanilla bean, cardamom, allspice, peppercorns, salt, and 1 cup water. Bring to a boil, then reduce the heat to medium-low, cover, and simmer for 15 minutes. Remove from the heat, add the orange zest; and set aside to cool.

2. Strain the spiced syrup through a fine-mesh sieve set over a 2-cup liquid measuring cup (discard the spices). You should have about 1 cup of syrup.

3. Fill a mug with hot coffee, leaving room for the syrup and milk. Stir in 1 to 3 tablespoons of the spiced syrup, depending on how sweet you like it. Top with the milk. Or if cold is your vibe, pour cold brew into an ice-filled glass, stir in the spiced syrup, and top with cold milk.

Champurrado

Hot corn and chocolate drink with cinnamon and dark brown sugar

Champurrado is the chocolate version of atole, which is a corn drink made from nixtamalized corn. I have this drink almost every morning when I go to the mercado—it's so warm, creamy, and chocolaty. It is like hot chocolate but with the nuttiness of corn masa and the smoky-caramel richness from piloncillo. I have had it in almost every state in México and like it best in the center and south of the country (not to name any names). In my opinion, the star of champurrado is the chocolate. Many people use Abuelita, an iconic brand of Mexican chocolate, and I totally understand. I have nothing against it, my actual abuelita used it to make her hot chocolate at New Year's and served it with her buñuelos. However, some of the best chocolate in the world grows in México and specifically, in Comalcalco, Tabasco. So why use a chocolate that has more sugar in it than cacao? From moles to champurrados, a dark bitter chocolate from Comalcalco is my go-to.

SERVES 4

- 5.64 ounces (160 g) grated piloncillo or dark brown sugar
- 1 3-inch stick canela or cassia cinnamon
- ½ teaspoon Morton kosher salt (0.14 oz/4 g)
- 5.64 ounces (160 g) fresh white fine-grind corn masa for tortillas
- 3.88 ounces (110 g) dark chocolate (72% cacao), preferably from Tabasco, chopped

1. In a medium saucepan, bring 5 cups water, the piloncillo, canela, and salt to a boil. Cover the pot, reduce the heat to medium-low, and simmer for 20 minutes.

2. Remove the cinnamon stick if using; it's okay to leave the canela. Pour half of the piloncillo infusion into a blender. Add the masa and process until smooth and no lumps of the masa remain.

3. Add the masa puree to the remaining piloncillo infusion in the saucepan and add the chocolate. Increase the heat to medium-high and cook, whisking frequently, until the mixture boils and the chocolate is completely melted, for about 3 minutes. Serve hot.

Chilpachole de Jaiba

Blue crab stew with tomato, jalapeños, and chipotles

I once worked in a restaurant that had a lot of incredible crab dishes on the menu. I loved them all but always felt that we were pulling back some of the more intense flavors to let the crab flavor shine. Here in México, most foods, including ones I thought were subtle—like crab—are actually really flavorsome and can take a lot of more aggressive pairings. The crabs on the Gulf Coast are especially robust in flavor, and here in this tomato-based stew they are matched with bold ingredients like chiles jalapeños, smoky chiles chipotles, cinnamon, and allspice. One of the ways to up the crab flavor is to use whole crabs like you would bones in a stock. Brown the crab shells and simmer them with your aromatics to create a beautifully flavored stew. If you can't find whole crabs, jumbo lump crabmeat will work just fine!

SERVES 4

- 8 large Roma tomatoes (2 lb/ 906 g), cored and quartered
- 1 large white onion (13.2 oz/ 376 g), quartered
- 1 chile jalapeño (1.1 oz/33.2 g), stemmed
- 5 garlic cloves, unpeeled
- 4 large chiles chipotles, stemmed (0.38 oz/10.8 g)
- 3 baked Tostadas de Maíz, p. 40, plus more for serving
- 1 2-inch stick canela or cassia cinnamon
- 6 allspice berries
- ¼ cup rendered lard or extra-virgin olive oil
- 3 blue crabs (1 lb/453 g), halved (optional)
- 6 cups fish stock or clam juice
- 1 fresh epazote or oregano sprig
- 1½ pounds (680 g) jumbo lump crabmeat, picked over for shells
- Morton kosher salt

FOR SERVING
- → Lime wedges
- → Chopped onion
- → Cilantro

1. Line a large cast-iron skillet with a sheet of foil and heat over high. Add the tomatoes, onion, chile jalapeño, and garlic and roast, turning occasionally, until charred on all sides, for about 3 minutes for the garlic, 4 to 5 minutes for the jalapeño, 6 to 8 minutes for the onion, and 8 to 10 minutes for the tomatoes. As the garlic, chile jalapeño, and vegetables char, use tongs to transfer to a large plate.

2. When cool enough to handle, peel the garlic and transfer to a blender. Add the tomatoes, onion, chile jalapeño, chiles chipotles, tostadas, canela, and allspice. Puree until smooth.

3. In a large heavy pot over medium-high heat, heat the lard. Cook the blue crabs (if using), turning once, until deep red all over, for 5 to 6 minutes. Transfer to a bowl.

4. Into the same pot over medium-high heat, carefully pour the tomato mixture; it will spit and sputter, so stand back. Cook, stirring occasionally, until the flavors have come together and the mixture is slightly thicker, for about 10 minutes.

5. Return the cooked whole crabs to the pot along with the stock and epazote and bring to a boil. Cover the pot, reduce the heat to medium-low, and simmer for 15 minutes. Add the crabmeat, stir to combine, and cook for about 5 minutes to heat through. Season with salt.

6. Serve with lime wedges, onion, cilantro, and more tostadas.

Pambazos Rellenos de Huevos y Chorizo

Chorizo, egg, and refried bean breakfast sandwiches

Pambazos are amazing, and for the record I love both styles, Veracruzanos and estilo CDMX (Mexico City style). In Veracruz, a round white bread dusted with flour called a pambazo is used—it gets split open and layered with refried beans, chorizo, and jalapeños. In Mexico City , a soft, white oval roll called a telera is often used; it is halved and bathed in a thin chile guajillo sauce then fried on a comal and stuffed with chorizo and potatoes.

In my version, I have taken the things that I like best about each one and made my own ultimate breakfast pambazo that uses beans and chorizo but no potatoes and a telera bathed in a slightly thicker salsa guajillo and fried in butter before stuffing.

MAKES 4 PAMBAZOS

- 3 large chiles guajillos (0.7 oz/ 20 g) or dried New Mexico chiles, stemmed and seeded
- 1 large chile morita (0.09 oz/2.7 g) or 1 canned chipotle pepper in adobo sauce
- 1 garlic clove, peeled
- 3 allspice berries or 1 whole clove
- ½ teaspoon dried oregano, preferably Mexican
- ¼ teaspoon cumin seeds
- 3 tablespoons unsalted butter (1.5 oz/42 g), cut into pieces
  Morton kosher salt

- 4 teleras, pan para pambazos, bolillos, or hoagie rolls, split horizontally
- 5 tablespoons extra-virgin olive oil, divided
- 8 ounces (226 g) Chorizo Rojo, p. 266
- 4 large eggs
- 2 cups Frijoles Refritos, p. 55

FOR SERVING
→ Sliced white onion
→ Sliced avocado
→ Cilantro leaves
→ Salsa de Tomatillo, p. 62
→ Crumbled Cotija

1. In a medium saucepan, boil the chiles guajillos, chile morita, garlic, allspice, oregano, cumin, and 1¼ cups water. Reduce to medium-low, cover, and simmer until the chiles are tender, about 10 minutes. Remove from heat and let sit for 5 minutes to soften completely. Transfer the chile mixture to a blender and puree until smooth. Add the butter, season with salt, and puree until sauce has emulsified. Brush ¼ cup of the salsa over the top, bottom, and both cut sides of each telera.

2. Arrange a rack in the center of the oven and preheat to 200°F. Heat a large skillet over medium-high heat. Working in batches, toast the teleras, pressing down with a spatula to flatten and make contact with the pan until brick red and browned on both sides, for about 3 minutes per side. Transfer to a sheet pan and keep warm in the oven. Repeat with the remaining teleras.

3. In the same skillet over medium-high, heat 2 tablespoons of the oil. Add the chorizo and cook, until browned and cooked through, 7 to 9 minutes. Using a slotted spoon, transfer to a medium bowl and set aside.

4. Meanwhile, in a large nonstick skillet over medium-high, heat the remaining 3 tablespoons oil. Crack the eggs into the skillet and cook until the whites are set and the edges are crisp, about 4 minutes. Season with salt.

5. Layer beans, chorizo, an egg, onion, avocado, cilantro, salsa, and Cotija on the bottom of each telera. Top and serve.

Tamales con Chicharrones y Frijoles Negros

Unfilled masa dumplings with black beans, chicharrones, and fresh chiles

There are so many different kinds of tamales—rolled, flat, grilled, fried, steamed, buried, and smoked, some even made out of rice and not corn. When I drove into Tabasco, I had heard about a tamal that was not filled, but rather what would have been the filling was mixed into the masa. I was intrigued. I had tried a black bean tamal in Campeche and a mussel tamal in Guerrero, where both of those ingredients were folded into the masa. But the tamal in Tabasco had black beans, chicharrones, and a lot of sautéed vegetables with a lot of habanero. They are traditionally made with ground fresh corn rather than dried. Their flavor was incredible— rich from the pork fat and chicharrones, earthy from the beans, while the chiles, onions, garlic, and herbs added a fresh sweet finish. When I developed this recipe, I was surprised how easy they were to assemble because you don't have to stuff them; you simply add the masa and wrap them up. This is a great starter tamal to practice the assembly and cooking method. And once you've mastered it, move right on over to the Tamales Oaxaqueños (p. 111) and they will be a cinch!

MAKES 14 TAMALES

- 1¼ cups rendered lard or vegetable oil, melted, divided
- 1 medium red onion (10.1 oz/ 287 g), chopped
- 1 large green bell pepper (8.8 oz/ 252 g), stemmed, seeded, and chopped
- 4 large chiles jalapeños (7.05 oz/ 200 g), stemmed and chopped
- 4 large scallions (2.1 oz/60 g), root end trimmed and chopped, white and green parts kept separate
- 3 large chiles habaneros (1.05 oz/ 30 g), stemmed, seeded (for less heat), and chopped
- 6 garlic cloves, finely chopped
- 5¾ teaspoons Morton kosher salt (1.41 oz/40 g)
- ¾ cup (packed) fresh cilantro leaves and tender stems (0.7 oz/20 g)
- ¾ cup (packed) fresh parsley leaves and tender stems (0.7 oz/20 g)
- 3 cups cooked Frijoles de Olla, p. 54, and 2 cups cooking liquid, or three 15-ounce cans black beans and 2 cups of their liquid (or stock or water), divided
- 3 pounds (1.36 kg) fresh coarse-grind corn masa for tamales, "unprepared" (see Cook's Note, p. 112, or fresh masa for tortillas
- 1½ cups chicharrones, cut into ½-inch pieces
- 1½ cups Carnitas estilo Ciudad México, p. 82, cut into ½-inch pieces (or substitute more chicharrones if desired)
- 1 pound (453 g) fresh or thawed frozen banana leaves, washed and patted dry

FOR SERVING
→ Lime wedges
→ Your favorite salsa

1. In a large skillet, preferably cast-iron, over medium, heat ¼ cup of the lard. Add the onion, bell pepper, jalapeños, scallion whites, chiles habaneros, garlic, and salt and cook, stirring occasionally, until the vegetables are just tender but have not taken any color (if they start to brown, reduce the heat), for 12 to 14 minutes. Stir in the scallion greens, cilantro, and parsley. Remove the skillet from the heat.

2. In a blender, puree 1 cup of the beans and 2 cups of the bean cooking liquid (or stock or water) until smooth.

3. If your masa is hard or crumbly, you can use a stand mixer to help you get a

RECIPE CONTINUES →

smooth consistency without a lot of work! In a large bowl, mix the masa, bean puree, and remaining 1 cup lard with your hands well incorporated, shiny, and smooth; the consistency of thick cake batter, and is easily spreadable, for about 5 minutes.

4. To the dough, add the cooked vegetables, remaining beans, chicharrones, and carnitas and mix well until incorporated and all of the ingredients are distributed throughout the masa. Cover the bowl with plastic wrap and set aside for at least 30 minutes and up to 2 hours at room temperature. The masa will thicken slightly as it sits.

5. Time to prepare the banana leaves. Unfold a banana leaf (it should be 2 to 3 feet long). If you have gas burners, heat 1 gas burner on high. Hold a leaf at each end and very slowly move the leaf over the flame, leaving it in one place until you see charring coming through the top. Continue moving the leaf slowly for 3 to 7 seconds to see char marks in one spot, or until the entire leaf is charred. Repeat with the remaining banana leaves.

6. If you don't have gas burners, unfold the leaves and place them in a large stockpot. Cover with water and bring to a boil. Cook for 5 minutes to soften, then drain, cool, and pat dry.

7. Remove the tough center rib and cut the leaf into 12-inch-long pieces; reserve the scraps. The leaves will vary in width from 10 to 16 inches depending on the age and type of tree they came from. Ideally you want a piece that's at least 12 × 10 inches. If your leaves are narrow or have holes in them, you can double up and slightly offset the leaves to get the right length.

8. Arrange the leaf so a long side is facing you. Spoon 1 heaping cup masa into the center of the leaf and shape it into a 6-inch log.

9. Fold one long side of the leaf over the filling, then fold the other long side over the filling to completely cover. Holding the tamal seam-side up, fold the two short sides over the tamal. Set the tamal on a sheet pan seam-side down. Repeat with the remaining tamales.

10. Place a basket insert or steaming rack into a tamal pot, stockpot, or pasta pot. Fill with water so that it comes up to just below the basket. Line the bottom of the basket with the reserved leaf scraps to cover up any exposed metal. Arrange and stack the tamales, seam-side down, in the lined basket. Cover loosely with several pieces of plastic wrap and place a damp clean kitchen towel over the plastic. Cover the pot and bring the water to a boil over high heat. Reduce the heat to medium-low and simmer the tamales, undisturbed and adding more water as needed to keep some liquid in the pot, for 40 minutes.

11. Remove a tamal from the pot and let cool for 5 minutes. (If you don't let it rest before checking, the masa will stick to the leaf and appear gummy.) Unfold the leaf, and if the masa sticks, it's not ready. Carefully refold and return the tamal to the pot. Cook for 5 minutes more, then check again. If, after the 5-minute rest, the leaf peels back easily and no masa sticks, your tamales are done. Remove from the heat, uncover the pot, and let sit for 10 minutes before unwrapping.

12. Serve warm with a squeeze of lime and salsa.

Jaibas Enchilpayadas

Jumbo lump crabmeat
in a garlic cream sauce
with crushed red chiles

*I had often read about
enchilpayada, a chile sauce
made with chiles chilpayas,
cream, and mayonnaise
paired with seafood, before
I got to Veracruz and knew
that I had to try it . . . but
to be honest, I was not
expecting to like it. I wouldn't
normally pair seafood with
such a luxuriously, rich
sauce. I went to the Mercado
de Mariscos in the city of
Veracruz and ordered the
jaibas enchilpayadas (crabs
in chile cream sauce) and
I loved it. The chiles chilpayas—
also known as chiltepín or
pequín in other parts of the
country—were spicy but fruity
in flavor, and they effortlessly
cut through all of the fat in
the sauce and balanced out
the sweetness of the crab.
I literally could not stop eating
it, and I came close to licking
the sauce off the plate. This
recipe is my take on that
surprisingly incredible sauce
that could—and should—be
used on anything.*

SERVES 4 TO 6

- 4 tablespoons unsalted butter (2 oz/57 g)
- 3 blue crabs (1 lb/453 g), halved (optional)
- ½ large white onion (6.6 oz/188 g), chopped
- 10 chiles chilpayas/pequines/chiltepines, crushed, or 1 teaspoon red chile flakes (0.14 oz/4 g), plus more for serving
- 4 garlic cloves, finely grated
- Morton kosher salt
- 1½ cups crema or heavy cream
- 1½ pounds (680 g) jumbo lump crabmeat, picked over for shells
- ¾ cup mayonnaise

FOR SERVING
- → Sliced scallion
- → Sliced tomato
- → Sliced cucumber
- → Arroz Blanco con Mantequilla, *p. 50*

1. In a large skillet over medium-high heat, melt the butter. Add the crabs (if using) and cook, turning occasionally, until very fragrant and bright red in color, for about 5 minutes.

2. Add the onion, chiles chilpayas, garlic, and ½ teaspoon salt (0.14 oz/4 g) and cook, tossing occasionally, until the onions are just beginning to brown, for about 5 minutes. Add the crema and ½ cup water and cook, stirring occasionally, until the mixture returns to the consistency of the crema. (The addition of water allows for a longer cook time and more flavor development.) As soon as the sauce has reduced to the same consistency as when you started, for about 5 minutes, move on to the next step.

3. Add the crabmeat and mayonnaise, stir to combine, and cook until just heated through, for about 4 minutes. Season with salt if necessary.

4. Top with crushed chiles chilpayas and sliced scallion and serve with sliced tomato, sliced cucumber, and arroz blanco con mantequilla.

Pescado a la Veracruzana

Red snapper fillets in a tomato-bell pepper sauce with capers and olives

This iconic dish combines pre-Hispanic ingredients like tomatoes and jalapeños with ingredients the Spanish brought into the country from the Mediterranean such as olives, capers, thyme, and parsley. For this recipe, when cooking the fish, the timing will depend on its thickness. Increase or reduce the heat slightly if needed, but don't rush it; less fatty fish won't release as much fat on its own, so you may need to add a splash more olive oil to the skillet if the skin isn't getting crisp enough.

SERVES 4

- 4 large skin-on red snapper, black bass, or striped bass fillets (6 oz/170 g each)
- Morton kosher salt
- ¼ cup plus 1 tablespoon extra-virgin olive oil, divided
- ½ large white onion (7 oz/200 g), thinly sliced
- 1 medium red bell pepper (6.34 oz/180 g), stemmed, seeded, and thinly sliced
- 1 medium green bell pepper (6.34 oz/180 g), stemmed, seeded, and thinly sliced
- 3 chiles de árbol (0.09 oz/2.4 g), stemmed and crushed (optional; I like heat)
- 4 garlic cloves, thinly sliced
- 3 fresh thyme sprigs
- 2 bay leaves
- ½ teaspoon dried oregano, preferably Mexican
- 4 large Roma tomatoes (1 lb/453 g), cored and cut into ½-inch cubes
- ½ cup fish stock or water
- 8 pickled chiles güeros, pepperoncini, or banana peppers
- ½ cup sliced Spanish green olives
- ¼ cup capers, rinsed and drained
- ¼ cup fresh flat-leaf parsley leaves and tender stems (1.41 oz/ 40 g), chopped

FOR SERVING
→ Steamed rice

1. Season the fish generously on both sides with salt; set aside. In a large skillet over medium-high, heat ¼ cup of the oil. Cook the onion, bell peppers, chiles de árbol (if using), garlic, thyme, bay leaves, oregano, and ½ teaspoon salt (0.14 oz/ 4 g), tossing occasionally, until the vegetables are tender but have not taken any color, for 6 to 8 minutes. Reduce the heat to medium. Add the tomatoes and stock and cook, stirring occasionally, until the tomatoes are very tender and have released their juices, for about 15 minutes.

2. Add the pickled chiles, olives, and capers and cook, stirring occasionally, until the flavors have been released, for about 5 minutes. Remove the skillet from the heat. Stir in the parsley just before serving.

3. Meanwhile, swirl the remaining 1 tablespoon oil to coat a large nonstick skillet. Add the fish, skin-side down. Place the skillet over medium heat and let it gradually heat up until the fat starts to render out of the fish, for about 4 minutes. Press down gently on the fish so the skin is flat against the pan. Continue to cook until the skin is super-crisp and the flesh is mostly opaque, for 8 to 12 minutes. Turn the fish and continue to cook just until opaque all the way through, for about 1 minute.

4. Divide the sauce in the pan among four plates. Top with the fish skin-side up. Serve with steamed rice.

THE MIGRATION OF PEOPLE IN MÉXICO

✕

WHEN THE PIXAR movie *Coco* came out, I visited an art exhibit centered around it and was struck by an eight-foot painting of one of those spectacular lit-up towers in the Land of the Dead. At the bottom of the towers are pyramids, representing the indigenous groups—Mayans, Aztecs, Zapotecs, and so many more—who make up the foundation of México's history. Then come the colonial cities of the Spanish and French, then all the generations that follow up through the present day, a modern city skyline topped with construction cranes to show that the process continues; the towers are still being built.

Seeing this piece, painted by the Mexican American artist Ernesto Nemesio, I was struck by the idea that, in the Land of the Dead, nothing is ever destroyed. Spanish colonizers tried to wipe out indigenous culture and religion, but they didn't succeed—the cultures just blended and built upon one another, like towers all the way to the sky.

This is how I like to think about Mexican cuisine. Take tacos al pastor (p. 73), for example, and their lesser-known cousins, tacos árabes (p. 93). If it weren't for the Lebanese and Iraqi people who entered the country through Veracruz in the 1930s—bringing with them lamb shawarma and the rotating spit it's cooked on, called a trompo—we wouldn't have these iconic tacos at all. In both cases, Mexicans substituted their preferred protein, pork, for the lamb. For tacos árabes, they kept the traditional Middle Eastern flavors mostly intact (thyme, parsley, garlic) and served the meat on pan árabe, a yeasted flatbread that resembles the Middle Eastern pita but is cooked on a Mexican comal like a tortilla. Al pastor, on the other hand, evolved into a more quintessentially Mexican dish, served in a corn tortilla, made spicy with red chiles, annatto seeds and sweet with pineapple. Like the towers in Coco, it's a dish of ingredients that evolved and built on one another as different groups of people brought their influence. And today, you'll find tacos al pastor everywhere, from Chetumal in Quintana Roo to Nogales in Sonora, on the border with Arizona.

Part of the reason I wanted to make a regional Mexican cookbook was to show how these different influences live on in different parts of the country. In Tepoztlán, just outside México City, you'll find indigenous dishes like Tlaltequeadas (p. 78): vegan fritters made with nuts and seeds and flowers and leaves and held together with chia and flaxmeal. They remain exactly as the

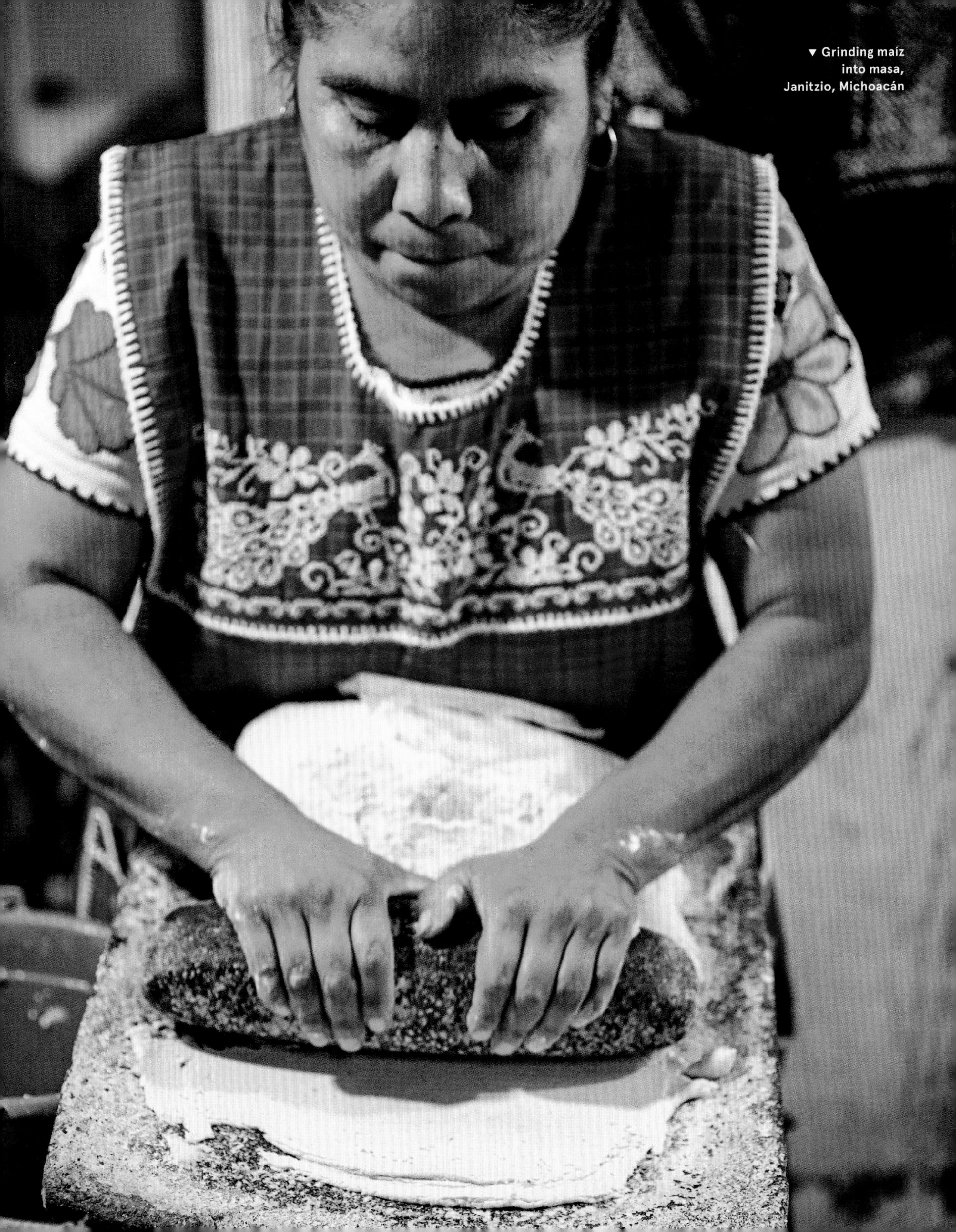

▼ Grinding maíz into masa, Janitzio, Michoacán

Aztec Tlahuica people were making them hundreds of years ago, before the Spanish came and brought pork and wheat and dairy and limes and so many of the other foods considered quintessentially Mexican today. In the Yucatán, ancient Mayan dishes like poc chuc (p. 159) and ha' sikil p'ak (p. 163) exist right alongside dishes rooted in these colonial Spanish ingredients, like chicharrón en salsa verde.

In Tabasco, you'll find a large African population because Spanish colonizers brought enslaved people in through the Gulf Coast to build their colonial cities. Many of them migrated west to Guerrero, and today in both places you'll find a rich blend of African, Caribbean, Cuban, and Mexican cultures, which means you'll also find a rich variety of dishes like pollo encacahuatado (chicken stewed in a rich peanut sauce) and tamales de tichinda (masa filled with raw mussels that open up as they steam).

Up north in Baja and Sonora, a wave of Chinese immigrants poured in from California at the turn of the twentieth century as the result of growing anti-Chinese sentiment in the US. Because México had railroads that needed to be built, Chinese immigrants were mostly welcomed, and so they spread out across the country, northwest to southeast, as the tracks were laid. This is why you'll find green tortillas de harina made with matcha and tamal chinos or zongzi filled with rice and carnitas in the city of Mexicali. As the tracks were laid eastward, the Chinese workers took with them their cooking techniques and ingredients like soy sauce, black bean paste, and Asian chiles all the way to the Gulf Coast. Across the northern states, I met many taqueros who used Chinese ingredients in their carne asada marinades.

Even the soft, stretchy cheese famous in Chihuahua originally came from Canadian Mennonites who established settlements there in the 1920s; locally, the cheese is still referred to as queso menonita.

I think the reason immigrant food spreads so quickly and thoroughly in México is because here, food is an equalizer. Yes, like any country it has its fair share of expensive restaurants that only rich people can go to, but there are a lot of towns in México that don't have expensive restaurants at all, even if they do have rich people. I've seen three guys making tacos with a mini grill and folding table in the parking lot of a México City convenience store attract everyone from wealthy businessmen in limos to skater kids to random visitors like me. Here, people don't look at a stand on the street and say, "Oh, that might be sketchy or unclean." They just say, "Oh, those oysters look good. I'm gonna order some." "Oh, you made a good taco? I'll take three."

This diversity, and the seamlessness of how different food cultures intermingle here, is something I wish we'd see more of in the States, where food is so often ranked by class or divorced from its origins.

When I set off on my trip, immigration in the US was always spoken about in a negative way. It was an "issue," no matter which side of the "issue" you were on. It meant border camps and xenophobia and kids in cages. But I want to talk about the positive side, which has always existed, since the first groups of humans started to walk across continents. Because some of the most iconic and delicious dishes (here and everywhere) exist because of immigration and because of immigrants. And these dishes are—and should be—for everyone.

> **Some of the most iconic and delicious dishes exist because of immigration and because of immigrants.**

▼ Trompo árabe,
Puebla, Puebla

▼ Carne Asada, p. 212

EL NORTE

THE NORTHERN
STATES

The northern region of México

is where I've learned the most about myself, as both an American and as a descendant of Mexican immigrants. This is where so many of the foods I ate growing up came from, and they have helped me understand who and what I am. As I traveled the region, I discovered the roots of my family's sazón and why our food tastes like it does—dishes like my mom's chile colorado and her tamales and my dad's refried beans. When they immigrated to Austin, my great-grandparents on my mom's side brought these culinary traditions back with them from their dairy farm in Torreón, Coahuila. Recipes were passed down to my grandmother, who passed them to my mother who passed them on to me, just like the hundreds of thousands of other immigrant families during the nineteenth and twentieth centuries. We created Tex-Mex food. We created Cal-Mex food. We created all of the Mexican food north of the border. Our families brought it to the United States, we cooked it for our families, and we cooked it for our communities. We cooked it to support ourselves and it caught on. This region, El Norte, is the birthplace of what we call "Mexican food" in the United States. And to me, this food is family.

El Norte is known for its deserts, cattle ranches, and vaqueros—the cowboys. It was via their cattle drives north into the Mexican territories of Alta California and Nuevo México and the Mexican state of Tejas that the vaqueros spread their grilling and pit-roasting techniques. Their families brought barbacoa, carne asada, and chile colorado into what is now the southwestern US, dishes that would later become fajitas and chili. Lebanese immigrants settled in northern México and brought with them their own ingredients, dishes, and techniques, like wheat flatbread and spit-roasting—both responsible for the creation of the pan árabe and al pastor. This intermingling of food, families, and culture created the food that I grew up with and ignited my—and so many others'—love of Mexican food and culture.

THE RECIPES

Frijoles con Veneno
slow-roasted pork shanks with chiles anchos over refried beans, p. 208

Carne Asada
marinated beef grilled with chorizo and jalapeños and served with grilled quesadillas, p. 212

Birria estilo Aguascalientes
slow-roasted goat in a rich guajillo-ancho broth with tomato and roasted cashews, p. 216

Caldillo Durangueño
braised oxtails with roasted poblanos and tomatillos, p. 219

Tacos Envenenados
crispy fried corn tortillas filled with potatoes, chorizo, refried beans, and steak, p. 220

Fideo Seco
toasted pasta with poblano, serrano, and potatoes simmered in chicken stock, p. 223

Chicharrones en Salsa Verde
toasted chicharrones simmered in a roasted tomatillo and jalapeño sauce, p. 224

Burritos de Chilorio
pasilla and allspice-braised pork, avocado, and cheese wrapped in toasted tortillas, p. 226

Torta de Lechón
garlic and lime slow-roasted pork sandwiches with salsa and pickled jalapeños, p. 230

Rajas con Crema
roasted poblanos in a garlic-cream sauce, p. 232

EL NORTE

States: Sonora, Chihuahua, Coahuila, Durango, Zacatecas, Aguascalientes, Nuevo Leon, Tamaulipas

▲ Hermosillo, Sonora

▲ Santa Catarina, Nuevo Leon

▼ Torreón, Coahuila

▼ Navojoa, Sonora

Frijoles con Veneno

Slow-roasted pork shanks with chiles anchos over refried beans

This is another side that steals the show. I first tried it when I was eating cabrito (roasted young goat) in Monterrey. The goat was served with several sides, including this very porky frijoles refritos con veneno (poison). The "poison" refers to the fat that is released by the pork as it cooks and stained red by chiles anchos and guajillos—and that red poison happens to be the best part. I ate it with flour tortillas and made taquitos. Yeah, I love cabrito, but I could easily eat this as a main dish instead— and I did. I promise, the only thing the veneno will kill is your hunger.

SERVES 4 TO 6

2 tablespoons rendered lard or extra-virgin olive oil

2¼ pounds (1 kg) pork shanks (about 2 large), ribs, or bone-in shoulder

4 large chiles anchos (2.4 oz/ 70 g), stemmed and seeded

6 large chiles guajillos (1.26 oz/ 36 g), stemmed and seeded

8 garlic cloves, chopped

3 cups fresh orange juice (about 8 oranges)

1¾ teaspoons Morton kosher salt (0.42 oz/12 g)

1 teaspoon cumin seeds

1 teaspoon dried oregano, preferably Mexican

2 bay leaves

1 tablespoon apple cider vinegar

FOR SERVING
→ Frijoles Refritos, *p. 55*; preferably made with pinto beans
→ Baked Tostadas de Maíz, *p. 40*
→ Warm Tortillas de Harina estilo Sinaloa, *p. 47*

1. Arrange a rack in the lower third of the oven and preheat to 275°F.

2. In a large heavy pot over medium-high heat, heat the lard. Add the pork and cook, turning occasionally, until browned on all sides, for 8 to 10 minutes. Transfer to a plate.

3. To the same pot, add the chiles anchos and chiles guajillos and toast, turning frequently, until the chiles are toasted, nutty, and very fragrant, for 1 to 2 minutes. Transfer to another plate.

4. To the same pot, add the garlic and cook, stirring occasionally, until very fragrant, about 1 minute. Add the reserved pork and chiles, the orange juice, salt, cumin, oregano, and bay leaves and bring to a boil.

5. Cover the pot and transfer it to the oven. Braise until the meat is falling off the bone, for 2 to 2½ hours.

6. Remove the pork (and any meat that has fallen from the bones) from the pot and transfer to a large bowl. Let sit until cool enough to handle, then shred it into bite-size pieces (discard the bones).

7. Working in baches if necessary, transfer the braising liquid and all the solids to a blender and puree until smooth. Return the chile puree to the pot. Stir in the meat and vinegar and serve over refried beans with tostadas and tortillas de harina.

▼ Grilling Carne Asada
at Rancho Los Olivos,
El Huajote, Sinaloa

▲ Carne Asada,
p. 212

Carne Asada

Marinated beef grilled with chorizo and jalapeños served with grilled quesadillas

Carne asada is a part of a larger ritual called la parrillada norteña (the northern barbecue) in the northern states of México, much in the same way that a backyard cookout or barbecue is a ritual in the southern United States. There is a fire, some meat, plentiful beer, a grillmaster, and always family and friends. Even in my adopted hometown of Mazatlán, on Sundays families roll their grills right onto the street, seemingly to attract the neighbors. The meaty smoke wafting down my block, laughter, and later into the evening, singing, fills the neighborhood. For this reason, everyone knows to always grill more than you think you need, because friends and neighbors—even if not invited, will always show up.

If you haven't tried carne asada inside a quesadilla, get ready for a life-changing experience. Quesadillas are always served at parrilladas norteñas and at taquerías that serve carne asada. In this recipe, you and your guests have the option of making tacos with the carne asada or stuffing the meat inside a toasted quesadilla with all of that melted cheese goodness.

SERVES 8

- ⅓ cup fresh lime juice (about 3 limes), plus more for grilling
- ⅓ cup fresh orange juice (about 2 oranges)
- ⅓ cup extra-virgin olive oil, plus more for grilling
- 2 teaspoons dried oregano, preferably Mexican
- 1¾ teaspoons Morton kosher salt (0.42 oz/12 g), plus more for grilling
- 1 teaspoon freshly ground black pepper
- 1 medium white onion (12.6 oz/ 358 g), thinly sliced
- 4 garlic cloves, finely grated
- 3.3 pounds (1.5 kg) mixed cuts of beef, such as flanken-cut short ribs, rib-eye, New York strip, skirt, and/or flank (see Cook's Note)
- 1 pound (453 g) fresh chorizo links (about 4) or your favorite sausage
- 8 large chiles jalapeños (8.8 oz/ 266 g), left whole
- 8 large scallions
- 8 Tortillas de Maíz, *p. 38*
- 1 pound (453 g) quesillo, Chihuahua, or Monterey Jack, shredded

FOR SERVING
→ Grilled Tortillas de Maíz, *p. 38* or Tortillas de Harina con Mantequilla, *p. 46*
→ Guacamole, *p. 64*
→ Salsa Tatemada, *p. 58*
→ Chopped cilantro
→ Frijoles Refritos, *p. 55*
→ Lime wedges

1. In a large bowl, whisk together the lime juice, orange juice, oil, oregano, salt, and pepper. Add the onion and garlic and toss with your hands to combine. Add the beef and toss to coat. Cover the bowl tightly with plastic wrap and refrigerate for at least 1 hour and up to 12 hours.

2. Prepare a gas grill for two-zone heat: Set one burner at medium-high and one or two burners at high. (Alternatively, prepare a charcoal grill for high heat.)

3. Remove the steaks from the marinade, shaking off any excess and brushing off and reserving any onions that are stuck to the meat. Drain the onions in a fine-mesh sieve set over the sink—discard the marinade and save the onions.

4. Grill the beef over high heat, turning once, for 2 to 3 minutes per side for medium-rare. Transfer to a cutting board and let rest for 10 minutes.

5. If the onions have fallen apart, they will be easier to sauté rather than grill, unless you have a vegetable grill basket—and if you do, I recommend using it (even if the onions didn't fall apart, a grill basket will help prevent them from slipping through the grill grates). Grill or sauté the onions until they are charred on all sides, for 4 to 8 minutes. Transfer to a plate.

6. Grill the chorizo, turning occasionally, until charred on all sides and cooked through, for 2 to 3 minutes per side.

7. Grill the whole jalapeños and scallions over medium-high heat, turning occasionally, until charred and tender, for 4 to 8 minutes. Transfer to a large bowl and toss with a squeeze of lime juice, a drizzle of oil, and a pinch of salt.

8. To make the quesadillas, toast one side of the tortillas over the medium-high side of the grill until lightly charred, for about 1 minute. Flip and place a small mound of cheese on the charred side, then fold in half like a taco, and continue to grill until the cheese begins to melt and the tortilla is lightly charred, for about 1 minute. Flip again to char the other side. Transfer to a platter.

9. Serve the quesadillas along with grilled tortillas and you can make tacos or stuff the quesadillas with carne asada, chorizo, chiles jalapeños, scallions, guacamole, salsa tatemada, and cilantro. Serve with the refried beans and lime wedges for squeezing.

COOK'S NOTE: Ask your butcher to slice the steaks lengthwise into ⅓-inch-thick steaks. These thin cuts are typical in México and take to the marinade quicker and also cook faster on the grill. If you're grilling flanken short ribs, strip, or rib eye, cut into 2-inch-wide pieces. If you're grilling flank or skirt, slice against the grain into ½-inch-thick strips.

▲ Birria estilo
Aguascalientes, p. 216

Birria estilo Aguascalientes

Slow-roasted goat in a rich guajillo-ancho broth with tomato and roasted cashews

Cocula, Jalisco, is considered to be the birthplace of birria, a dish originally made by braising goat with herbs, spices, and dried chiles in earthen ovens or in pits underground. Today there are countless variations of this dish, some made with guajillo and chile de árbol, which make a rich, velvety broth, and others that have an almost clear brown broth flavored with herbs and spices but few or no dried chiles. I drove to Aguascalientes, a state adjacent to Jalisco, where it's common to add tomatoes to birria, which adds body, sweetness, and acidity. I walked up to a puesto (food stall) in Mercado Juarez and saw the owner pulling huge pieces of meat out of a steaming pot and putting it down onto a round wooden board that was slightly hollowed out from years of wear from his knives. His hands moved so quicky, chopping mounds of beautifully tender cooked goat. He added the birria to bowls and topped it off with a hot brick red consommé. He served it with both hot tostadas and tortillas de maíz. It was incredible. The tomatoes were such a good counterpoint to the richness of the goat and added a touch of sweetness that balanced out the heat of the chiles. It was a beautiful morning.

SERVES 10

- 2 large bone-in goat or lamb shoulders (8 lb/3.6 kg)
- 3 tablespoons Morton kosher salt (2.11 oz/60 g), plus more to taste
- 8 large Roma tomatoes (1¾ lb/ 801 g), cored and left whole
- 1 large white onion (14 oz/400 g), quartered
- 6 large chiles guajillos (1.26 oz/ 36 g), stemmed and seeded
- 2 medium chiles cascabeles (0.5 oz/16 g), stemmed and seeded
- 2 chiles moritas (0.2 oz/5.8 g), stemmed
- 1 corn tortilla
- 8 garlic cloves, peeled
- ¼ cup raw cashews or peanuts (1.5 oz/44 g)

- 1 tablespoon black peppercorns
- 1 teaspoon allspice berries
- 1 3-inch stick canela or cassia cinnamon
- 5 whole cloves
- 1 tablespoon dried oregano, preferably Mexican
- 1 tablespoon chopped fresh thyme
- 1 teaspoon cumin seeds

FOR SERVING
- → Chopped onion
- → Cilantro
- → Lime wedges
- → Salsa de Chile de Árbol, *p. 62*
- → Warm Tortillas de Maíz, *p. 38* or baked Tostadas de Maíz, *p. 40*

1. Rub the goat shoulders with the salt, working it into the flesh and fat. Wrap tightly in plastic and refrigerate for at least 3 hours and up to 3 days.

2. Arrange a rack in the lower third of the oven and preheat to 475°F.

3. In a large roasting pan (a turkey roasting pan works great), roast the tomatoes and onion, tossing occasionally, until the tomato skin is dark brown in places and starting to peel away from the flesh, for 30 to 35 minutes.

4. Carefully add the chiles guajillos, chiles cascabeles, chiles moritas, tortilla, garlic, cashews, peppercorns, allspice, canela, and cloves and continue to roast until the chiles are very fragrant and begin to smell like toasted nuts, for about 5 minutes.

5. Remove the pan from the oven and add the oregano, thyme, and cumin (the residual heat of the pan will quickly toast them). Place a roasting rack over the roasted vegetables so the juices from the goat flavor the vegetables and spices as it cooks.

6. Reduce the oven temperature to 350°F.

7. Unwrap the goat shoulders and set on the rack. Pour 12 cups water into the pan and cover the pan tightly with foil, carefully crimping around the pan (take care, as the pan will still be hot).

8. Return to the oven and continue to bake until the meat pulls away from the bone and shreds easily with a fork, for 4½ to 5 hours.

9. Remove the pan from the oven and set aside, covered, until the goat is cool enough to handle, for about 1 hour. Shred the meat into small pieces and place in a large bowl (discard the bones).

10. Working in batches, transfer the liquid and aromatics from the pan to a blender and puree until smooth. As you work, transfer the puree to a large bowl or pot and stir to combine the batches. Taste and season the consommé with more salt if desired.

11. Divide the meat among shallow bowls and pour the consommé over. Top with onion and cilantro. Serve with lime wedges for squeezing and salsa de chile de árbol and tortillas or tostadas alongside.

Caldillo Durangueño

Braised oxtails with roasted poblanos and tomatillos

I tried several versions of this regional stew of beef and rajas (strips of roasted chiles poblanos) while I was in Durango. In most of the ones that I tried, the cooks had used tomatoes in the braising liquid, which is the norm—but there was this one restaurant where tomatillos were used instead . . . and it was incredible! This version stood out among the others. The acidity of the tomatillos cut through the richness of the beef broth in a way that tomatoes can't. I also liked the play of the rajas with the tomatillos. My caldillo durangueño calls for lots of tomatillos; I also use oxtails because I love them and because I wanted an incredibly rich stock to balance out the tomatillos.

Cook's Note

To roast the chiles in the broiler: Arrange a rack in the top position and preheat the broiler to high. Set the chiles poblanos on a sheet pan; position under the broiler, turning occasionally, until all sides are charred, for 2 to 4 minutes per side.

To roast the chiles on a grill: Prepare a charcoal or gas grill for high heat. Set the chiles poblanos directly on the grate and grill, using tongs to turn them as they char on all sides, for about 4 minutes per side.

SERVES 6 TO 8

- 8 large chiles poblanos (2.25 lb/1 kg) (see Cook's Note)
- 2 tablespoons extra-virgin olive oil
- 4 pounds (2 kg) beef oxtails or beef neck bones
- 10 medium tomatillos (1 lb/453 g), husked, rinsed, and chopped
- 1 medium white onion (10 oz/ 300 g), chopped
- 4 garlic cloves, finely grated
- 1 tablespoon plus 1 teaspoon Morton kosher salt (0.9 oz/28 g)
- 1½ teaspoons cumin seeds
- 1 teaspoon dried oregano, preferably Mexican
- 1 teaspoon freshly ground black pepper

FOR SERVING
→ **Warm Tortillas de Maíz,** *p. 38*

1. To roast the chiles on a gas stove, turn all of the burners to high and set 2 chiles poblanos on each grate. Char, using tongs to turn them occasionally, until all sides are charred, for about 4 minutes per side.

2. Transfer the chiles to a large bowl, cover the bowl tightly with plastic wrap, and let the chiles steam for 20 minutes.

3. Carefully remove the stems, peel, and seeds from each chile (use gloves if you have them—poblanos can be spicy; don't be tempted to rinse with water, or you'll wash off all of the flavor). Cut the chiles into ½-inch-wide strips and set the rajas aside until ready to use.

4. In a large heavy pot over medium-high heat, heat the oil. Working in batches so not to crowd the pan, add some of the oxtails or neck bones (they should not be touching each other in the pot) and cook until browned, for 4 to 5 minutes. Use tongs to turn the pieces over and brown the other side for an additional 4 to 5 minutes. Transfer to a plate and repeat with the remaining pieces.

5. To the same pot, add the tomatillos, onion, garlic, salt, cumin, oregano, and pepper and cook, scraping up any browned bits from the bottom of the pot, until the vegetables are tender and just beginning to brown, for 8 to 10 minutes.

6. Add the rajas and the browned beef along with any accumulated juices to the pot. Add 6 cups water and bring to a boil. Reduce the heat to low, cover, and simmer until the meat is very tender and easily comes off the bone, for 2½ to 3 hours.

7. Serve in bowls with warm corn tortillas on the side.

Tacos Envenenados

Crispy fried corn tortillas filled with potatoes, chorizo, refried beans, and steak

Another poisonous dish from the north! Tacos envenenados (poisoned tacos) is a dish (which was created in Zacatecas) that I am in absolutely in love with. In 1940, Don Lauro, a taquero in Zacatecas, became a local celebrity thanks to his potato, bean, cheese, and chorizo tacos—which he fried, filling and all, in lard. As you can imagine, the tacos were insanely good and attracted a following of very loyal customers. As his popularity grew, he hung a sign outside his puesto that read "si quiere envenenarse, coma tacos" (if you want to poison yourself, eat tacos). And from that came the name that clearly did not stop anyone from eating his tacos, least of all me.

MAKES 12 TACOS

FOR THE FILLING

- 1 large Yukon Gold potato (9.31 oz/ 264 g), peeled and chopped
  Morton kosher salt
- 1 tablespoon rendered lard or vegetable oil
- 8 ounces (226 g) Chorizo Rojo, *p. 266*, casing removed if using chorizo in links
- ¼ medium white onion (3.45 oz/ 98 g), finely chopped
- 1 small chile serrano (0.85 oz/ 24.3 g), stemmed and finely chopped
- 2 garlic cloves, finely grated
- 1 cup Frijoles Refritos, *p. 55*
- 12 Tortillas de Maíz, *p. 38*

FOR THE TACOS

- 2 cups vegetable oil or rendered lard
- ½ medium white onion (7 oz/200 g), thinly sliced
- 4 medium chiles jalapeños (4.4 oz/132.8 g) or chiles serranos, or more to taste
- 2 cups warm Carne Asada, *p. 212*
- 8 ounces (226 g) quesillo, queso Chihuahua, or Monterey Jack cheese, shredded

FOR SERVING

→ Salsa de Chipotle y Chile de Árbol, *p. 62*
→ Lime wedges

1. MAKE THE FILLING: In a medium saucepan, cover the potato with cold water by 1 inch. Generously season the water with salt and bring to a boil. Reduce the heat to medium-low and simmer until the potatoes are tender, for 10 to 15 minutes. Drain; transfer the potatoes to a plate. Let sit for 15 minutes to dry.

2. In a large skillet over medium-high, heat the lard. Cook the chorizo, onion, chile serrano, and garlic, breaking up the chorizo with a wooden spoon, until browned, 7 to 9 minutes. Add the potatoes and use a potato masher to smash them. Stir in the frijoles refritos; the mixture should be a smooth, dry paste. Divide the filling among the tortillas.

3. FRY THE TACOS: Line a baking sheet with paper towels. In a medium skillet over high, heat the oil. Add the onion a little bit at a time to avoid spattering and carefully fry, reducing the heat if necessary, until all of the onion is added and is tender and beginning to brown, about 5 minutes. Transfer the fried onion to the paper towels. Repeat the process with the jalapeños, cooking for about 5 minutes. Transfer to the same baking sheet with the onion.

4. Line a separate baking sheet with paper towels. Add 2 tacos to the pan, laying them on one side, and fry, until both sides are deep golden brown and crispy, 1 to 2 minutes on each side. Transfer to the paper towels and let cool for 10 minutes. Repeat with the remaining tacos. Fill each taco with the carne asada, onion, and queso. Serve with fried jalapeños, salsa, and lime wedges.

Fideo Seco

Toasted pasta with poblano, serrano, and potatoes simmered in chicken stock

I adore fideo seco—toasted bits of pasta simmered with a rich chicken broth until the pasta absorbs every last drop of liquid. Growing up, it was always served as a side dish. When I got to Monterrey I saw it in a taco! I couldn't believe that I had eaten it for so many years of my life and never put it inside of a tortilla. So of course I had to try it. And yes, it was amazing carb on delicious carb. While it was delicious, in all honesty, my favorite way to eat fideo seco is straight out of the pan. In fact, when I was in college, I would make huge batches for me and my roommate. It was cheap and easy and the perfect meal to make after a night out drinking. Between the two of us, we'd devour a whole skillet! Now I skip the bar and go straight to the skillet. Feel free to stuff it into a tortilla if you are needing a little carb pick-me-up!

SERVES 4

- 8 ounces (226 g) fideo, vermicelli, or angel hair pasta, broken into 2-inch pieces
- 2 tablespoons rendered lard or extra-virgin olive oil
- 2 large tomatoes (8 oz/226 g), cored and chopped
- ½ medium white onion (5.43 oz/ 154 g), chopped
- 1 medium chile poblano (4 oz/ 125 g), stemmed, seeded, and chopped
- 1 chile serrano (0.85 oz/24.3 g), stemmed and thinly sliced
- 3 garlic cloves, thinly sliced
- 2½ cups homemade chicken stock or store-bought low-sodium chicken broth
- 1 large Yukon Gold potato (8.25 oz/234 g), peeled and chopped
- 2 teaspoons Morton kosher salt (0.56 oz/16 g)

FOR SERVING
→ **Warm Tortillas de Harina estilo Sinaloa**, *p. 47*
→ **Sliced avocado**
→ **Cilantro leaves and tender stems**
→ **Salsa Tatemada**, *p. 58*

1. Heat a large skillet over high heat for 2 minutes. Add the fideo and toast, tossing constantly, or until most of the fideo has browned, for 3 to 4 minutes. Transfer to a medium bowl.

2. Reduce the heat to medium-high. In the same skillet, heat the lard. Add the tomatoes, onion, chile poblano, chile serrano, and garlic and cook, tossing occasionally, until the onions and chile poblano are tender and just beginning to brown, for 6 to 8 minutes.

3. Add the stock, potato, salt, and toasted fideo and bring to a boil. Reduce the heat to low, cover, and simmer until all of the liquid has been absorbed, for 20 to 25 minutes. Remove from the heat and let sit, still covered, for 5 minutes.

4. Make tacos with the fideo and topped with the avocado slices, cilantro, and salsa. Or, eat the fideo straight from the pan.

Chicharrones en Salsa Verde

Toasted chicharrones simmered in a roasted tomatillo and jalapeño sauce

This was a total staple of my travel diet during my entire journey. I tried this dish in every city that I visited—research is such hard work! Growing up, my mom and dad would make theirs using tomatoes in a slightly thicker sauce. I liked it, but I discovered on my trip that salsa verde and chicharrón is a heavenly combination that I cannot get enough of. Tomatillos are much more acidic than tomatoes and can cut through the richness of the chicharrón, leaving your palate cleansed and ready for more. Luckily for me, there are many places near my home that sell it, but every now and then I will invite friends over for my version stuffed inside hot and crispy gorditas.

SERVES 4 TO 6

- 1.1 pounds (500 g) chicharrón, broken into bite-size pieces
- 7 medium tomatillos (12 oz/ 340 g), husked and rinsed
- ¼ medium white onion (3.45 oz/ 98 g), coarsely chopped
- 2 chiles jalapeños (2.2 oz/66 g), stemmed and halved
- 4 garlic cloves, unpeeled
- ¾ teaspoon Morton kosher salt (0.14 oz/4 g), plus more to taste

FOR SERVING
→ **Gorditas de Maíz,** *p. 43*

1. Line a large skillet, preferably cast-iron, with two sheets of foil and heat over high for about 2 minutes, or until the pan is very hot. Add the chicharrones and cook, using tongs to turn occasionally, until browned in spots, for about 5 minutes. Transfer to a medium bowl.

2. In the same lined skillet, char the tomatillos, onion, jalapeños, and garlic, turning occasionally, until everything is charred on all sides, for about 3 minutes for the garlic, 4 to 5 minutes for the jalapeños, and 6 to 8 minutes for the onion and tomatillos. Transfer to a plate and let cool. Once cool enough to handle, peel the garlic.

3. In a blender on low speed, puree the tomatillos, onion, jalapeños, garlic, and salt until the salsa is almost smooth but some small bits remain.

4. Transfer the tomatillo mixture to a large saucepan. Add 2 cups water and bring to a boil over high heat. Reduce the heat to medium-low and simmer, uncovered, stirring occasionally, until the salsa is olive green and the flavors have mellowed and come together, for about 20 minutes.

5. Add the chicharones and cook, stirring occasionally, until softened and tender, for 5 to 10 minutes. Taste and season with salt if desired.

6. Serve stuffed inside warm gorditas.

Burritos de Chilorio

Pasilla and allspice-braised pork, avocado, and cheese wrapped in toasted tortillas

Because I live on the tropical Sinaloan coast, a lot of what I eat is caught in the Pacific or grown along the shoreline. Further inland, the terrain gets more rugged, hotter, and drier and the food becomes more land animal–based and flavored with things that can be preserved in the hot desert sun, like dried chiles and spices. Chilorio is a staple dish on the rancher's table—pieces of boneless pork shoulder that get braised for hours with chiles pasilla, guajillo, and ancho. It's often served with beans and rice, but I decided to pair it with queso Chihuahua (a gloriously creamy and smooth-melting cheese from the state of the same name), and wrap it in tortillas de harina, the iconic tortilla of the north and also of my hometown, Austin, Texas. I then take them a step further and brown them in lard in a skillet. The result, a crisp porky shell holding back oozing melted cheese and rich chile-braised pork.

SERVES 8

- 1 cup homemade chicken stock or store-bought low sodium chicken broth
- 4 large chiles pasillas (1.4 oz/41 g), stemmed and seeded
- 3 large chiles guajillos (0.63 oz/ 18 g), stemmed and seeded
- 1 large chile ancho (0.61 oz/ 17.5 g), stemmed and seeded
- 2 tablespoons apple cider vinegar
- 1¾ teaspoons Morton kosher salt (0.42 oz/12 g)
- 1 teaspoon dried oregano, preferably Mexican
- ¾ teaspoon cumin seeds
- ½ teaspoon black peppercorns
- 5 allspice berries
- 2 bay leaves
- 1 whole clove

- 2 tablespoons rendered lard or vegetable oil, plus more for toasting
- 2¼ pounds (1 kg) boneless pork shoulder, cut into 2-inch pieces
- ½ large white onion (7.1 oz/201 g), finely chopped
- 6 garlic cloves, finely grated Tortillas de Harina con Mantequilla *p. 46*
- 8 ounces (226 g) queso Chihuahua, quesillo, or Monterey Jack, shredded

FOR SERVING
→ Sliced avocado
→ Cebolla Morada Encurtida, *p. 59*
→ Salsa de Chile de Árbol, *p. 62*
→ Lime wedges

1. In a medium saucepan, combine the stock, chiles pasillas, chiles guajillos, chile ancho, vinegar, salt, oregano, cumin, peppercorns, allspice, bay leaves, and clove. Bring to a boil. Cover the pot, remove from the heat, and let sit until the chiles have softened, for about 30 minutes. Transfer the chiles, liquid, and spices to a blender and puree until smooth. Set aside until ready to use.

2. Arrange a rack in the lower third of the oven and preheat to 275°F.

3. In a large, heavy ovenproof pot over medium-high, heat the lard. Add the pork and cook, turning occasionally, until browned on at least 2 sides, for 8 to 10 minutes. Use a slotted spoon to transfer the pork to a medium bowl.

4. To the same pot, add the onion and garlic and cook, stirring occasionally and scraping up any browned bits, until the onion is browned and tender, for 6 to 8 minutes.

5. Return the pork to the pot and pour in the chile mixture. Bring to a boil, cover the pot, and transfer it to the oven to braise until the pork is completely tender and easily shreds, for 2 to 2½ hours. Remove the pot from the oven and let sit, covered for 30 minutes to cool slightly. Uncover and using a potato masher, smash the pork into the sauce and stir to completely combine the chilorio.

6. To assemble the burritos, arrange ⅓ cup chilorio down the center of each tortilla. Sprinkle with 2 tablespoons queso and top with avocado, cebolla morada encurtida, salsa, and a squeeze of lime. Fold the sides of the tortilla over the ends of the filling, then roll up tightly from the bottom.

7. Brush a large skillet, preferably cast-iron, with some lard and heat over medium-high heat until very hot and wisps of smoke are visible, for about 2 minutes. Working in batches, place the burritos in the skillet seam-side down and cook, turning occasionally, until all the sides are golden brown in spots, for about 5 minutes. Repeat with the remaining burritos and lard. Slice in half and serve.

▲ Burritos de
Chilorio, p. 226

▼ Torta de Lechón,
p. 230

Torta de Lechón

Garlic and lime slow-roasted pork sandwiches with salsa and pickled jalapeños

There is a man named Rudy in Aguascalientes who is famous for his lechón—this incredibly succulent, marinated, slow-roasted pig. He serves it by the pound, or in tacos, or in a torta. I asked which he thought I should try and he said torta. This thing was almost obscene, completely loaded with tender and juicy pork and almost drowning in a salsa verde.

SERVES 8

- 2 heads garlic, cloves separated and peeled
- ⅓ cup fresh lime juice (about 3 limes)
- ⅓ cup white wine vinegar
- ¼ cup plus 1½ teaspoons Morton kosher salt (3.38 oz/96 g)
- ¼ cup chopped fresh flat-leaf parsley (1.4 oz/40 g)
- 2 tablespoons chopped fresh oregano or 1 tablespoon dried
- 2 tablespoons chopped fresh thyme
- 2 tablespoons extra-virgin olive oil, plus more for roasting
- 1 to 4 tablespoons crushed chiles de árbol or red chile flakes (depending on how hot you like it)
- 1 tablespoon black peppercorns
- 1 8- to 10-pound (3.6 to 4.5 kg) skin-on, bone-in pork shoulder
- 12 ounces (354 ml) lager, preferably Mexican
- 8 bolillos or hoagies, split and toasted

FOR SERVING
→ Double batch of Salsa de Aguacate, *p. 60*
→ Chiles Jalapeños en Escabeche plus brine, *p. 64*
→ Curtido, *p. 59*

1. In a blender, puree the garlic, lime juice, vinegar, salt, parsley, oregano, thyme, oil, chiles de árbol, and peppercorns until smooth.

2. Push a small paring knife (about 3½ inches long) into the pork through the skin, working the blade all the way in and twisting the knife to make a small hole in the meat. Repeat, making holes spaced about 1½ inches apart on all sides of the pork.

3. Set the pork on a sheet pan and rub it all over with the lime/herb mixture, pushing it into the holes and covering any exposed meat and skin. Try to get as much of the mixture into the meat as possible, and not just on the surface, where it may burn when roasting. Be sure to use all of it! Wrap the pork tightly in a few layers of plastic wrap, wipe the sheet pan clean, set the pork back on the sheet pan, and refrigerate for at least 3 hours and up to 3 days.

4. Arrange a rack in the lower third of the oven and preheat to 275°F.

5. Line a large roasting pan with two layers of heavy-duty foil. Place a roasting rack on top. Set the pork, skin-side up, on the rack. Scrape any lime/herb mixture off the skin and thoroughly pat the pork dry with paper towels. Liberally brush the cleaned skin with some oil.

6. Transfer the pan to the oven and carefully pour the beer and 3 cups water into the pan. Roast until an instant-read thermometer inserted into the thickest part of the shoulder registers 195°F, the meat pulls away from the bone and easily shreds, and the skin is crisp, for 8 to 9 hours.

7. Remove the roasting pan from the oven and let the pork sit, uncovered, at room temperature for at least 1 hour and up to 5 hours to cool.

8. Just before serving, preheat the oven to 500°F.

9. Set the pork in the oven and reheat until the skin gets very crispy, like a chicharrón (but don't let it take on any more color), for 5 to 10 minutes.

10. Remove the chicharrón (crispy skin) and cut or break into smaller pieces (chicharrones). Slice or pull the lechón and transfer to a platter.

11. Build your sandwiches on the bolillos with the lechón, chicharrones, lots of salsa de aguacate, chiles jalapeños en escabeche, curtido, and extra brine from the jalapeños splashed on top.

Rajas con Crema

Roasted poblanos in a garlic-cream sauce

I was in Durango at a small restaurant in which they served a dish of rajas con crema as a condiment with other assorted salsas and chiles en escabeche. I tasted it and was so completely taken, I kept asking them to bring me more. It was creamy and spicy, with a tiny bit of sweetness from the charred chiles and the onion. The poblanos here in the northern states seem to be hotter than those in the US, so it does read a little more like a hot condiment, but I love the extra heat and am crazy for these rajas as a taco filling or as a side dish for grilled meat or fish. But honestly, I could eat this right out of the skillet wrapped in a warm flour tortilla. This to me is pure comfort food.

SERVES 4

8 large chiles poblanos (2.2 lb/1 kg)
2 tablespoons unsalted butter (1 oz/28 g)
½ large white onion (6 oz/180 g), thinly sliced
1 garlic clove, thinly sliced
1⅛ teaspoons Morton kosher salt (0.28 oz/8 g)

1 cup whole milk
¾ cup crema, crème fraîche, or sour cream

FOR SERVING
→ Tortillas de Harina con Mantequilla, p. 46

1. To roast the chiles on a gas stove: Turn all of the burners on to high and set 2 chiles poblanos on each grate. Char, using tongs to turn them occasionally, until all sides are charred, for about 4 minutes per side.

To roast the chiles in the broiler: Arrange a rack in the top position and preheat the broiler to high. Arrange the chiles poblanos on a sheet pan and char under the broiler, turning occasionally, until all sides are charred, for 2 to 4 minutes per side.

To roast the chiles on a grill: Preheat a charcoal or gas grill for high heat. Set the chiles poblanos directly on the grate. Char, using tongs to turn them as they char on all sides, for about 4 minutes per side.

2. Transfer the chiles poblanos to a large bowl, cover the bowl tightly with plastic wrap, and let the chiles steam for 20 minutes.

3. Carefully remove the stems, peel, and seeds from each chile (use gloves if you have them—poblanos can be spicy; don't be tempted to rinse with water, you'll wash off all of the flavor). Cut the chiles lengthwise into ½-inch-wide strips and set the rajas aside until ready to use.

4. In a large skillet, preferably cast-iron, over medium heat, melt the butter. Add the onion, garlic, and salt and cook, tossing occasionally, until the onion is lightly browned, for 6 to 8 minutes.

5. Add the rajas, milk, and crema and stir to combine. Reduce the heat to medium-low and simmer until the mixture thickens slightly, for about 10 minutes.

6. Make tacos with the warm tortillas de harina and rajas con crema.

MY ORIGIN STORY

—✕—

WHEN I WAS RESEARCHING the food for this book and would drive into a new town, I always had a detailed list of all of the dishes I needed to try, all of the chefs I wanted to meet, and all of the historical sites I had to visit. Something that was never written on that list but, deep down, was really the most important thing, was my desire to find people that looked like me. Let me explain.

When I was twenty-seven, I met a group of vacationing Mexicans in Barra de Navidad, Jalisco. We had been hanging out for a few days. One night, we were at a bar on the beach drinking, talking about living in México versus the US and where each of us was born and raised. We were all about the same age, same build, and same color. One of them looked at me and said "Pareces de Michoacán" (you look like you are from Michoacán). I didn't really know what that meant. Imagine if someone said to you, you look like you are from Idaho. Was that a compliment, an insult, or just an observation? I didn't know. Michoacán is a state west of Mexico City. I hadn't been there but was super curious. But I also had

never really considered that different states and regions had different defining looks. But now it makes sense given all of the different groups of indigenous people that have populated México before the arrival of people from Africa, Asia, and Europe.

That statement stuck with me all these years, and I became more and more excited to explore Michoacán. I think part of me expected or hoped to find an enclave of Martínez or Castruita or, at the very least, a state full of people with a similar complexion, cheekbones, and eyes. I started to wonder, was that where my family was from? One of my cousins had done a lot of research collecting church records in México and found birth and death certificates of my great-great-grandparents, but even still, we could only trace the family back to the mid-1800s. It seemed strange to me to have lived half (hopefully) of my life and only now wonder where I came from. But I think that happens to many immigrant families; you try so hard to fit into your new country that you forget where you came from. I needed to find my origins.

▲ My dad and me cooking breakfast for the team, New York, New York

I finally made it to Michoacán in October 2019—nearly twenty years after being told I looked like I was from there. And I loved it. The carnitas in Michoacán are some of the best in the country (and you know how much I love pork!). Most of the avocados grown in México come from Michoacán and are so sweet, flavorful, and luxurious. However, despite the fact that the people were so generous, warm, and welcoming, I didn't feel that connection that I desperately longed to feel. I still didn't see people who looked like me. I felt slightly let down, but I had twenty-nine states left to visit; surely I would find myself, my family, and that connection in one of them.

Weeks passed, many state lines were crossed, with the odometer in my car spinning higher and higher, and I still hadn't found what I was looking for.

I HAD JUST driven into Monterrey, Nuevo León, the second largest city in México just one hundred miles from the Texas border. My paternal grandmother, María de Jesús de León, was born there and in 1913, when she was one year old, she and her family moved to Waco, Texas, where they worked picking cotton in the fields around Waco, a migrant job that some of their children would do as well. My great-grandmother brought to Texas the recipes and cooking style unique to Monterrey.

When I was a kid, we would go to my grandmother's house every Sunday evening for dinner. My grandmother would open the front door, grab my cheeks, give me a hug and kiss, and bring me into the house. I can still remember the smell of the porky pinto beans cooking in the kitchen

> **But I think that happens to many immigrant families; you try so hard to fit into your new country that you forget where you came from. I needed to find my origins.**

and what seemed to me like several hundred warm homemade flour tortillas, each a perfect round and stacked to the ceiling. And the smell of stewed pork, dried chiles, and cumin. This was home, this was the food of my family. And after seven months and seventeen thousand miles I still hadn't found it.

As I drove west across the northern states just below Texas, I'd stop and eat in the small towns between Ciudad Victoria, Tamaulipas, and Monterrey, and as I got closer to the city where my grandmother was born, the food became progressively more familiar. In Santiago, just outside the Monterrey city limits, I stopped for lunch at the mercado and went to one of the puestos serving comida corrida, a prix-fixe choose-your-own quick and hot meal. I chose one of the red pork guisos. The stew came with beans and rice and tortillas de harina. When the plate landed in front of me I had an instant flashback to my grandmother's table on Briarwood Lane in North Austin—it looked exactly like the food she made. The pinto beans were mashed with lots of rich pork fat. The flour tortillas were thick and made with baking powder to get a better rise and were perfect for soaking up the rich red chile and pork guiso next to it. This was my grandmother's food. I took a bite, teared up, and sat there almost unable to finish eating. I called my dad and cried.

I grew up thinking that we were Mexican not because my family self-identified as Mexican but because that was the word others used to describe us. One day when I was probably about twelve years old, we were at the grocery store and were buying cornmeal to make cornbread muffins for a delicious beef stew my mom used to make. The woman standing behind us in the check-out line asked, leaning in and speaking very slowly, exaggerating each consonant and syllable, "A-r-e y-o-u m-a-k-i-n-g t-o-r-t-i-l-l-a-s?" I looked at her, puzzled by the way she was speaking and also because, as everyone knows, you don't make tortillas from cornmeal.

I have always been put into a very small box because of the way I look. Many people have a rigid, preconceived notion of what it is to be Mexican and everyone they encounter with that "Mexican look" gets assigned an arbitrary list of attributes and a predefined past, present, and future. So I grew up thinking that everything that we ate was Mexican because of those labels others put on us. We were expected to represent México even though we had never lived there and I had only ever been to the border towns—Matamoros, Juárez, and Nuevo Progreso.

The first time that I traveled to the central states in México, far away from the Texas border, the food was *nothing* like the food I ate growing up. I remember calling my mom and telling her about what I had eaten as if I had made a discovery. A foolish college boy had discovered that central Mexican cuisine is nothing like the Tex-Mex food he ate growing up. I was conditioned to believe we were the "poster family" representing all of México, and that belief had just been obliterated. I was so confused but desperately wanted to understand my connection to this culture. I had to know why we ate what we ate and where we came from.

It only took twenty years, but sitting at this little puesto in the middle of the mercado, after so many miles, and so many plates of food, here it was. Something that looked and tasted exactly like my grandmother's food.

I had found a food connection. But the people in Monterrey didn't look like me.

My father had blond hair up until he was about five years old and then it turned light brown. The Martínez side of my family are light skinned and have lighter hair than my mother's side, the Castruitas. I have more of my maternal grandfather's features—darker hair, darker skin, darker eyes, sharper features in my face, more moreno (brown). The people in Monterrey looked a lot like my dad's side of the family.

A few days later I drove into Saltillo, Coahuila, about an hour southwest of Monterrey. I parked in el centro, the historic center, and walked the cobblestone streets into one of the colonial Spanish plazas. There was a little girl, about three years old in a little white dress and little black Mary Jane shoes dancing between her parents. I sat on one of the wooden benches to watch this beautiful moment. She turned toward me and I was able to see her face. My heart sank and I could feel the tears welling up in my eyes. She looked exactly like a photo of my mother when she was about the same age. I sat there frozen and I watched, almost in shock at the striking resemblance. I walked to the mercado. Everyone who I saw looked familiar, like when you are at a wedding and you see relatives you haven't seen for years; you can't remember their names, but you know their faces (well, at least in a big Mexican American family this is what weddings are like).

Finally, I found the people who looked like me.

I had now found the flavors of my childhood and had found people who look like me, but still, I didn't feel the personal sense of belonging that I expected—that I desperately wanted. I felt comfortable in Saltillo, and I felt the love and the nostalgia in the food in Monterrey, but I still hadn't found that deeper connection that I longed for. My connection. A connection to a place.

This was just before the world turned upside down in March 2020, when the pandemic came to the US and México. Naturally I assumed that I would finish the research for the book and return to my life in New York City after having discovered my origin and finding that deeper connection. But lockdown kept me in the country for longer than expected, which was the gift that eventually allowed me to find that coveted connection. One month later in Mazatlán, a city in the state of Sinaloa, a city by the sea—I found me.

▼ Tortas Ahogadas, p. 248

PACÍFICO

CENTRAL

Mazatlán in Sinaloa is my home.

It is my chosen home. I have been traveling up and down the Pacific coast for the last twenty-five years. When I was in my twenties, hiking up the rocky coast in Puerto Escondido, I fantasized about buying a house on the coast and eventually retiring there one day, eating freshly caught shrimp, octopus, and lobster every day. That's why I ended up here, buying a house ten minutes from the beach and where I do eat freshly caught shrimp, octopus, and lobster often (though not every day—I still need my pork!). The idea of moving to México had always been in the back of my mind. The Mexican Pacific coast is incredibly beautiful and nothing compares to the freshness and flavor of the seafood and produce, especially the coconuts, mango, and papaya.

As you travel south into Nayarit from Mazatlán, through the coconut forests and mango farms, tropical seafood vibes continue and evolve into Jalisco's colonial Spanish Mexican scene with mariachis, birria, pozole, and tequila. I recently drove from Mexico City to Mazatlán and decided to stop in Guadalajara, the capital of Jalisco. On my way I passed through miles and miles of agave fields glowing silvery-blue in the Mexican sun. And even though Guadalajara is a large city with over 1.5 million people, it still retains so much Old World charm. The first time I visited Guadalajara was in 1999. I remember walking around the centro historico and sitting in awe of the Catedral de la Asunción de María Santísima (Cathedral of the Assumption of Our Lady), built in 1618 in the Spanish renaissance architectural style. I went back to Guadalajara earlier this year and took my rescue lab Choco to play in the plaza in front of the cathedral, and I was struck with the same feeling of awe that I felt twenty-two years ago.

THE RECIPES

Aguachile
fresh butterflied shrimp with avocado, cucumber, lime, and a spicy serrano salsa, p. 242

Pipián Rojo estilo Jalisco
pumpkin seed, peanut, and sesame seed sauce served over roasted chicken, p. 244

Tortas Ahogadas
slow-roasted pork sandwiches bathed in a tomato sauce, p. 248

Carne en su Jugo
sirloin steak simmered in a roasted tomatillo salsa with bacon and served over beans, p. 251

Langosta con Salsa Guajillo
garlic-and-herb fried lobster tossed in a buttery guajillo and agave sauce, p. 252

Tamales Barbones de Camarón
steamed shrimp and corn dumplings with chiles and roasted tomato, p. 256

Pozole Rojo
rich hominy and pork stew with guajillos, anchos, and chipotles, p. 260

Tacos Gobernador
buttery shrimp tacos with toasted flour tortillas and melted cheese, p. 262

Tlayuda con Chorizo Rojo
homemade chorizo on a large corn tostada topped with refried beans, p. 266

PACÍFICO CENTRAL

States: Jalisco, Nayarit, Sinaloa, Colima

▲ Tamazula, Jalisco

▲ Manzanillo, Colima

▼ San Ignacio Cerro Gordo, Jalisco

▼ Guadalajara, Jalisco

Aguachile

Fresh, butterflied shrimp with avocado, cucumber, lime, and a spicy serrano salsa

I love Pacific-caught shrimp. The first time I tried them I was in a town called Barra de Navidad. Every morning the shrimp dinghies and the young fisherman would come in with their haul. They sold fresh shrimp ceviche with crispy tortillas and fresh coconut water harvested from the trees along the beach. And for the ten days I was there, that was my breakfast.

Twenty years later, I walk the beaches in Mazatlán with a mission to try aguachile at just about every puesto I find. I had forgotten until I moved here how much I love fresh shrimp. Mazatlán is known around the country for its sweet shrimp and this dish is iconic—and, I believe, the best way to showcase the gorgeousness of this ingredient. If you follow my social, you know how much aguachile I eat and how much I love it. Whenever I make ceviche or aguachile, I look for the freshest shrimp possible. Find a fishmonger with a reputation for high quality—usually the one where the best seafood restaurants source their seafood. Look for shrimp that is translucent and shiny. They should have a subtle fresh smell, like the sea, nothing harsh or strong. Ask the fishmonger when they were caught and when they arrived. Look for the shrimp that were caught nearest the date you are making aguachile.

SERVES 4

FOR THE SALSA DE SERRANO
- 2 medium tomatillos (3.4 oz/97 g), husked, rinsed, and quartered
- 4 chiles serranos (3.4 oz/97.2 g), stemmed and coarsely chopped
- 1 large garlic clove, lightly crushed
- ¼ cup fresh cilantro leaves with tender stems (1.41 oz/30 g)
- ¾ teaspoon Morton kosher salt (0.14 oz/4 g), plus more to taste

FOR THE AGUACHILE
- 1 pound (453 g) large shrimp, shelled, deveined, and butterflied
- ¼ teaspoon finely grated lime zest
- ¾ cup fresh lime juice (about 6 limes)

- Morton kosher salt
- ½ medium cucumber (4.9 oz/ 140 g), peeled, seeded, and thinly sliced
- ½ medium red onion (5.4 oz/154 g), thinly sliced
- ½ medium avocado (2.9 oz/84 g), peeled, seeded, and thinly sliced
- Freshly ground black pepper

FOR SERVING
- → Fried or baked Tostadas de Maíz, *p. 40*
- → Totopos
- → Saltine crackers

1. MAKE THE SALSA DE SERRANO: In a blender on medium-low speed, puree the tomatillos, chiles serranos, garlic, cilantro, salt, and ½ cup ice water (this keeps it very green) until smooth. Do not be tempted to blend above medium speed or your salsa will get airy and will have the texture of a smoothie. Taste and season with more salt if desired.

2. ASSEMBLE THE AGUACHILE: In a medium bowl, toss the shrimp with the lime zest and lime juice. Season with salt and arrange on a platter in an even layer.

3. Arrange the cucumber around the edges, then arrange the onion inside the cucumber ring. Arrange the avocado in the center and season with pepper. Serve with tostadas, totopos, saltines, and the salsa de serrano.

Pipián Rojo estilo Jalisco

Pumpkin seed, peanut, and sesame seed sauce served over roasted chicken

There is a pottery workshop I love in a town in Jalisco called Tlaquepaque. They make beautifully glazed plates, bowls, and platters in rich, vibrant colors. I went to visit, and Santi Padilla, the ceramicist, gave me some beautiful tableware to take back to Mazatlán with me. I told her that I wanted her to choose the first meal that I ate on her plates and she told me to make a pipián from her town. So that's what this is—a rich sauce thickened with toasted pumpkin seeds, peanuts, and sesame seeds, flavored with allspice and cloves, and spiced from the heat of chiles anchos and chiles de árbol.

SERVES 6

1¼ cups raw pepitas (5.5 oz/157 g)

⅓ cup salted roasted peanuts (1.9 oz/54 g)

¼ cup raw sesame seeds (1.4 oz/41 g)

5 allspice berries

3 whole cloves

1 teaspoon dried oregano, preferably Mexican

½ teaspoon cumin seeds

¼ teaspoon black peppercorns

4 large chiles anchos (2.4 oz/ 70 g), stemmed and seeded

3 chiles de árbol (0.07 oz/2 g), stemmed and seeded

3 large Roma tomatoes (11 oz/ 314 g), cored and left whole

½ large white onion (6.6 oz/188 g)

1 2-inch piece bolillo (1.2 oz/35 g) or baguette, halved

3 garlic cloves, unpeeled

6 cups homemade chicken stock or store-bought low-sodium chicken broth

2¾ teaspoons Morton kosher salt (0.74 oz/21 g), plus more to taste

¼ cup lard or vegetable oil

1 tablespoon dark or light agave syrup or honey

1 roast chicken, carved

1. Heat a large skillet over medium-high heat. Toast the pumpkin seeds and peanuts, tossing frequently, until very fragrant and browned in spots, for 3 to 4 minutes. Reserve about ¼ cup of toasted pepitas for serving (it's okay if there is a peanut or two mixed in). Transfer the remaining seeds and nuts to a large heavy pot.

2. In the same skillet over medium-high heat, toast the sesame seeds, tossing frequently, until fragrant and browned, for 2 to 3 minutes. Transfer to the pot with the pumpkin seeds.

3. In the same skillet over medium-high heat, toast the allspice, cloves, oregano, cumin, and peppercorns, tossing frequently, until browned and fragrant, for 1 to 2 minutes. Transfer to the pot with the pumpkin seeds.

4. Line the skillet with two large sheets of foil to prevent the chiles and tomatoes from burning and sticking to the bottom of the skillet. Cook the chiles, pressing down on them with a metal spatula to make contact with the pan, until lightly toasted on both sides, for about 30 seconds total. The chiles will burn easily, so press down and turn them quickly. Transfer the toasted chiles to the pot with the pumpkin seeds.

5. Add the tomatoes, onion, bolillo, and garlic and char on all sides, turning occasionally, for about 3 minutes for the bolillo (it will char quickly), about 5 minutes for the garlic, about 9 minutes for the onion, and about 16 minutes for the tomatoes. Transfer to the pot with the pepitas.

6. To the pot, add the stock and salt and bring to a boil over high heat. Reduce the heat, cover, and simmer until the seeds and chiles have softened and the flavors have come together, for about 30 minutes. Remove from the heat and let sit covered for 20 minutes to cool slightly before blending.

7. Working in batches, carefully add the cooked pumpkin seed mixture and liquid to a blender and puree until smooth. Transfer each batch to a large bowl, stirring to combine the batches of pipián each time.

8. Rinse and wipe the pot clean and dry. Set the pot over medium-high and heat the lard until it's very hot. Carefully pour the blended pipián into the hot lard (it will spit and sputter, so wearing an apron and long sleeves are a good idea). Stir, scraping up any fried bits from the bottom of the pot, reduce the heat to medium-low, and simmer, stirring frequently, until the top of the pipián is glossy and thick, for about 10 minutes. Stir in the agave. Taste and season with more salt if desired.

9. Serve over roasted chicken and sprinkled with the reserved toasted pepitas.

▲ Pipián Rojo estilo Jalisco, p. 244

▼ Tortas Ahogadas, p. 248

Tortas Ahogadas

Slow-roasted pork sandwiches bathed in a tomato sauce

It's amazing to me to see how many riffs there are on this torta around the country. I have tried many of them, but nothing comes close to the original in Guadalajara, where the star of the show is the bread, the birote—a deep golden-brown, crusty roll with a slight tang from lime juice. Panaderos (bakers) will tell you that the birote can only be made properly in Guadalajara because of the high altitude (5,138 feet) and climate of the city. The birote has such a crispy crust that you have to bathe it in a salsa in order to soften it up enough to eat without cutting your mouth. But that crust soaks up all of those delicious flavors from the salsas and melts in your mouth when you take a bite. The torta is filled with slow-braised pork carnitas that fall apart and melt into the torta and sit atop of a thin layer of refried beans. Two salsas, one tomato-based and the other made from spicy chile de árbol, allows you to control the level of heat in each torta.

MAKES 6 SANDWICHES

FOR THE SALSA DE JITOMATE
- 3 pounds (1.3 kg) Roma tomatoes, cored and left whole
- ¼ medium white onion (3.45 oz/ 98 g), coarsely chopped
- 3 whole cloves
- 2 garlic cloves, peeled
- 2 teaspoons dried oregano, preferably Mexican
- 2 teaspoons Morton kosher salt (0.56 oz/16 g)
- ¾ teaspoon cumin seeds
- 2 tablespoons rendered lard or extra-virgin olive oil

FOR THE SALSA PICANTE
- 8 chiles de árbol (0.22 oz/6.4 g), stemmed
- ¼ medium white onion (3.45 oz/ 98 g), coarsely chopped
- 2 garlic cloves, peeled
- 2 tablespoons rendered lard or extra-virgin olive oil
- ½ cup distilled white vinegar
- ½ teaspoon Morton kosher salt (0.14 oz/4 g)

FOR THE TORTAS
- 6 birotes salados, bolillos, or hoagie rolls
- 2 cups Frijoles Refritos, *p. 55*
- 1.3 pounds (600 g) Carnitas estilo Ciudad Mexico, *p. 82*

FOR SERVING
- → Cebolla Morada Encurtida, *p. 59*
- → Quartered radishes
- → Lime wedges

1. MAKE THE SALSA DE JITOMATE: In a large pot over medium-high heat, bring the tomatoes, onion, cloves, garlic, oregano, salt, cumin, and 2 cups water to a boil. Cover and cook until the skin starts to peel away from the tomatoes, for about 10 minutes. Working in batches if necessary, transfer the tomatoes, aromatics, and cooking liquid to a blender and carefully puree until smooth.

2. Wipe the pot dry with paper towels. Heat the lard over high heat. Strain the tomato puree through a fine-mesh sieve (discard the solids) and pour the strained puree into the hot lard (be careful—the mixture will spit and splatter). Reduce the heat to medium and cook, stirring occasionally, until the mixture has thickened slightly and the flavors have come together, for about 20 minutes. Keep in the pot until ready to serve.

3. MAKE THE SALSA PICANTE: In a medium saucepan over medium heat, bring the chiles de árbol, onion, garlic, and 2 cups water to a boil. Cook until the chiles are softened, for about 10 minutes. Transfer to the blender and puree until smooth.

4. Wipe the pot dry with paper towels. Heat the lard over high heat. Strain the chile de árbol puree through a fine-mesh sieve, discard the solids, and pour the strained puree into the hot lard (be careful—the mixture will spit and splatter). Reduce the heat to medium and stir in the vinegar and salt. Cook, stirring occasionally, until the mixture has thickened slightly and the flavors have come together, for about 15 minutes.

5. ASSEMBLE THE TORTAS: Warm the salsas. Split the birotes horizontally, keeping the roll attached on one long side. Spread about ⅓ cup frijoles on the bottom of each birote, then top with the carnitas.

6. TO SERVE: Carefully dip each torta into the pot of warm salsa de jitomate (you can also ladle the salsa de jitomate over each torta, but I prefer to dip the torta so that the salsa gets into every nook and cranny and the carnitas and the cut sides of the bread get good and soaked). Transfer to a deep plate or wide bowl and spoon a bit more salsa over each torta; it should pool around the edges. Top with salsa picante and cebolla morada encurtida. Serve with the radishes and lime wedges on the side.

Carne en su Jugo

Sirloin steak simmered in a roasted tomatillo salsa with bacon and served over beans

I have always been fascinated by the name of this dish: meat served in its own juices. I saw it on signs and menus all across Jalisco. And this dish actually surpassed my expectations. Tapatíos (people from Guadalajara) love a brothy dish. Tortas Ahogadas (p. 248), the iconic torta from Guadalajara, is drowned in tomato and chile de árbol salsas. Birria, braised goat, is served shredded and covered with the braising liquid or consommé it was cooked in. So it's not surprising that carne en su jugo is a dish of meat and beans and their broth covered in a charred salsa. There is something very comforting about a dish that is close to being a soup or stew. I think you tend to eat it more slowly, with a spoon and not just in a taco. I end up savoring each spoonful like I would chicken soup. Carne en su jugo has so many layers of flavor from the meat, the bacon, the charred salsa, and the beans that every bite is always a little different.

SERVES 8

- 7 medium tomatillos (12 oz/ 340 g), husked and rinsed
- ½ medium white onion (7.01 oz/201 g), halved
- 2 to 4 chiles serranos (0.85 oz/ 24.3 g each), stemmed
- 6 garlic cloves, unpeeled
- ¼ cup (packed) fresh cilantro leaves with tender stems (1.41 oz/40 g)
- 1.1 pounds (453 g) thick-cut smoked bacon, cut into 2-inch pieces
- 2¼ pounds (1 kg) boneless sirloin steak
- 12 large scallions (10.8 oz/ 306 g), ends trimmed, cut into ½-inch pieces
- 3 cups homemade chicken stock or store-bought low-sodium chicken broth
- 1 tablespoon Morton kosher salt (0.7 oz/20 g)
- 4 cups Frijoles de Olla, p. 54, and their cooking liquid, warm

FOR SERVING
→ Chopped onion
→ Chopped cilantro
→ Lime wedges
→ Warm Tortillas de Maíz, p. 38

1. Line a large skillet, preferably cast-iron, with foil. Heat over high heat for about 2 minutes, or until very hot. Cook the tomatillos, onion, chiles serranos, and garlic, turning occasionally, until all sides are charred, for about 3 minutes for the garlic, 4 to 5 minutes for the chiles serranos, and 6 to 8 minutes for the onion and tomatillos. Transfer to a plate and let cool. Peel the garlic.

2. In a blender on medium-low speed, puree the tomatillo, onion, chiles serranos, peeled garlic, and the cilantro until smooth. Set aside.

3. In a large heavy pot, arrange the bacon in an even layer. Cook over medium-high heat and let the bacon slowly render, stirring occasionally, until crispy, for 9 to 11 minutes. Transfer to a paper towel-lined plate, leaving the fat in the pan.

4. Carefully place the steak in the bacon fat. Cook over medium-high heat until browned, for 5 to 6 minutes per side. Transfer to a cutting board and let rest for 10 minutes. Cut into ¼-inch-thick strips.

5. In the same skillet, cook the scallions over medium-high heat, stirring, until browned and tender, for 6 to 8 minutes. Return the steak and half of the bacon to the pot. Stir in the salsa verde, stock, and salt; bring to a boil. Reduce the heat to medium; simmer until the steak is very tender, for about 20 minutes.

6. Serve the steak and salsa over the hot frijoles de olla and garnish with the onion, cilantro, and remaining bacon. Serve lime wedges and tortillas alongside.

Langosta con Salsa Guajillo

Garlic-and-herb fried lobster tossed in a buttery guajillo and agave sauce

One morning I headed to an island just off the coast of Mazatlán for a hike to the top of one of the mountains. I had only intended to go for the morning and then hike back to the city for a late breakfast. After the hike, as I was walking back to the beach to find the boat to go back to town, a guy came up to me and said that if I was hungry, he had fresh fish and coconuts at his stand on the beach. I was very hungry after the hike so I decided to see what he had. I assumed I'd get a fried or grilled fish, but when I asked what he had, he pulled out three live langostas that he had just caught and asked if I wanted them. Obviously I said yes. He took them to a table under a palapa on the beach and split them in half and fried them in a pot full of smashed garlic and hot oil. They were incredible—rich and tender from the oil bath and full of garlic flavor. We made tacos from some hot tortillas he warmed up and topped with a pico de gallo his wife made. It was the most perfect beachside breakfast.

SERVES 6 TO 8

12 garlic cloves, lightly crushed, divided
8 large chiles guajillos (1.69 oz/ 48 g), stemmed and seeded
3 medium chiles cascabeles (0.84 oz/24 g), stemmed and seeded
3 cups fish stock or clam juice
1 tablespoon apple cider vinegar
2 teaspoons agave syrup or honey
1 teaspoon coriander seeds
4 allspice berries
1 whole clove
2 bay leaves

Morton kosher salt
6 tablespoons unsalted butter (3 oz/85 g), cut into pieces
3 live lobsters (1½ lb/680 g each)
2 cups vegetable oil
4 fresh thyme sprigs

FOR SERVING
→ Warm Tortillas de Maíz, *p. 38*
→ Chopped onion
→ Chopped cilantro
→ Crushed chiles de árbol
→ Lime wedges

1. To make the salsa guajillo, in a large saucepan, combine 6 of the garlic cloves, the chiles guajillos, chiles cascabeles, stock, vinegar, agave, coriander, allspice, clove, bay leaves, and ½ teaspoon salt (.1 oz/4 g). Bring to a boil over high heat, cover, and remove from the heat. Let sit until the chiles have softened, for about 30 minutes.

2. Transfer all of the chile mixture to a blender and carefully puree until smooth. Wipe the saucepan clean with a paper towel. Pour the chile puree into the pan and cook over medium heat until slightly thickened and the salsa turns brick red in color, for about 10 minutes. Add the butter and stir until melted. Remove the salsa from the heat. Taste and season with salt if desired.

3. Meanwhile, chill the lobsters in the freezer for 15 minutes (this will slow down their nervous system and is apparently a more humane way to kill a lobster).

4. Working with one at a time, transfer a lobster to a cutting board, belly-side down, and arrange lengthwise in front of you. Using a kitchen towel, hold the tail (it shouldn't be very active now) and, pointing the tip of a sharp chef's knife at the point where the tail meets the body, halve the lobster through the body and head lengthwise in one clean, firm, powerful cut. Turn the lobster around and cut lengthwise through the tail—you should have 2 halves of the lobster from claw to tail. Remove any tomalley or eggs (and reserve, if you'd like). Repeat with the remaining lobsters. Or you can ask your fishmonger to do it for you.

5. In a large cold skillet, preferably cast-iron, combine the oil, the remaining 6 garlic cloves, and the thyme. Set over medium heat and allow the oil to slowly infuse with the flavor of the thyme and garlic. Cook until the thyme is browned, for about 5 minutes, and until the garlic is lightly browned, for about 10 minutes. The oil should be about 300°F—if it isn't, either turn up or turn down the heat until it registers 300°F on an instant-read thermometer.

6. Fry two lobster halves at the same time. Grip one lobster half firmly by the tail fin and carefully lower the head and claw side first into the skillet, making sure to lay it down with the end of the tail away from you. Repeat with another lobster half. Fry until the exposed flesh on the bottom side is just beginning to brown, for 3 to 4 minutes. Use tongs to carefully turn each lobster half over, making sure to lay it down away from you. Fry until the shells on the second side is bright red, for 3 to 4 minutes. Transfer to a large bowl and season the flesh side with salt. Repeat with the remaining lobster halves, returning the oil to 300°F between each if necessary.

7. Toss the lobsters in the salsa guajillo. Transfer to a large platter. Serve with warm tortillas, onion, cilantro, chiles de árbol, and lime wedges.

▲ Langosta con
Salsa Guajillo, p. 252

▼ Tamales Barbones
de Camarón, p. 256

Tamales Barbones de Camarón

Steamed shrimp and corn dumplings with chiles and roasted tomato

Tamales barbones de camarón are an iconic dish in Sinaloa. The barbones are the antennae of the shrimp and peek out from the corn husk, making them very distinctive and easily identifiable. I had never eaten a shrimp tamal until I came to Sinaloa. The shrimp that are normally used are very large, usually super jumbo or colossal size. The larger size ensures that they do not overcook in the steamer. When they steam wrapped in chile-flavored masa, the shrimp pick up the flavor of chile with a hint of the corn and the masa absorbs all of the sweet shrimp flavor. If you can't find shrimp with the heads still on, no worries, the tamales will be great with the shrimp you can find. Just use the biggest shrimp you can buy!

MAKES 16 TAMALES

2¼ pounds (1 kg) head-on (if possible) super colossal shrimp (about 16), peeled, deveined, and tails removed
Morton kosher salt
10 large chiles guajillos (2.11 oz/ 60 g), stemmed and seeded
6 chiles de árbol (0.18 oz/4.8 g), stemmed (seeded for mild)
5 Roma tomatoes (17.8 oz/505 g), cored and left whole
¼ large white onion (3.4 oz/98 g)
6 garlic cloves, peeled
1 teaspoon dried oregano, preferably Mexican
1 teaspoon dried thyme

3 pounds (1.36 kg) fresh coarse-grind corn masa for tamales, "unprepared" (see Cook's Note, *p. 112*), or fresh masa for tortillas
¼ cup ground dried shrimp (optional)
1 cup rendered lard or vegetable oil
30 dried corn husks (from a 1-pound bag)

FOR SERVING
→ Lime wedges
→ Your favorite salsa

1. In a medium bowl, toss the shrimp with 1¼ teaspoons salt (0.28 oz/8 g). Cover the bowl with plastic wrap and refrigerate for at least 30 minutes and up to 3 hours.

2. In a large saucepan, cover the chiles guajillos and chiles de árbol with 3 cups water and bring to a boil. Cover the pot, remove from the heat, and let sit until the chiles have softened, for about 30 minutes.

3. Line a medium skillet, preferably cast-iron, with a sheet of foil and heat over high heat. Cook the tomatoes and onion, undisturbed, until charred on all sides, for 4 to 5 minutes for the onion and 10 to 12 minutes for the tomatoes.

4. Transfer the tomatoes and onion to a blender and add the garlic, oregano, thyme, ½ teaspoon salt (0.14 oz/4 g), the softened chiles, and 2 cups of their cooking liquid. Puree until smooth.

5. In a large bowl, mix the masa, ground shrimp (if using), lard, 1¾ teaspoons salt (0.42 oz/12 g), and half of the chile puree with your hands until well incorporated and the mixture looks shiny and smooth and is the consistency of thick cake batter and easily spreadable (if your masa is hard or crumbly before you start

to mix, you can use a stand mixer instead of mixing by hand to help you get a smooth consistency), for about 5 minutes. Cover the bowl with plastic wrap and set aside for at least 30 minutes and up to 2 hours at room temperature. The masa will thicken slightly as it sits.

6. Fill a large bowl with hot water, add the husks, and soak until soft and pliable, for about 15 minutes. Using your hands, swirl the husks in the water to loosen any strands of corn silk or dirt. Drain, rinse, and shake off any excess water.

7. Place a husk on a work surface and gently stretch out the wide end; it should be at least 5 inches wide. The width doesn't have to be exactly 5 inches, but if you go any narrower, your husk might not fully cover the shrimp. If the husk is really wide, you can trim it to 5 inches, but remember to save the scraps. This recipe makes about 16 tamales, so you will have extra husks in case you need it, as some may tear.

8. Arrange a husk so the wide end is closest to you. Spoon ¼ cup of the masa onto the husk about 4 inches from the wide end. Using a spoon, small offset spatula, or butter knife, spread the masa into a thin, even layer, covering the width of the husk by 5 inches up the length of the husk; leave the narrow end uncovered. If you mess up, just scrape off the masa and start over. Repeat with the remaining husks and masa.

9. Keeping the wide end closest to you, place 1 shrimp in the center of the masa on each husk so that the head is pointing toward the wide end of the husk. The head and antenna should be just off the edge of the husk. Spread a tablespoon or two of the remaining chile puree over the shrimp.

10. Fold one side of the husk over the shrimp, then fold the other side over to cover. Holding the tamal seam-side up, fold the narrow, pointed end of the husk away from you and under the tamal. Set on a sheet pan seam-side up. Repeat with the remaining tamales.

11. Place a basket insert or steaming rack into a tamal pot, stockpot, or pasta pot. Fill with water so that it comes up to just below the basket. Line the bottom of the basket with the reserved husk scraps to cover up any exposed metal. Crumple a large sheet of foil to form a 3-inch-diameter ball. Place the ball in the center of the pot. Using the foil ball as support, prop 4 to 7 tamales upright and around and leaning against the ball with the folded end down and seam-side facing up.

12. Continue placing the tamales around the ball, stacking and leaning them against one another until all of the tamales are in the pot. Cover the tamales loosely with several pieces of plastic wrap and place a damp clean kitchen towel over the tamales. Cover the pot and bring the water to a boil over high heat. Reduce the heat to medium-low and simmer the tamales, undisturbed, for 30 minutes, checking the pot occasionally to make sure there is still water in the pot, and if not, adding more as needed.

13. After 30 minutes, remove the cover and use tongs to remove a tamal from the pot; let it cool for 5 minutes. (If you don't let it rest before checking, the masa will stick to the husk and appear gummy.) Unfold the husk—if the masa sticks, the tamal is not ready. Carefully refold and return it to the pot. Cook for 5 minutes more, then check again. If the husk peels back easily and no masa sticks, your tamales are done. Remove from the heat, uncover the pot, and let sit for 10 minutes before unwrapping.

14. Serve warm with a squeeze of lime and salsa.

▼ Pozole Rojo, p. 260

Pozole Rojo

Rich hominy and pork stew with guajillos, anchos, and chipotles

This is a very different style of pozole than the pozole verde from Guerrero (see p. 116). Whereas the one from Guerrero is green from the fresh chiles, tomatillos, herbs, and pepitas, this one, from Jalisco, is deep brick red from the dried chiles, which offer a warm, gentle heat. What makes this version special is the amount of chiles in the broth, which, when pureed, act as a thickener and give the stew its velvety body. For this recipe I wrote an oven-toasting method for the chiles, which is easier for most home cooks. The method is fast, easy, and almost foolproof (unless you walk away!). In México, the toasting of chiles usually happens on a comal or over a direct flame, both of which take a lot of practice to get right without burning them.

SERVES 8

- 6 large chiles guajillos (1.3 oz/ 37 g), stemmed and seeded
- 2 large chiles anchos (.7 oz/20 g), stemmed and seeded
- 2 chiles chipotles (0.2 oz/5.8 g), stemmed
- 4 15.5-ounce cans white or golden hominy, rinsed and drained
- 2 tablespoons rendered lard or vegetable oil
- 3 pounds (1.3 kg) boneless pork shoulder
- 16 garlic cloves (about 2 heads), lightly crushed
- 1 large white onion (14.9 oz/424 g) Morton kosher salt
- 2 teaspoons dried oregano, preferably Mexican
- 1 teaspoon fresh thyme leaves
- 1 teaspoon black peppercorns
- 1 whole clove
- 1 star anise
- 2 large dried bay leaves

FOR TOPPING
→ Chicharrones
→ Sliced avocado
→ Crema
→ Crumbled queso fresco
→ Thinly sliced green cabbage
→ Chopped white onion
→ Sliced radishes
→ Totopos
→ Dried oregano
→ Crushed chiles de árbol
→ Lime wedges

1. Arrange a rack in the center of the oven and preheat to 350°F.

2. On a sheet pan, arrange the chiles guajillos, chiles anchos, and chiles chipotles in an even layer. Transfer to the oven and roast until the chiles are beginning to brown (be careful not to char) and are very fragrant and smell almost like toasted nuts, for about 5 minutes. Remove the pan from the oven and set aside to cool.

3. Increase the oven temperature to 450°F. On a foil-lined sheet pan (move the chiles to a large plate if you only have one sheet pan), spread the drained hominy in an even layer. Roast, tossing once, until lightly toasted, very fragrant, and just beginning to brown on the edges, for 15 to 20 minutes. Remove from the oven and set aside until ready to use.

4. Meanwhile, in a large Dutch oven or heavy pot over medium-high, heat the lard. Add the pork and cook, turning occasionally, until browned on the 2 largest sides, for 10 to 12 minutes. Transfer to a large plate and set aside until ready to use.

5. In the same pot over medium-high heat, cook the garlic, onion, and ½ teaspoon salt (0.14 oz/4 g), stirring occasionally, until the onion is tender and beginning to brown, for 8 to 10 minutes.

6. Add the toasted chiles, oregano, thyme, peppercorns, clove, anise, bay leaves, and 10 cups water to the onion mixture and bring to a boil. Nestle the pork into the pot (the liquid should come halfway up the sides of the pork; if it doesn't, add more). Cover the pot, reduce the heat to low, and simmer until the pork is very tender and shreds easily, for 2 to 2½ hours.

7. Transfer the pork to a large plate. Once it is cool enough to handle, shred the pork into large pieces. Cover loosely with plastic wrap and set aside until ready to serve.

8. Working in batches, transfer the cooking liquid and aromatics from the pot to a blender and puree until smooth and no large pieces of chile remain.

9. Wipe the pot clean. Return the chile puree to the pot and add the toasted hominy. Bring to a simmer over medium heat and cook, uncovered, until the flavors meld, the broth is rich, and the hominy has plumped up and is tender, for about 20 minutes. Stir the reserved pork into the pozole and cook to heat through, for about 5 minutes.

10. Divide the pozole among eight bowls. Top with your desired toppings and a squeeze of lime.

COOK'S NOTE: Here's a way to master roasting chiles on the stove: Heat a comal or skillet over medium heat for about 2 minutes. Set a timer, put one chile down on the comal, and use a metal spatula to press it down. Pay close attention to the smell and the color of the chile. When it starts to smell toasted and nutty, look at the clock and note the time. But keep going. When the chile starts to smell burnt and you can see smoke, look at the time. Now you know how long to toast the chile and how long you have before it burns.

Tacos Gobernador

Buttery shrimp tacos with toasted flour tortillas and melted cheese

In 1987, the governor of Sinaloa, Francisco Labastida, planned a visit to Mazatlán and made a reservation to eat at Los Arcos. Eduardo Angulo, the owner, began to plan a menu and remembered that the governor loved his wife's shrimp tacos. Trying to outdo the governor's wife, Eduardo and his chef created this taco, and when the governor asked the name of the taco, he replied, tacos gobernador.

MAKES 8 TACOS

- 2 tablespoons extra-virgin olive oil
- 1 pound (453 g) large shrimp, peeled, deveined, and tails removed
- 3 tablespoons unsalted butter (1.5 oz/42 g)
- ½ medium white onion (5.4 oz/ 154 g), thinly sliced
- 1 medium chile poblano (4 oz/ 125 g), stemmed, seeded, and thinly sliced into strips
- 1 medium celery stalk (1.72 oz/ 49 g), thinly sliced crosswise on the diagonal
- 1 medium chile serrano (0.85 oz/ 24.3 g), stemmed and thinly sliced into rings
- 2 garlic cloves, finely grated
- 1 teaspoon dried oregano, preferably Mexican
- ¾ teaspoon Morton kosher salt (0.14 oz/4 g), plus more to taste
- ½ teaspoon crushed or ground coriander seeds
- 1 medium Roma tomato (3.9 oz/ 113 g), cored and chopped
- 8 Tortillas de Maíz, p. 38
- 6 ounces (170 g) queso asadero, quesillo, or Monterey Jack cheese, grated

FOR SERVING
→ Lime wedges
→ Your favorite salsa

1. In a large skillet over high, heat the oil. Arrange the shrimp in an even layer in the skillet and cook, turning once, until just starting to brown, for about 1 minute per side. Transfer to a medium bowl and set aside.

2. Reduce the heat to medium and melt the butter. Cook the onion, chile poblano, celery, chile serrano, garlic, oregano, salt, and coriander, tossing occasionally, until the onion and chile poblano are beginning to brown, for 6 to 8 minutes.

3. Add the tomato and cook, tossing occasionally and scraping up any browned bits, until the tomato begins to break down, for about 5 minutes more. Transfer to the bowl with the shrimp and toss to combine. Taste and season with salt.

4. Wipe the skillet clean with a paper towel. Working with 2 or more tortillas at a time (if you can fit 2 tortillas in your skillet), cook the tortillas until lightly toasted on one side, for 2 to 3 minutes.

5. Flip and add a small mound of cheese in the center of the toasted side. Top with some of the shrimp filling and fold over like a taco. Cook the untoasted side until the cheese is beginning to melt and the tortilla is lightly toasted, for 2 to 3 minutes. Flip to toast the second half. Continue with the remaining tortillas, cheese, and shrimp.

6. Serve with a squeeze of lime and your favorite salsa.

▲ Tlayuda con Chorizo
Rojo, p. 266

Tlayuda con Chorizo Rojo

Homemade chorizo on a large corn tostada topped with refried beans

Another thing that I have tried in every state that makes it is chorizo rojo. And it is different in each part of the country. Sometimes you see it in casings, sometimes it's smoked, and sometimes it's grilled. My favorite style is fresh and marinated for several days—four, to be exact. Four days allows for maximum flavor development and the chorizo will start to straddle the line between fresh and cured sausage, and I think it is absolutely necessary. If you cook the sausage without a marinating time, it will just taste like spiced ground pork. The marinade time allows the pork to meld with the flavors of the spices, and the vinegar gives a slight bratwurst-like funk to develop. When I make sausage I make a big batch, and after four days I freeze half of it so that I always have homemade chorizo on hand. Then I cook and eat the other half—usually in breakfast tacos. But if I am serving a larger crowd, I make tlayudas topped with frijoles refritos and chorizo so that we can all dig in together. In this recipe I am giving you both the chorizo and the tlayuda. You can choose to make just the chorizo or both. But I definitely recommend freezing half of it after it's been marinated so that you have homemade chorizo for whenever the mood strikes.

SERVES 8 (ABOUT 2 POUNDS CHORIZO)

FOR THE CHORIZO
- 1 tablespoon black peppercorns
- 1 teaspoon allspice berries
- 2 whole cloves
- 2 teaspoons cumin seeds
- 10 large chiles guajillos (2.11 oz/ 60 g), stemmed and seeded
- 2 large chiles anchos (1.2 oz/35 g), stemmed and seeded
- ¾ cup apple cider vinegar
- 6 garlic cloves, peeled
- 4 teaspoons dried oregano, preferably Mexican
- 2¾ teaspoons Morton kosher salt (0.42 oz/18 g)
- 1 teaspoon dried thyme
- ¼ teaspoon ground canela or cinnamon
- 2¼ pounds (1 kg) ground pork, preferably not lean (see Cook's Note)

FOR THE TLAYUDAS (OPTIONAL)
- 6 tablespoons rendered lard, divided
- 2 tlayudas oaxaqueñas or 6 baked Tostadas de Maíz, p. 40, warm
- 1½ cups Frijoles Refritos, p. 55
- 12 ounces (340 g) queso Oaxaca or fresh mozzarella, pulled into thin strands or shredded
- 6 ounces (170 g) queso fresco, crumbled

FOR SERVING
- → Chiles Jalapeños en Escabeche, *p. 64*
- → Salsa de Aguacate, *p. 60*

1. MAKE THE CHORIZO: In a small skillet over medium heat, toast the peppercorns, allspice, and cloves, swirling the pan often, until very fragrant, for about 1½ minutes. Add the cumin seeds and cook until the cumin smells earthy and fragrant, for about 30 seconds. Set aside.

2. In a large saucepan, cover the chiles guajillos and chiles anchos with water. Bring to a boil. Cover the pot, remove from the heat, and let sit until the chiles have softened, for about 30 minutes. Drain and discard the liquid.

3. Transfer the chiles to a blender. Add the toasted spices, the vinegar, garlic, oregano, salt, thyme, and canela and puree until smooth. Transfer to a large bowl.

4. Add one-quarter of the pork to the bowl and mix together (combining just a small amount of meat in the beginning makes it easier to incorporate the rest without overmixing). Add the remaining pork and mix well to thoroughly combine, but don't overwork it or it will get tough and sticky. Cover the bowl tightly with plastic wrap and refrigerate for at least 24 hours and up to 4 days. (I like to marinate the mixture for 4 days for maximum flavor.)

5. After it's marinated, you can use half of it (1 pound) right away to make these tlayudas or any other recipe that calls for fresh chorizo. And you will still have another pound to freeze for later! Divide the chorizo in half and place one half (a little over 1 pound or ½ kilo) in a freezer bag and freeze for up to 3 months.

6. MAKE THE TLAYUDAS: *(You will only be using 1 pound of the chorizo for the tlayudas.)* In a large skillet, preferably cast-iron, over medium-high heat, heat 2 tablespoons of the lard until hot. Cook half of the chorizo, breaking it up with a wooden spoon and stirring often, until browned and cooked through, for 7 to 9 minutes. Transfer the chorizo to a plate and repeat with another 2 tablespoons of the lard and the remaining meat.

7. Arrange a rack in the center of the oven and preheat to 475°F.

8. Brush one side of each of the tlayudas with the remaining 2 tablespoons lard. Place on a sheet tray and bake until just beginning to brown, for about 5 minutes. Remove from the oven and carefully spread a thin layer of frijoles on top of each tlayuda. Sprinkle with the chorizo, queso Oaxaca, queso fresco, and sliced jalapeño en escabeche (including carrot and onions). Serve with the salsa de aguacate. I like to drizzle with the jalapeño brine from the escabeche instead of a squeeze of lime!

COOK'S NOTE: Ideally, when you make sausage, you want 25 percent of the weight of the meat to be fat. It's difficult—if not impossible—to find 75/25 pork in the supermarket. But if you ask your butcher at the meat counter nicely, he or she will be more than happy to take some of the trimmings in the back and grind them into your pork. If not, you can mix in ½ cup cold lard into the pork and spice mixture, and this will add more flavor and a bit of richness to leaner ground pork.

MAZATLÁN

><

I WAS DRIVING ACROSS the Mexican desert just as COVID-19 was bearing down on the US. There were very few cases in México when numbers in New York started to spike—it seemed safer here than back home. I was scared that if I went back to New York I'd get stuck; having lived through 9/11, rolling blackouts of the 2000s, and Hurricane Sandy, I wasn't ready to go through this in my Harlem apartment, whatever "this" was about to become. So I moved my flights back and decided to wait it out in México, where there had only been sixty-six cases so far. It was time to stop traveling and hunker down like the rest of the planet. And if I was going to have to quarantine by myself I had one nonnegotiable requirement—to be by the sea.

I had heard a lot about Mazatlán, the first major city on the open Pacific Ocean, just below the Baja California peninsula. It had a reputation for having some of the best shellfish in the country and for being a city that loves a good party, like Carnival before Easter. While it's not a big international tourist destination, or even a big national destination, for families and twenty-something Mexicans in the north and central part of the country, it's a big draw. So I booked an Airbnb, packed up my car, and drove eight hours across the desert and through the mountains— arriving a week before the city locked down.

Living in a tropical flower–covered apartment in the center of the city's historic district, I got a glimpse of what life was like in the before times. At sunset on the Malecón—a long stretch of boardwalk along the public beaches—bikers, skaters, and joggers shared space with families, locals, and the few tourists who stuck around. Friends and lovers sipped bottles of beer or micheladas, setting up portable speakers and picnics, waiting for the sky to stain pink and orange with the setting sun. I found the positive energy and love of the sea and desire to be outside with friends and family so compelling. There are a few cities that I have fallen in love with instantly. New York City is one of them. I felt something very similar that night in Mazatlán. Watching my first Mazatlecan sunset, I knew I'd made the right decision.

Every morning I would wake up and go to the mercado to buy food to cook for this book. I can tell a lot about a city by the mercado: how many vendors there are, how big it is, the quality of what is being sold and prepared. Mazatlán has a great market. In the area surrounding the city there are farms delivering fresh and, more important, ripe (not hard and flavorless) coconut, mango, limes, peaches, pears, tomatoes, beans, corn, chiles, and wheat to mercados within twenty-five miles from where they were

▼ Las Casas de Colores,
Mazatlán, Sinaloa

harvested. That alone was enough to keep me happy, well fed, and busy developing the recipes for the book for most of quarantine.

THERE IS SOMETHING about beaches in any country that call to me and tug at my soul, but I have to say that Mexican beaches are particularly stunning. When I was in my twenties, I'd come to México to explore the beaches on the Pacific coast, and came up with a wild boyish fantasy that one day, I would buy a house on the beach and retire there. I have always been calmed and centered by the ocean. Things that bother me seem less significant when I am watching the waves crash against the shore. Alone in a town where I knew no one from March until July, my only human contact was a food exchange with the owner of my Airbnb and the food vendors at the mercado and Zoom calls with friends and co-workers. I cried myself to sleep more than once in that little apartment. But then I would wake up early in the morning as the sun was coming up, open the house, and breathe in the cool salty sea air.

Because of the pandemic, the beaches were closed and no one was allowed on the sand or in the water. I managed to find a few hidden (at least from the police) cliffs along the coast near my apartment, and I would sit there and watch the waves crashing on the rocks. All of my anxieties and COVID fears seemed to get washed away with each passing wave. The ancient ocean and cliffs were a powerful reminder that life goes on. They gave me the energy to keep going, knowing that everything—both good and bad—has a beginning and an end.

LIVING IN NEW YORK CITY for twenty years made me a bit suspicious of my fellow humans. I am not one given to instant trust when I meet someone new. But when I arrived in Mazatlán, I posted about it on social media and was overwhelmed with offers of places to stay. A stranger named Juan Carlos Lopez was attending classes at a university in México City when the pandemic shut down the city. His family is from Mazatlán and he was on his way home when he saw on Instagram that I was planning to hunker down for a month. So he DM'd me and said that if I needed anything—food, a place to stay, help navigating the city, anything—his family would be there to help.

At first I was suspicious; why would I take the help of a stranger and what did he want from me? Then he said that if I needed any kitchen tools or equipment, his mom was a great cook and would love to lend me some. Because of this book and all the recipes I needed to develop, I decided to take him up on his offer. The next day a courier showed up with huge boxes. His mom had sent me her KitchenAid stand mixer, a Le Creuset Dutch oven, sheet pans, a pasta machine, bags of flour, a bottle of mezcal, and chile mango candy. Their generosity overwhelmed me with gratitude—and they were not the only ones. There have been so many people who have done so much to welcome me and help me settle into my new home. México is a country full of kind, loving people. But Mazatlecos are some of the best.

I had no intention of staying here in Mazatlán. But every day that passed I fell a little more for this city, its people, the beaches, and, of course, the food. Then, finally, on my birthday, I decided to make an offer on a house. By August I had moved in, and by December I had a dog.

Now, after almost two years in Mazatlán, soy Mazatleco.

> # México is a country full of kind, loving people. But Mazatlecos are some of the best.

▲ Eating shrimp on the beach

▲ Casa de Color

▼ Playa Olas Altas

▼ Mercado Municipal Pino Suarez

▼ Ostiones a la Parrilla
con Chicharrones, p. 281

BAJA

—

CALIFORNIA
PENINSULA

When I think of Baja, I think of the beach, fish tacos,

almejas chocolatas (chocolate clams), pristine oysters, and wine. The rocky peninsula, which extends south of California and stretches into the Pacific, is surrounded by the sea and has a climate similar to the Mediterranean. The landscape morphs from salt marshes to coastal dunes to forest-covered mountains. Here, the concept of sencillo (simple) is key to creating this food and to life. The ingredients that grow in this region, specifically the Guadalupe Valley, are so incredibly delicious—grapes, olives, dates, lemons, limes, and oranges—and they find their way into the many iconic dishes.

Mexicali, a city on the California border, is the home of a large population of Chinese immigrants who worked to build the US transcontinental railroad but were expelled after its completion. They migrated south to México, where they worked on the Mexican transcontinental railroad, and as the railroad progressed across the continent, they left their culinary influence across the northern states. Mexicali has the largest population of Chinese-Mexicans of any city in México. Over the last 140 years, a food culture has developed around Chinese techniques and foods, like wok stir-frying, soy sauce, and zongzi, which have fused with traditional Mexican dishes like carnitas, carne asada tacos, and salsa macha.

THE RECIPES

Ceviche de Almejas Chocolatas
briny fresh clams with mandarin orange, lime, serrano, and fresh mint, p. 277

Arrachera y Tacos Norteños
chipotle- and beer-marinated steak in a toasted flour tortilla with cheese, p. 278

Ostiones a la Parrilla con Chicharrones
grilled oysters with chicharrones in an herby orange-lime sauce, p. 281

Burritos de Langosta
burritos filled with lobster tossed in garlic butter and herbed rice and beans, p. 282

Camarones al Tamarindo
stir-fried shrimp with coconut and cashews in a sweet tamarind sauce, p. 284

Pulpo Kung Pao
stir-fried octopus with peanut and poblano in a soy-agave sauce, p. 288

Huevos Rancheros con Arrachera
fried egg tostada with a refried salsa, steak, and beans, p. 291

Nopales Enchilados
pan-roasted cactus strips in a spicy guajillo and chile de árbol sauce, p. 292

Tacos Capeados
corn-fried fish tacos with papaya, tomatillo, and a spicy cream sauce, p. 295

BAJA CALIFORNIA PENINSULA

States: Baja California, Baja California Sur

▲ Valle de Guadalupe, Baja California

▲ Mercado Negro, Ensenada, Baja California

▼ Puerto Nuevo, Baja California

▼ Ensenada, Baja California

Ceviche de Almejas Chocolatas

Briny fresh clams with mandarin orange, lime, serrano, and fresh mint

SERVES 4

Almejas chocolatas (or chocolate clams) are so named for their beautiful brown shells, not because they taste like chocolate. One of the things that I love about this country is the almost cult-like culture that can grow around ridiculously delicious local ingredients that don't really exist anywhere else—chocolate clams are one of them. They are sweet and meaty and can be found in the high-end restaurants as well as little ceviche stands on the beach. Families have dedicated generations to catching, selling, and eating these clams, and now I can add myself to the fanbase.

In addition to the clams, this dish offers another one of my favorite ingredients that is also loved and eagerly anticipated once they come into season: mandarinas (mandarin oranges). I love their sweet-tart flavor, and they pair so well with the sweet meat of the almejas. This dish screams Baja beach to me—citrus and fresh clams, it doesn't get much better.

24 almejas chocolatas or littleneck clams, rinsed and scrubbed

2 medium mandarins (8 oz/226 g), tangerines, or clementines, chilled

½ small shallot (0.5 oz/15 g), cut crosswise into very thin slices

2 chiles serranos (1.7 oz/48.6 g), stemmed, halved lengthwise, and cut into very thin slices

¼ cup fresh lime juice (about 2 limes), chilled

¼ teaspoon Morton kosher salt (0.07 oz/2 g)

FOR SERVING
→ Extra-virgin olive oil
→ Flaky sea salt
→ Torn mint leaves

1. Using an oyster knife, gently pry the clam shells apart starting at the hinge, then scrape the top shell under the muscle to disconnect the meat from the shell; discard any gritty dark parts. Repeat with the bottom shell and meat. Cut the meat into ½-inch pieces. Scrub and thoroughly clean the shells or wash them in the dishwasher; chill until ready to serve.

2. Slice off the very top and bottom of the mandarins so they stand upright. Then cut away the peel and pith, starting at the top and following the curve of the fruit as you slice toward the bottom. You want to remove the rind and white pith but not too much of the fruit. Once the mandarin is peeled, hold it in your hand and, over a medium bowl (to catch the juices), cut between the membranes to release the individual citrus segments. Place them in the bowl. Once the fruit has been segmented, squeeze the juice from the membranes over the segments.

3. Add the shallot, chiles serranos, lime juice, and kosher salt to the mandarins and gently stir to combine. Add the clams to the mandarin mixture and toss to combine. Let sit for at least 5 minutes and up to 30 minutes (this is long enough to "cook" the raw clams in the acidic dressing).

4. Fill a platter with crushed ice. Divide the ceviche among the chilled shells and set them in the ice. Drizzle with olive oil and sprinkle with a few pinches of flaky sea salt and the mint.

Arrachera y Tacos Norteños

Chipotle- and beer-marinated steak in a toasted flour tortilla with cheese

This dish reminds me of Texas-style fajitas and the memories I have of both eating and grilling fajitas back home. However, the recipe is very northern Mexican. It is a celebration of many of the best ingredients in northern Baja—beef, cheese, beer, plus Chinese flavors like fish sauce and soy sauce, which are used in this marinade. If you have the time, I highly recommend marinating the meat for the arrachera overnight, as the flavors have more time to develop and penetrate the steak. Serve with tortillas, guacamole, and your favorite salsa (I can think of at least five that I would definitely put on these tacos!).

SERVES 4

FOR THE ARRACHERA
- 4 canned chipotle peppers in adobo sauce, smashed
- 4 garlic cloves, finely grated
- 1 cup Mexican-style pale lager beer
- ½ cup fresh lime juice
- ¼ cup fish sauce
- ¼ cup fresh orange juice
- ¼ cup soy sauce
- 2 teaspoons dried oregano, preferably Mexican
- 1 teaspoon crushed cumin seeds
- ¾ teaspoon Morton kosher salt (0.14 oz/4 g)
- 1½ pounds (680 g) skirt or flank steak

FOR THE TACOS NORTEÑOS
- ¼ cup lard or extra-virgin olive oil
- ½ medium white onion (6.3 oz/ 179 g), thinly sliced
- 1 medium chile poblano (4 oz/ 125 g), stemmed and seeded, thinly sliced
- 3 chiles jalapeños (3.3 oz/99.6 g), stemmed and chopped
- 3 garlic cloves, thinly sliced
- ¾ teaspoon Morton kosher salt (0.14 oz/4 g)
- 8 medium Roma tomatoes (1.5 lb/ 680 g), cored and chopped
- 12 ounces (340 g) queso asadero, queso Chihuahua, quesillo, or Monterey Jack, shredded
- Tortillas de Harina con Mantequilla *p. 46*

FOR SERVING
→ Your favorite salsa
→ Guacamole, *p. 64*
→ Lime wedges

1. MARINATE THE ARRACHERA: In a medium bowl, whisk the chipotle peppers, garlic, beer, lime juice, fish sauce, orange juice, soy sauce, oregano, cumin, and salt. Add the steak, turn to coat, and wrap tightly with plastic wrap. Refrigerate for at least 1 hour and up to 12 hours.

2. MAKE THE TACOS NORTEÑOS: In a large skillet over medium-high heat, heat the lard. Cook the onion, poblano, jalapeños, garlic, and salt until the onion and chiles are tender and beginning to brown, for 5 to 7 minutes. Add the tomatoes and cook, stirring, until they release their juices and start to break down, for 6 to 8 minutes. Remove from the heat. Sprinkle with the queso. Cover to keep warm.

3. Meanwhile, prepare a gas grill for high heat. (Alternatively, prepare a charcoal grill for high heat.) Grill the steak, turning occasionally, until charred, for 2 to 3 minutes per side for medium-rare. Transfer to a cutting board and let rest for 10 minutes. Slice against the grain into ½-inch-thick strips.

4. Grill the tortillas until lightly charred, for about 1 minute per side.

5. TO SERVE: Top the tortillas with the steak, cheese, vegetables, salsa, and guacamole. Serve lime wedges on the side.

Ostiones a la Parrilla con Chicharrones

Grilled oysters with chicharrones in an herby orange-lime sauce

There is something about pork and oysters that frankly makes my mouth water (even as I type this headnote). I have only had grilled ostiones and chicharrones once at a street stall—but that's all it took to leave a forever-delicious impression. The combination is simply amazing. I used to be leery of the seafood street vendors, until I found myself at the fish market in Ensenada at 5:30 in the morning looking to buy the freshest oysters and clams. As I walked through the market, I recognized many of the street vendors who were also in the mercado buying ultrafresh mariscos for the day. After that, I had no fear of street vendor seafood and started fully enjoying raw seafood on the street.

MAKES 3 DOZEN OYSTERS

½ cup extra-virgin olive oil
¼ medium white onion (3.1 oz/ 89 g), finely chopped
6 garlic cloves, finely grated
¾ teaspoon Morton kosher salt (0.14 oz/4 g) plus more
3 ounces (84 g) chicharrones, finely crushed
1 teaspoon ground coriander seeds
½ teaspoon freshly ground black pepper
½ to 1 teaspoon crushed chiles de árbol, plus more for serving

3 dozen large oysters, scrubbed
¼ cup finely chopped fresh basil (1.05 oz/30 g)
¼ cup finely chopped fresh flat-leaf parsley (1.05 oz/30 g)
¼ teaspoon finely grated orange zest
2 tablespoons fresh orange juice
2 tablespoons fresh lime juice

FOR SERVING
→ Lime wedges

1. In a large skillet over medium-high heat, heat the oil. Cook the onion and garlic, stirring occasionally, until the onion is tender and just beginning to brown, for about 5 minutes. Add the chicharrones, coriander, pepper, and chiles de árbol and cook, stirring to combine, until very fragrant, for about 1 minute. Transfer the chicharrón mixture to a medium bowl and let sit until ready to assemble.

2. Prepare a grill for medium-high heat (if you have wood chips, use them!). Place the oysters, rounded-side down, on the grate. Cover the grill and grill until the oysters begin to open, for about 3 minutes.

3. Transfer the opened oysters to a platter (discard any that do not open), taking care not to spill their juices onto the grill. Let them cool slightly, then hold the oyster rounded-side down in a doubled kitchen towel in your non-dominant hand and use an oyster knife or screwdriver to pry open the shells, retaining as much liquid as possible. Slide an oyster knife or paring knife beneath the oyster to sever the muscles connecting the oysters to the shells. Remove the flat top shell and discard. Keeping the loosened oyster in the cupped half of the shell, sprinkle a generous amount of salt on a sheet pan and nestle the oysters in the salt so that they remain level and stable.

4. To the chicharrón mixture, add the basil, parsley, orange zest, orange juice, and lime juice and toss until combined. Top each oyster with some of the chicharrón mixture. Serve with lime wedges and more crushed chiles de árbol.

Burritos de Langosta

Burritos filled with lobster tossed in garlic butter and herbed rice and beans

While a lobster burrito sounds decadent (and it is!), in Baja, during lobster season in the late fall and winter, the waters cool and the markets are full of ice-covered baskets topped with beautiful black, spiny lobsters. I debated whether to use Arroz Rojo (p. 49) or Arroz Verde (p. 51) for this burrito. In Puerto Nuevo, it's made with rojo, but I really love it with verde along with any of the salsa verdes in the essentials chapter: Salsa de Chile de Àrbol (p. 62), Salsa de Tomatillo (p. 62) or Salsa de Aguacate (p. 60). If you want to really go crazy, instead of a burrito make a mollete: Butter and toast both halves of a bolillo, spread some frijoles on top, add the langosta and garlic butter, and sprinkle a little chorizo and queso fresco over top.

MAKES 12 BURRITOS

Morton kosher salt
2 live lobsters (1½ lb/680 g each)
6 tablespoons unsalted butter (3 oz/85 g)
5 chiles de árbol (0.15 oz/4 g), stemmed
4 garlic cloves, finely grated
Freshly ground black pepper
2¼ cups Frijoles de Olla, p. 54, drained

12 Tortillas de Harina estilo Sinaloa, p. 47, warm
2¼ cups Arroz Rojo, p. 49, or Arroz Verde, p. 51

FOR SERVING
→ Your favorite salsa
→ Lime wedges

1. Pour 2 inches of cold water into a large stockpot or pasta pot. Season generously with salt and bring to a boil.

2. Add the lobsters to the pot, cover, and steam (they should not be completely covered with water) until the shells are bright red (they should be slightly undercooked because the meat gets cooked in garlic butter just before serving), for about 8 minutes. Transfer the lobsters to a large sheet pan and let them sit until cool enough to handle.

3. Cut or tear off the small legs. Use a skewer to push the meat out of each into a medium bowl (or just eat it). Use kitchen shears to snip the tender underside portion of the tail open, then remove the tail meat. Cut the tail meat in half lengthwise, then cut each half into bite-size pieces and transfer to the bowl.

4. Crack the knuckles and claws with lobster crackers, pliers, a nutcracker, or the back of a heavy chef's knife and remove the meat. It's okay if the claw and knuckle meat breaks up on you; it's going into a burrito! Add the knuckle and claw meat to the bowl with the tail meat.

5. In a large skillet over medium heat, melt the butter. Add the chiles de árbol and garlic and cook, stirring occasionally, until the butter begins to brown, for about 5 minutes. Add the lobster meat and toss to coat. Season with salt and pepper to taste. Cook for 3 to 4 minutes to heat the lobster through. Remove the skillet from the heat.

6. To assemble the burritos, arrange 3 tablespoons frijoles down the center of a warm tortilla. Top with 3 tablespoons arroz, the lobster meat, and a drizzle of garlic butter. Add the salsa and roll into a burrito. Repeat with the remaining tortillas, frijoles, arroz, lobster, butter, and salsa. Serve with a lime wedge.

Camarones al Tamarindo

Stir-fried shrimp with coconut and cashews in a sweet tamarind sauce

Tamarind is native to tropical Africa but was brought to México by the Spanish and Portuguese in the 16th century. It grows on both the east and west coasts. Its ripe, sticky, reddish-brown pulp is slightly sweet and very tart and is used to make drinks, candies, and salsas. In parts of Chiapas and many of the northwestern states where there are large populations of Chinese-Mexicans and Chinese immigrants, tamarind paste is used to add a sweet-and-sour flavor to many regional dishes.

This dish, a popular menu item in many Chinese restaurants in Mexicali, is one of my favorites. I love how the sweet, sour, spicy, and slightly funky flavors come together. It's a really fun, fast, and unique way to treat stir-fried shrimp. This salsa would also be great with clams, octopus, or even chicken or pork.

SERVES 4

FOR THE SALSA TAMARINDO
- ¼ cup fish sauce
- ¼ cup tamarind paste
- 2 tablespoons piloncillo or dark brown sugar
- 2 tablespoons sambal oelek or chili sauce
- 1 star anise
- 1 tablespoon cornstarch

FOR THE STIR-FRY
- 5 tablespoons virgin coconut oil or vegetable oil, divided
- 1½ pounds (680 g) large shrimp, peeled, deveined, and tails removed
- ½ large white onion (7 oz/200 g), thinly sliced
- 6 medium chiles jalapeños (6.98 oz/198 g), stemmed, halved lengthwise, seeded, and sliced lengthwise into thin strips
- ½ cup unsalted roasted cashews
- 5 garlic cloves, thinly sliced
- 3 tablespoons finely grated fresh ginger
- 1 large scallion (0.84 oz/24 g), ends trimmed and sliced
- ¼ cup fresh basil leaves (1.41 oz/30 g)
- ¼ cup fresh cilantro leaves with tender stems (1.41 oz/30 g)

FOR SERVING
- → Toasted unsweetened coconut flakes
- → Steamed rice
- → Lime wedges

1. MAKE THE SALSA TAMARINDO: In a medium saucepan over medium heat, bring the fish sauce, tamarind paste, piloncillo, sambal, star anise, and ¼ cup water to a boil. Whisk until smooth and cook, stirring occasionally, until reduced by half and very fragrant, for about 10 minutes.

2. In a small bowl, stir the cornstarch and 1 tablespoon water together until smooth. Whisk the slurry into the tamarind sauce, increase the heat to medium-high, and bring to a boil. Cook until thickened, about 1 minute. Remove the saucepan from the heat.

3. MAKE THE STIR-FRY: In a large nonstick skillet or wok over high, heat 2 tablespoons of the oil. Working in two batches, cook the shrimp in an even layer, turning once, until lightly browned, for about 1 minute per side. Transfer to a large bowl.

4. Pour 2 tablespoons of the oil into the same skillet, then add the onion, jalapeños, and cashews. Cook, tossing frequently, until the onion is just beginning to brown but is crisp-tender, for about 2 minutes. Transfer to the bowl with the shrimp.

5. In the same skillet, heat the remaining 1 tablespoon oil. Add the garlic and ginger and cook, stirring frequently, until the garlic is beginning to get fragrant and brown, for about 1 minute. Return the shrimp mixture to the skillet and toss to combine. Pour the tamarind sauce over top, stir to combine, and bring to a boil. Remove the saucepan from the heat.

6. Top with the scallions, basil, cilantro, and toasted coconut. Serve the rice and lime wedges alongside.

▼ Camarones al
Tamarindo, p. 284

▲ Pulpo Kung
Pao, p. 288

Pulpo Kung Pao

Stir-fried octopus with peanut and poblano in a soy-agave sauce

This dish frankly blew my mind when I first tasted it. I love octopus so much and thought that grilled octopus was the only way I wanted to eat it. That was before I went to Mexicali and ate my way through the Chinese-Mexican neighborhoods. Spicy kung pao chicken was my first taste of Chinese flavors when I was a boy in Texas and was what I ordered every time we went to a Chinese restaurant. I still have a great affinity for the flavors and textures in this dish, and when I saw it on the menu but with pulpo, I had to have it. The velvety sauce grabs hold of the pulpo and won't let go. And every bite is meaty, sweet, and spicy.

SERVES 4

FOR THE OCTOPUS
- 2 pounds (907 g) octopus, cleaned, head and tentacles separated
- ½ teaspoon Morton kosher salt (0.14 oz/4 g)
- 1 tablespoon cornstarch
- 1 tablespoon Mexican-style pale lager beer, Shaoxing wine, sake, or mirin
- 1 tablespoon soy sauce

FOR THE STIR-FRY
- 3 tablespoons seasoned rice vinegar
- 2 tablespoons soy sauce, plus more to taste
- 2 teaspoons agave syrup or honey
- ½ cup unsalted roasted peanuts
- 4 tablespoons rendered lard or vegetable oil, divided
- 1 medium chile poblano (4.4 oz/ 127 g), stemmed, seeded, and cut into 1-inch pieces
- 8 to 15 chiles de árbol (0.03 oz/0.8 g each), Thai bird chiles, or 1 teaspoon crushed red chile flakes
- 4 large scallions (1.69 oz/48 g), ends trimmed, coarsely chopped
- 2 large chiles jalapeños (2.2 oz/ 66.4 g), stemmed and sliced crosswise into ¼-inch-thick rings
- 1 1-inch piece fresh ginger, peeled and finely grated
- 3 garlic cloves, thinly sliced
- ½ teaspoon Sichuan peppercorns or cracked black peppercorns

FOR SERVING
→ Steamed rice
→ Cilantro leaves and tender stems

1. **PREPARE THE OCTOPUS:** In a large heavy pot, combine the octopus, salt, and water to cover. Bring to a boil over high heat. Reduce the heat to medium-low, cover, and simmer until the octopus is very tender and a knife passes through the thickest tentacle with little resistance, for 1 to 1½ hours.

2. Remove from the heat and let the octopus cool in the liquid, still covered. Using a paper towel, wipe the purple skin off the tentacles, leaving the suckers intact. Cut the tentacles into 1-inch pieces and cut the head into bite-size pieces. Transfer both to a large bowl. Discard the cooking liquid.

3. In a small bowl, whisk together the cornstarch, beer, and soy sauce. Pour over the octopus and toss to coat. Let sit for at least 10 minutes or up to 30 minutes.

4. **MAKE THE STIR-FRY:** In a small bowl, whisk together the vinegar, soy sauce, and agave. Set the stir-fry sauce aside.

5. In a large dry skillet over medium-high heat, toast the peanuts, tossing frequently, until browned in spots, for about 5 minutes. Transfer to a heatproof bowl.

6. In the same skillet over high heat, heat 2 tablespoons of the lard. Add the octopus and the marinade clinging to it and cook, tossing occasionally, until lightly browned on all sides, for 3 to 4 minutes. Transfer to a plate.

7. In the same skillet still over high heat, heat the remaining 2 tablespoons lard. Cook the chile poblano, tossing occasionally, until browned and crisp-tender, for about 2 minutes. Stir in the chiles de árbol, scallions, jalapeños, ginger, garlic, and peppercorns. Cook, tossing frequently, until very fragrant and the chiles de árbol are lightly toasted, for about 1 minute.

8. Return the octopus to the pan and add the reserved stir-fry sauce and cook, tossing, until the liquid is nearly evaporated and coats the octopus, for about 1 minute more. Add the toasted peanuts and toss to combine. Taste and season lightly with more soy sauce if needed.

9. Serve with steamed rice and cilantro.

Huevos Rancheros con Arrachera

Fried egg tostada with a refried salsa, steak, and beans

I am not certain why but I never really ate huevos rancheros growing up, nor did I eat them in México until I got to the northern part of the country. Though this breakfast dish is on the menu of nearly every restaurant in the country, for some reason huevos rancheros seem to be made with a bit more pride in the north. I also have to admit that they have been a part of my daily book writing routine since I started working in earnest. Luckily for me, almost all of the restaurants around me deliver huevos rancheros from very early in the morning until late in the day. That said, home-cooked huevos rancheros are so satisfying and give me the energy I need for shoots and a day full of Zoom calls and recipe edits.

Cook's Note

Follow the directions in Arrachera y Tacos Norteños, p. 278, for marinating, grilling, and slicing the arrachera.

SERVES 6

- 8 medium Roma tomatoes (2 lb/907 g), cored and left whole
- ½ medium white onion (6.31 oz/ 179 g), halved
- 3 chiles serranos (2.55 oz/72.9 g), stemmed
- 4 garlic cloves, unpeeled
- ¾ teaspoon Morton kosher salt (0.14 oz/4 g), plus more to taste
- 6 tablespoons rendered lard or extra-virgin olive oil, divided
- 6 large eggs
- 6 fried Tostadas de Maíz, p. 40 Arrachera (see Cook's Note) Frijoles Refritos, p. 55
- 4 ounces (113 g) queso Cotija or fresco, crumbled

1. Line a large skillet, preferably cast-iron, with two sheets of foil and heat over high heat for about 2 minutes, or until the pan is very hot. Cook the tomatoes, onion, chiles serranos, and garlic, turning occasionally, until charred on all sides, for about 3 minutes for the garlic, 4 to 5 minutes for the chiles serranos, 6 to 8 for the onion, and 8 to 10 for tomatoes. Transfer to a plate and let cool. Peel the garlic.

2. In a blender on low speed, puree the tomatoes, onion, chiles serranos, garlic, and salt until almost smooth but some small pieces remain. Taste and season with more salt if desired.

3. Remove the foil from the skillet and heat 3 tablespoons of the lard over medium-high heat. Working in two batches, crack the eggs into the skillet, leaving space around each one, and cook until the egg whites are set and the edges are crisp but the yolk is still soft, for about 4 minutes. Season with salt to taste. Transfer to a large plate.

4. In the same skillet over medium-high heat, heat the remaining 3 tablespoons lard. Carefully pour the salsa into the hot oil (it will spit and splatter, so stand back). Stir to calm the bubbles and cook, stirring occasionally, until the salsa has slightly thickened, for about 5 minutes.

5. Divide the tostadas among plates. Top each with an egg and cover in salsa. Serve with the arrachera and frijoles refritos. Sprinkle with the queso.

Nopales Enchilados

Pan-roasted cactus
strips in a spicy guajillo
and chile de árbol sauce

I have to admit something: I've hated nopales for most of my life. When I was really little, my grandmother made me nopales con huevo (nopales with scrambled eggs and onions). I vividly remember the texture and flavor—and didn't love it. I am pretty sure my grandmother (whom I adore and love) undercooked the onions so they were sharp and kind of crunchy. And the nopales made the eggs really slimy. Three-year-old Rick was not into it. I didn't eat another nopal for about twenty years, until I tried the duck and nopal enchiladas at Fonda San Miguel in Austin. They were amazing and nothing like what I had remembered as a child.

I tried this dish, nopales enchilados, when I was in La Paz, Baja California Sur. I had been hiking and exploring the beautiful waterfalls, and the friend who I was with said he wanted to take me to a place that had the best grilled fish. One of the condiments they sent to accompany the fish was a bowl of nopales enchilados. I could not stop eating them. I generally have an aversion to slimy-textured foods, but these nopales were cooked until most of the liquid had been evaporated and were left with the most delicious flavor of the nopal. Serve as a filling for tacos, a side dish, or over eggs and frijoles refritos.

SERVES 4

- 2 large chiles guajillos (0.49 oz/14 g) stemmed and seeded
- 2 chiles de árbol (0.06 oz/1.6 g), stemmed
- ¼ teaspoon dried oregano, preferably Mexican
- 1 dried bay leaf
- 5 tablespoons extra-virgin olive oil, divided
- 2 large nopales (cactus paddles; about 8 oz/225 g each), spines removed (see Cook's Note), cut into ½-inch-wide strips
- 1 teaspoon Morton kosher salt (0.21 oz/6 g), divided
- ½ large white onion (6.63 oz/188 g), chopped
- 2 garlic cloves, finely grated

1. In a medium saucepan, bring 1 cup water, the chiles guajillos, chiles de árbol, oregano, and bay leaf to a boil. Cover the pot, remove from the heat, and let sit until the chiles have softened, for about 30 minutes. Transfer to a blender and puree until smooth. Set aside until ready to use.

2. In a large skillet over medium-high, heat 2 tablespoons of the oil. Add half of the nopales and ½ teaspoon of the salt and cook, tossing occasionally, until tender and all of the rendered juices have evaporated, for 6 to 8 minutes. Transfer to a medium bowl. Repeat with 2 more tablespoons of the oil and the remaining nopales and salt.

3. In the same skillet still over medium-high, heat the remaining 1 tablespoon oil. Add the onion and garlic and cook, stirring occasionally, until tender and just beginning to brown, for 5 to 7 minutes. Reduce the heat to medium, add the guajillo mixture, and cook until thick and the liquid has almost completely evaporated, for 8 to 10 minutes. Stir in the nopales and any accumulated juices and cook for about 3 minutes to heat through.

COOK'S NOTE Most nopales you will find in the grocery stores or markets in both the US and México will have the spines removed. But it's a good idea to inspect the paddle before you cook it to make sure. If you see any, you can use a vegetable peeler or a paring knife to remove any spines and a bit of the green skin under the spine. Think of it like removing the eye growing on a potato.

Tacos Capeados

Corn-fried fish tacos with papaya, tomatillo, and a spicy cream sauce

For crispy fried fish, I use a mixture for the batter that has a 50/50 mix of wheat flour to corn flour or masa harina because the corn adds extra flavor but also creates a crispier crust that actually will hold its crunch even when cooled to room temperature. Before I started eating tacos capeados here in Baja and in México generally, I was guilty of over-spicing my batter. I think I was trying to make the crust pull more than its fair share of the flavor lifting. However, the real artistry of taco-making is in the layering of flavor and texture. Each element contributes to a different sensation in your mouth—hot, cold, soft, crunchy, sweet, savory, and spicy. The crust in this recipe does two things: gives crunch to the taco and preserves the juicy and flaky texture of the fish.

SERVES 4 TO 6

- 1½ pounds (680 g) skinless halibut, cod, or other white fish fillets, cut crosswise into 16 strips Morton kosher salt and freshly ground black pepper
- 1 cup (4.4 oz/125 g) all-purpose flour
- 1 cup (3.5 oz/100 g) masa harina or fine- or medium-grind cornmeal
- 2 teaspoons baking powder
- ¼ teaspoon baking soda
- 12 ounces Mexican-style pale lager beer
- ½ cup sparkling mineral water, club soda, or water
- 3 tablespoons apple cider vinegar Vegetable oil, for deep-frying (about 3 quarts)

FOR SERVING
- → Warm Tortillas de Maíz, *p. 38*
- → Salsa de Papaya y Tomatillo Cruda, *p. 60*
- → Salsa Blanca, *p. 58*
- → Lime wedges
- → Shredded red cabbage

1. Lightly season the fish with salt and pepper. Transfer to a wire rack set inside a sheet pan. Refrigerate, uncovered, for at least 1 hour or up to overnight (this air-dries the surface so the batter will adhere better to the fish).

2. In a medium bowl, whisk together the all-purpose flour, masa harina, baking powder, baking soda, and 1¼ teaspoons salt (0.28 oz/8 g). Add the beer, sparkling water, and vinegar and whisk just until combined and no lumps remain.

3. Pour 3 inches of oil into a large heavy pot and clip on a deep-fry thermometer. Heat over medium-high heat until the thermometer registers 375°F. Line a sheet pan with paper towels.

4. Working in batches, dip the fish into the batter, allowing any excess batter to drip back into the bowl. Lower the fish carefully into the oil and fry, using tongs to turn the fish occasionally, until light golden brown and just cooked through, for 3 to 4 minutes. Transfer the fish to the paper towels to drain.

5. Serve the pescado capeado with tortillas, both salsas, lime wedges, and cabbage.

AGRADECIMIENTOS

WHEN I STARTED WRITING this book, I had a clear vision of what it would be—the food, the text, and the design. But it was my creative team that took that vision and amplified it to a height I never could have imagined. This team inspired me to keep going, to work harder, and to fight to maintain the creative vision we all so fiercely believed in and worked so hard to create. This team toiled long hours, well beyond the jobs that they were contracted to do and well past the money that I could afford to pay them. I had never met many of them in person, but invited them into my home and challenged them to create a book in a restricted and frighteningly uncertain world. We spent weeks together, cooking, eating, building, shooting, laughing, and enjoying each other's company. We became great friends. Friends who shared ideas and grew them to greatness. I love you all so much. ¡Muchísimas Gracias!

Gracias a Chris Cristiano, who spent countless late nights and weekends directing and designing every page in this book. Chris, this is one of the most beautiful books I have ever seen and that is, in large part, because of you.

Gracias a Ren Fuller. Your photos bring light, love, and energy to every page. Gracias a Nidia Cueva. You brought color and joy to this book, and I still cannot believe you built a workshop on my roof and hand-painted sixteen surfaces on which to shoot the food, each in a more vibrant Mexican hue. Gracias a David Koung. Your positive energy, hard work, and creativity moved our shoot from beginning to end with effortless perfection. Caroline K. Hwang, you are a culinary master. I was enraptured to see you present my food with more sophistication and style than I thought possible. Jessica Darakjian and Sergio Gamboa, gracias for bringing us all treats from the market each morning, for cooking through the recipes, and for making sure they worked as written.

Gracias a Hilary Cadigan. You helped me to get my truth onto the page. You took my esoteric meanderings and honed them into poignant prose. You have been my light and my support in this long and lonely process.

▲ TOP ROW, FROM LEFT: Christopher Boccard, Juan Carlos Osuna Moreno, Socrates Figueroa, Barkley, Rick Martínez, Caroline K. Hwang, Chris Cristiano, Sara Jendusa, Penny Lu, Chris Boccard; CENTER: Brad Cromer, David Koung, Michelle Barrera, Jessica Darakjian, Nidia Cueva, Conchita Valades de Boccard, Ren Fuller; BOTTOM: Bruno, Sophia Boccard, Choco

Gracias a Jill Baughman. I haven't written a recipe in ten years without your eyes and edits and these recipes are thoughtful and concise because of you.

Gracias a Kate Gordon for amassing hundreds of pages of research about the food, culture, and history of each city and state. Gracias a Enrique Martínez for helping me buy a car in México and for organizing much of my travel around the country.

Gracias a Eric Kim for holding my hand and being a cheerleader through our parallel journeys to authorship. Gracias a Sohla El-Waylly, Priya Krishna, and Carla Lalli Music for validating my thoughts and feelings and for keeping me centered through the challenges of publishing a book.

Gracias a mi mamá y papá for surrounding me with love and great food. You taught me how to cook and through your nurturing and generosity, I learned to express my love to my friends, family, and followers with food.

Gracias a Katherine Cowels for your fierce dedication, guidance, and loyalty to me and to the integrity of this project.

Gracias a the hard-working team at Clarkson Potter for bringing this book to life.

Finalmente, gracias a my fans and followers, whose DMs, stories, reposts, tags, photos, videos, love, encouragement, excitement, and anticipation of this book kept me going during the development of the recipes and the writing of the manuscript.

INDEX

Note: Page references
in *italics* indicate recipe
photographs.

A

Aceite de Habanero
    Quemado, *61,* 63
Achiote paste
    Recado Rojo, 65
    Tikin Xic, *166, 167*
Aguachile, 242, *243*
Albóndigas en Chipotle, *125,*
    126–27
Annatto seeds
    Recado Rojo, 65
Arrachera y Tacos Norteños,
    278, *279*
Arroz
    Blanco con
        Mantequilla, *48,* 50
    a la Tumbada, 176, *177*
    Rojo, *48,* 49
    Verde, *48,* 51
Avocado leaves, about, 29
Avocados
    Aguachile, 242, *243*

Burritos de Chilorio,
    226–27, *228*
Cemita Poblana, *88,* 89
Ceviche de Pulpo
    y Habanero
    Quemado, 160, *161*
Guacamole, 64
Salsa de Aguacate,
    56, 60

B

Bacon
    Carne en su Jugo, *250,*
        251
Banana leaves
    Tamales con
        Chicharrones y
        Frijoles Negros,
        192, 193–94
    Tamales Oaxaqueños,
        110, 111–13
    Tikin Xic, *166, 167*
Bay leaves, about, 29
Beans
    Burritos de Langosta,
        282, *283*
    Carne en su Jugo, *250,*
        251

Frijoles con Veneno,
    208, *209*
Frijoles de Olla, *52,* 54
Frijoles Refritos, *53,* 55
Huevos Rancheros con
    Arrachera, *290,*
    291
Pambazos Rellenos de
    Huevos y Chorizo,
    190, 191
Pan de Cazón, 168, *169*
Tacos Envenenados,
    220, *221*
Tamales con
    Chicharrones y
    Frijoles Negros,
    192, 193–94
Tlayuda con Tasajo,
    118, 119
Tortas Ahogadas, *247,*
    248–49

Beef
    Albóndigas en
        Chipotle, *125,*
        126–27
    Arrachera y Tacos
        Norteños, 278, *279*
    Caldillo Durangueño,
        218, 219

Carne Asada, *211,* 212–13
Carne en su Jugo, 251
Huevos Rancheros con
    Arrachera, *290,* 291
Puchero Tabasqueño,
    180, *181*
Tacos Envenenados,
    220, *221*
Tlayuda con Tasajo,
    118, 119
Birria estilo Aguascalientes,
    214, 216–17
Bread. *See also* Tortillas
    Pan Árabe, 44, *45*
    Pan de Muerto,
        100–101, 102–3
Brochetas de Pulpo y
    Camarones, *121,*
    122–23
Burritos
    de Chilorio, 226–27, *228*
    de Langosta, 282, *283*

C

Cabbage
    Chileatole Verde, *140,*
        141
    Curtido, *56,* 59

Cactus. *See* Nopales
Café de Olla, 184, *185*
Caldillo Durangueño, *218*, 219
Camarones al Tamarindo, 284–85, *286*
Carne Asada, *211*, 212–13
Carne en su Jugo, *250*, 251
Carnitas estilo Ciudad México, 82, *83*
Carrots
　Arroz Blanco con Mantequilla, *48*, 50
　Arroz Rojo, *48*, 49
　Chiles Jalapeños en Escabeche, *61*, 64
　Curtido, *56*, 59
　Enchiladas Mineras, 74–75, *76*
　Salsa de Zanahoria y Habanero, *61*, 63
Cashews
　Birria estilo Aguascalientes, *214*, 216–17
　Camarones al Tamarindo, 284–85, *286*
　Salsa Macha, 60, *61*
Cebolla Morada Encurtida, *56*, 59
Cemita Poblana, *88*, 89
Ceviche
　de Almejas Chocolatas, *276*, 277
　de Camarón y Leche de Coco, 150, *151*
　de Pulpo y Habanero Quemado, 160, *161*
Champurrado, *186*, 187
Chayote
　Mole Amarillo con Chochoyotes, *133*, 134–35
　Puchero Tabasqueño, 180, *181*
Cheese
　Arrachera y Tacos Norteños, 278, *279*
　Burritos de Chilorio, 226–27, *228*

Carne Asada, *211*, 212–13
Cemita Poblana, *88*, 89
Enchiladas Mineras, 74–75, *76*
Tacos Envenenados, 220, *221*
Tacos Gobernador, 262, *263*
Tlayuda con Tasajo, *118*, 119
Chicharrones
　en Salsa Verde, 224, *225*
　Ostiones a la Parrilla con, *280*, 281
　y Frijoles Negros, Tamales con, *192*, 193–94
Chicken
　Empanadas de Mole Amarillo, *136*, 137
　Enchiladas Mineras, 74–75, *76*
　Mole Coloradito, *129*, 130–31
　Pipián Rojo estilo Jalisco, 244–45, *246*
　Pollo al Pastor, 72, *73*
　Pozole Verde estilo Guerrero, *115*, 116–17
　Relleno Negro, *155*, 156–57
　Salbutes, 164, *165*
　Sopa de Lima, *170*, 171
　Stock, 112
　Tamales Oaxaqueños, *110*, 111–13
　Uliche (Mole Blanco), *182*, 183
Chileatole Verde, *140*, 141
Chile powder, cooking with, 32
Chiles. *See also specific chiles below*
　dried, flavor and uses, 32
　dried, shopping for, 31
　dried, storing, 31

dried green, about, 31
dried red, about, 31
fresh, selecting, 31
freshly dried, about, 31
in ground chile powder, 32
Jaibas Enchilpayadas, *196*, 197
Mole Amarillo con Chochoyotes, *133*, 134–35
preparing, 32
Uliche (Mole Blanco), *182*, 183
Chiles anchos
　flavor and uses, 32
　Frijoles con Veneno, 208, *209*
　Horneado Tabasqueño, *178*, 179
　Mole Coloradito, *129*, 130–31
　Pozole Rojo, *259*, 260–61
　Relleno Negro, *155*, 156–57
　Salsa Macha, 60, *61*
Chiles cascabel
　flavor and uses, 32
　Salsa de Chipotle y Chile de Árbol, *61*, 62
　Salsa Macha, 60, *61*
Chiles Chipotle
　Albóndigas en Chipotle, *125*, 126–27
　Chilpachole de Jaiba, 188, *189*
　en Escabeche, *56*, 59
　flavor and uses, 32
　Pozole Rojo, *259*, 260–61
　Salsa Chipotle, *61*, 63
　Salsa de Chipotle y Chile de Árbol, *61*, 62
Chile(s) de Árbol
　Esquites, *84*, 85

flavor and uses, 32
Nopales Enchilados, 292, *293*
Salsa de, *61*, 62
Tortas Ahogadas, *247*, 248–49
y Chipotle, Salsa de, *61*, 62
Chiles guajillos
　Birria estilo Aguascalientes, *214*, 216–17
　Enchiladas Mineras, 74–75, *76*
　flavor and uses, 32
　Langosta con Salsa Guajillo, 252–53, *254*
　Mole Amarillo con Chochoyotes, *133*, 134–35
　Morisqueta Michoacana, 80, *81*
　Nopales Enchilados, 292, *293*
　Pescado a la Talla, 142, *143*
　Pozole Rojo, *259*, 260–61
　Relleno Negro, *155*, 156–57
　Tamales Barbones de Camarón, *255*, 256–57
　Tamales Oaxaqueños, *110*, 111–13
Chiles Habanero(s)
　Aceite de Habanero Quemado, *61*, 63
　Brochetas de Pulpo y Camarones, *121*, 122–23
　Cebolla Morada Encurtida, *56*, 59
　Encurtidos, *56*, 58
　Ha' Sikil P'ak, *162*, 163
　Pan de Cazón, 168, *169*
　Salsa de Zanahoria y Habanero, *61*, 63

Chiles Jalapeños
    Arroz a la Tumbada,
      176, *177*
    Carne Asada, *211,*
      212–13
    Chicharrones en Salsa
      Verde, 224, *225*
    Chilpachole de Jaiba,
      188, *189*
    Curtido, *56,* 59
    en Escabeche, *61,* 64
    Tlaltequeadas, *77,*
      78–79
Chiles pasillas
    Burritos de Chilorio,
      226–27, *228*
    flavor and uses, 32
    Mole Coloradito, *129,*
      130–31
Chiles poblanos
    Arroz Blanco con
      Mantequilla, *48,* 50
    Caldillo Durangueño,
      218, 219
    Chileatole Verde, *140,*
      141
    Esquites, *84,* 85
    Fideo Seco, *222,* 223
    Pozole Verde estilo
      Guerrero, *115,*
      116–17
    Pulpo Kung Pao, *287,*
      288–89
    Rajas con Crema, 232,
      233
    Salsa de Tomatillo,
      61, 62
Chiles serranos
    Aguachile, 242, *243*
    Chorizo Verde, 86, *87*
    Fideo Seco, *222,* 223
    Salsa Blanca, *56,* 58
    Salsa Tatemada, *56,* 58
Chilpachole de Jaiba, 188,
    189
Chocolate
    Champurrado, *186,* 187
    Mole Coloradito, *129,*
      130–31

Chorizo
    Rojo, *265,* 266–67
    Verde, 86, *87*
Cilantro
    Arroz Verde, *48,* 51
Clams
    Arroz a la Tumbada,
      176, *177*
    Ceviche de Almejas
      Chocolatas, *276,*
      277
Cochinita Pibil, *148,* 149
Coconut milk
    Ceviche de Camarón
      y Leche de Coco,
      150, *151*
Coffee
    Café de Olla, 184, *185*
Corn
    Arroz Blanco con
      Mantequilla, *48,* 50
    Chileatole Verde, *140,*
      141
    Esquites, *84,* 85
    Puchero Tabasqueño,
      180, *181*
Corn husks
Tamales Barbones de
    Camarón, *255,* 256–57
Crab
    Arroz a la Tumbada,
      176, *177*
    Chilpachole de Jaiba,
      188, *189*
    Jaibas Enchilpayadas,
      196, 197
Curtido, *56,* 59

D

Digital scale, 24
Drinks
    Café de Olla, 184, *185*
    Champurrado, *186,* 187
Dumplings
    Mole Amarillo con
      Chochoyotes, *133,*
      134–35

Tamales Barbones de
    Camarón, *255,*
      256–57
Tamales con
    Chicharrones y
    Frijoles Negros,
    192, 193–94
Tamales Oaxaqueños,
    110, 111–13

E

Eggs
    Huevos Rancheros con
      Arrachera, *290,* 291
    Pambazos Rellenos de
      Huevos y Chorizo,
      190, 191
    Papadzules, *152,* 153
    Relleno Negro, *155,*
      156–57
Empanadas de Mole
    Amarillo, *136,* 137
Enchiladas Mineras, 74–75, *76*
Equipment, 24
Esquites, *84,* 85

F

Fideo Seco, *222,* 223
Frijoles
    con Veneno, 208, *209*
    de Olla, *52,* 54
    Refritos, *53,* 55
Fritters. *See* Tlaltequeadas

G

Garlic
    Langosta con Salsa
      Guajillo, 252–53,
      254
    Mojarra Frita, 138, *139*
    Torta de Lechón, *229,*
      230–31
Gaspacho Moreliano, 90,
    91
Goat. *See* Birria

Gorditas
    de Maíz, *42,* 43
    Griddled, 43
Guacamole, 64

H

Ham
    Carnitas estilo Ciudad
      México, 82, *83*
    Cemita Poblana, *88,*
      89
Harina de Maíz
    Empanadas de Mole
      Amarillo, *136,* 137
    Gorditas de Maíz, *42,*
      43
    Mole Amarillo con
      Chochoyotes, *133,*
      134–35
    Salbutes, 164, *165*
    Tortillas de, *37,* 39
Ha' Sikil P'ak, *162,* 163
Herbs, 28–29
    Arroz Verde, *48,* 51
    dried, buying, 29
    fresh, storing, 28
    hardy, types of, 28
    Recado de Toda Clase,
      64
    tender, types of, 28
Hominy
    Pozole Rojo, *259,*
      260–61
    Pozole Verde estilo
      Guerrero, *115,*
      116–17
Horneado Tabasqueño, *178,*
    179
Huevos Rancheros con
    Arrachera, *290,* 291

J

Jaibas Enchilpayadas, *196,*
    197
Jícama
    Gaspacho Moreliano,
      90, *91*

K

Kitchen scale, 24

L

Langosta con Salsa
Guajillo, 252–53,
254
Lard, 25
Lime
Aguachile, 242, *243*
Ceviche de Almejas
Chocolatas, *276*,
277
Ceviche de Camarón
y Leche de Coco,
150, *151*
Cochinita Pibil, *148*, 149
Mojarra Frita, 138, *139*
Poc Chuc, *158*, 159
Torta de Lechón, *229*,
230–31
Lobster
Burritos de Langosta,
282, *283*
Langosta con Salsa
Guajillo, 252–53,
254

M

Mango
Gaspacho Moreliano,
90, *91*
Masa
Champurrado, *186*, 187
Gorditas de Maíz, *42*, 43
Tamales Barbones de
Camarón, *255*,
256–57
Tamales con
Chicharrones y
Frijoles Negros,
192, 193–94
Tamales Oaxaqueños,
110, 111–13
Tortillas de Maíz, *37*, 38
Uliche (Mole Blanco),
182, 183
Masa harina. *See* Harina de
Maíz

Meatballs
Albóndigas en
Chipotle, *125*,
126–27
Relleno Negro, *155*,
156–57
México
Baja Peninsula, 274
Central, 68–71
Chiapas, 109
Día de Los Muertos,
94–98
El Golfo Central, 174
El Norte, 206
Guadalajara, 240
Guerrero, 109
Mazatlán, 240, 268–70
Mexico City, 68–71
Michoacán, 234–36
migration patterns,
200–202
Monterrey, 236–37
Oaxaca, 106–9
Pacífico Central, 240
South Pacific, 106–9
Tabasco, 174
Teotihuacán, 71
Veracruz, 174
Yucatán Peninsula, 146
Mojarra Frita, 138, *139*
Mole
Amarillo, Empanadas
de, *136*, 137
Amarillo con
Chochoyotes, *133*,
134–35
Blanco (Uliche), *182*, 183
Coloradito, *129*, 130–31
Morisqueta Michoacana, 80

N

Nopales Enchilados, 292,
293

O

Octopus
Brochetas de Pulpo y
Camarones, *121*,
122–23

Ceviche de Pulpo
y Habanero
Quemado, 160, *161*
Pulpo Kung Pao, *287*,
288–89
Onions
Cebolla Morada
Encurtida, *56*, 59
Orange
Ceviche de Almejas
Chocolatas, *276*,
277
Cochinita Pibil, *148*, 149
Poc Chuc, *158*, 159
Oregano
about, 29
Recado de Toda Clase,
64
Ostiones a la Parrilla con
Chicharrones, *280*, 281
Oysters. *See* Ostiones

P

Pambazos Rellenos de
Huevos y Chorizo, *190*,
191
Pan
Árabe, 44, *45*
de Cazón, 168, *169*
de Muerto, *100–101*,
102–3
Pantry ingredients, 26
Papadzules, *152*, 153
Papaya
Tacos Capeados, *294*,
295
y Tomatillo Cruda,
Salsa de, *56*, 60
Pasta. *See* Fideo Seco
Peanuts
Pipián Rojo estilo
Jalisco, 244–45,
246
Pulpo Kung Pao, *287*,
288–89
Pepitas
Chorizo Verde, 86, *87*
Ha' Sikil P'ak, *162*, 163
Papadzules, *152*, 153

Pipián Rojo estilo
Jalisco, 244–45,
246
Pozole Verde estilo
Guerrero, *115*,
116–17
Uliche (Mole Blanco),
182, 183
Peppers. *See also* Chiles
Brochetas de Pulpo y
Camarones, *121*,
122–23
Pescado a la
Veracruzana, 198,
199
Puchero Tabasqueño,
180, *181*
Pescado
a la Talla, 142, *143*
a la Veracruzana, 198,
199
Pineapple
Gaspacho Moreliano,
90, *91*
Pollo al Pastor, *72*, 73
Pipián Rojo estilo Jalisco,
244–45, *246*
Plantains
Puchero Tabasqueño,
180, *181*
Poc Chuc, *158*, 159
Pollo al Pastor, *72*, 73
Pork. *See also* Bacon; Ham;
Sausage
Albóndigas en
Chipotle, *125*,
126–27
Burritos de Chilorio,
226–27, *228*
Carnitas estilo Ciudad
México, 82, *83*
Cemita Poblana, *88*, 89
Cochinita Pibil, *148*, 149
Frijoles con Veneno,
208, *209*
Horneado Tabasqueño,
178, 179
Morisqueta
Michoacana, 80,
81

Pork (cont.)
    Poc Chuc, *158*, 159
    Pozole Rojo, *259*,
        260–61
    Relleno Negro, *155*,
        156–57
    Salbutes, 164, *165*
    Tacos Árabes, *92*, 93
    Tamales con
        Chicharrones y
        Frijoles Negros,
        192, 193–94
    Torta de Lechón, *229*,
        230–31
    Tortas Ahogadas, *247*,
        248–49
Potatoes
    Enchiladas Mineras,
        74–75, *76*
    Fideo Seco, *222*, 223
    Puchero Tabasqueño,
        180, *181*
    Tacos Envenenados,
        220, *221*
Pozole
    Rojo, *259*, 260–61
    Verde estilo Guerrero,
        115, 116–17
Puchero Tabasqueño, 180,
    181
Pulpo Kung Pao, *287*, 288–89

R
Rajas con Crema, 232, *233*
Recado
    de Toda Clase, 64
    Rojo, 65
Red snapper
    Pescado a la Talla, 142,
        143
    Pescado a la
        Veracruzana, 198,
        199
    Tikin Xic, *166*, 167
Relleno Negro, *155*, 156–57
Rice
    Arroz a la Tumbada,
        176, *177*

Arroz Blanco con
    Mantequilla, *48*,
    50
Arroz Rojo, *48*, 49
Arroz Verde, *48*, 51
Burritos de Langosta,
    282, *283*

S
Salad. *See* Gaspacho
Salbutes, 164, *165*
Salsa
    Aceite de Habanero
        Quemado, *61*, 63
    Blanca, *56*, 58
    Chipotle, *61*, 63
    de Aguacate, *56*, 60
    de Chile de Árbol, *61*,
        62
    de Chipotle y Chile de
        Árbol, *61*, 62
    de Papaya y Tomatillo
        Cruda, *56*, 60
    de Tomatillo, *61*, 62
    de Zanahoria y
        Habanero, *61*, 63
    Macha, 60, *61*
    Tatemada, *56*, 58
Salt, 24–25
Sandwiches
    Cemita Poblana, *88*, 89
    Pambazos Rellenos de
        Huevos y Chorizo,
        190, 191
    Torta de Lechón, *229*,
        230–31
    Tortas Ahogadas, *247*,
        248–49
Sausage
    Carne Asada, *211*,
        212–13
    Chorizo Rojo, *265*,
        266–67
    Chorizo Verde, 86, *87*
    Pambazos Rellenos de
        Huevos y Chorizo,
        190, 191
    Tacos Envenenados,
        220, *221*

Seafood. *See also* Shrimp
    Arroz a la Tumbada,
        176, *177*
    Brochetas de Pulpo y
        Camarones, *121*,
        122–23
    Burritos de Langosta,
        282, *283*
    Ceviche de Almejas
        Chocolatas, *276*,
        277
    Ceviche de Pulpo
        y Habanero
        Quemado, 160,
        161
    Chilpachole de Jaiba,
        188, *189*
    Jaibas Enchilpayadas,
        196, 197
    Langosta con Salsa
        Guajillo, 252–53,
        254
    Mojarra Frita, 138, *139*
    Ostiones a la Parrilla
        con Chicharrones,
        280, 281
    Pan de Cazón, 168, *169*
    Pescado a la Talla, 142,
        143
    Pescado a la
        Veracruzana, 198,
        199
    Pulpo Kung Pao, *287*,
        288–89
    Tacos Capeados, *294*,
        295
    Tikin Xic, *166*, 167
Shrimp
    Aguachile, 242, *243*
    Arroz a la Tumbada,
        176, *177*
    Brochetas de Pulpo y
        Camarones, *121*,
        122–23
    Camarones al
        Tamarindo,
        284–85, *286*
    Ceviche de Camarón
        y Leche de Coco,
        150, *151*

Tacos Gobernador,
    262, *263*
Tamales Barbones de
    Camarón, *255*,
    256–57
Sopa de Lima, *170*, 171
Soup. *See* Sopa de Lima
Spice blends
    Recado de Toda Clase,
        64
    Recado Rojo, 65
Spices, buying and grinding,
    29
Spinach
    Chorizo Verde, 86, *87*
    Tlaltequeadas, *77*,
        78–79
Squash
    Chileatole Verde, *140*,
        141
    Mole Amarillo con
        Chochoyotes, *133*,
        134–35
    Puchero Tabasqueño,
        180, *181*
    Tlaltequeadas, *77*,
        78–79
Stews
    Arroz a la Tumbada,
        176, *177*
    Caldillo Durangueño,
        218, 219
    Chilpachole de Jaiba,
        188, *189*
    Pozole Rojo, *259*,
        260–61
    Pozole Verde estilo
        Guerrero, *115*,
        116–17
    Puchero Tabasqueño,
        180, *181*
    Relleno Negro, *155*,
        156–57
    Uliche (Mole Blanco),
        182, 183
Stock, Chicken, 112
Sweet potatoes
    Puchero Tabasqueño,
        180, *181*

Swordfish
  Pan de Cazón, 168, *169*

T
Tacos
  Árabes, *92*, 93
  Arrachera y Tacos
    Norteños, 278,
    279
  Capeados, *294*, 295
  Envenenados, 220, *221*
  Gobernador, 262, *263*
Tamales
  Barbones de Camarón,
    255, 256–57
  con Chicharrones y
    Frijoles Negros,
    192, 193–94
  Oaxaqueños, *110*,
    111–13
Tamarind
  Camarones al
    Tamarindo,
    284–85, *286*
Tikin Xic, *166*, 167
Tlaltequeadas, *77*, 78–79
Tlayuda con Tasajo, *118*, 119
Tomatillo(s)
  Caldillo Durangueño,
    218, 219
  Carne en su Jugo, *250*,
    251
  Ceviche de Pulpo
    y Habanero
    Quemado, 160, *161*
  Chicharrones en Salsa
    Verde, 224, *225*
  Pozole Verde estilo
    Guerrero, *115*,
    116–17
  Salsa de, *61*, 62
  Salsa de Aguacate,
    56, 60
  Salsa de Chile de Árbol,
    61, 62
  Tacos Capeados, *294*,
    295
  Tamales Oaxaqueños,
    110, 111–13

y Papaya Cruda, Salsa
  de, *56*, 60
Tomatoes
  Albóndigas en
    Chipotle, *125*,
    126–27
  Arroz a la Tumbada,
    176, *177*
  Arroz Rojo, *48*, 49
  Birria estilo
    Aguascalientes,
    214, 216–17
  Brochetas de Pulpo y
    Camarones, *121*,
    122–23
  Chilpachole de Jaiba,
    188, *189*
  Ha' Sikil P'ak, *162*, 163
  Horneado Tabasqueño,
    178, 179
  Huevos Rancheros con
    Arrachera, *290*,
    291
  Mole Coloradito, *129*,
    130–31
  Morisqueta
    Michoacana, 80,
    81
  Pan de Cazón, 168, *169*
  Pescado a la
    Veracruzana, 198,
    199
  Pipián Rojo estilo
    Jalisco, 244–45,
    246
  Relleno Negro, *155*,
    156–57
  Salsa de Chipotle y
    Chile de Árbol,
    61, 62
  Salsa Tatemada, *56*, 58
  Tamales Barbones de
    Camarón, *255*,
    256–57
  Tikin Xic, *166*, 167
  Tlaltequeadas, *77*,
    78–79
  Tortas Ahogadas, *247*,
    248–49

Torta de Lechón, 229,
  230–31
Tortas Ahogadas, *247*,
  248–49
Tortillas
  Arrachera y Tacos
    Norteños, 278,
    279
  Burritos de Chilorio,
    226–27, 228
  Burritos de Langosta,
    282, *283*
  Carne Asada, *211*,
    212–13
  de Harina con
    Mantequilla, *45*, 46
  de Harina de Maíz, *37*, 39
  de Harina estilo
    Sinaloa, *45*, 47
  de Maíz, *37*, 38
  Enchiladas Mineras,
    74–75, *76*
  Huevos Rancheros con
    Arrachera, *290*,
    291
  Pan de Cazón, 168, *169*
  Papadzules, *152*, 153
  Salbutes, 164, *165*
  store-bought,
    improving flavor
    of, 35
  Tacos Capeados, *294*,
    295
  Tacos Envenenados,
    220, *221*
  Tacos Gobernador,
    262, *263*
  Tlayuda con Tasajo,
    118, 119
  Tostadas de Maíz, 40,
    41
Tostadas
  de Maíz, 40, *41*
  Huevos Rancheros con
    Arrachera, *290*,
    291

U
Uliche (Mole Blanco), *182*,
  183

V
Ve getables. *See also
  specific vegetables*
  used most often, 28
Vegetarian recipe
  modifications, 25

W
Watermelon
  Ceviche de Camarón
    y Leche de Coco,
    150, *151*

Library of Congress
  Cataloging-in-Publication Data
Names: Martínez, Rick (Chef) author. | Fuller,
  Ren, photographer.
Title: Mi Cocina / by Rick Martínez; photography
  by Ren Fuller.
Description: New York City: Clarkson Potter,
  2022. | Includes index.
Identifiers: LCCN 2021034744 (print) | LCCN
  2021034745 (ebook) | ISBN 9780593138700
  (hardcover) | ISBN 9780593138717 (ebook)
Subjects: LCSH: Cooking, Mexican. | LCGFT:
  Cookbooks.
Classification: LCC TX716.M4 M3754 2022 (print)
  | LCC TX716.M4 (ebook) | DDC 641.5972—dc23
LC record: lccn.loc.gov/2021034744
LC ebook record: lccn.loc.gov/2021034745

ISBN: 978-0-593-13870-0
Ebook ISBN: 978-0-593-13871-7

Printed in China

Designer and creative director:
  Christopher Cristiano
Photographer: Ren Fuller
Photography assistant: David Koung
Food stylist: Caroline Hwang
Food styling assistant: Jessica Darakjian
Food styling assistant: Sergio Gamboa
Prop stylist: Nidia Cueva

Editor: Raquel Pelzel
Editorial assistant: Bianca Cruz
Production editor: Mark McCauslin
Copy editor: Kate Slate
Production manager: Jessica Heim
Compositors: Merri Ann Morrell and Nick Patton
Indexer: Elizabeth T. Parson

10 9 8 7 6 5 4 3 2 1

First Edition

Rick Martínez is the host of the
YouTube series *Pruébalo* on the Babish
Culinary Universe and the Food52
video series *Sweet Heat*. He cohosts
the *Borderline Salty* podcast with
Carla Lalli Music, is a regular
contributor to *Bon Appétit* magazine
and *The New York Times*, and teaches
live, weekly cooking classes for the
Food Network Kitchen. He currently
resides in Mazatlán with his dog,
Choco, where he cooks, eats, and
enjoys the Mexican Pacific coast.

Clarkson Potter/Publishers
New York
clarksonpotter.com

Cover design: Christopher Cristiano
Cover photographs: Ren Fuller